TABLE OF CONTENTS

Introduction

- **What is a "Mitch"**

The "Transformers": The "Flipping" of Sex/Gender Roles

- **Politics**
- **Popular Culture**

The Pimp/Prostitute Relationship Re-Defined
Birth Control and the Paradigm of "Sex for Sex's Sake"
How Women Get Laid and Paid: A Socio-Historical and Political Analysis

- PREFACE
- INTRODUCTION: "ALL OF ME"
- THE MYTH OF "THE PRETTY GIRL'S CURSE"
- THE TOP 20 TRAITS WOMEN WANT IN A MAN: A SURVEY ANALYSIS
- SIGNS THAT A MAN IS BAD-IN-BED: AN ANALYSIS
- THE FOUNDATION: DISGUISED "MISANDRY"

  - ❖ The Woman Hater's Club" – The 3 Stooges
  - ❖ On-Going Misandry Gets "Flipped"

- THE 'PUSSY PRINCIPLE': CONCEPTS AND CHARACTERISTICS

  - ❖ The Economic Reality of "Getting Laid and Paid"

  - ❖ It Begins With What is Called "Nigga-Shit"

- ❖ Professional Athletes and 'Mistresses'
- ❖ Politicians and "Mistresses"

  - ❖ George Washington & Venus
  - ❖ Abraham Lincoln & Joshua Speed
  - ❖ JFK & Mimi Alford
  - ❖ JFK & Marilyn Monroe
  - ❖ JFK & Judith Campbell Exier
  - ❖ JFK & Ellen Rometsch
  - ❖ Grover Cleveland & Maria Crofts Halpin
  - ❖ Bill Clinton & Monica Lewinsky
  - ❖ James Buchanan a& William Rufus King
  - ❖ Warren G. Hardin & Nan Britton
  - ❖ Warren G. Harding & Carrie Fulton Phillips
  - ❖ Dwight D. Eisenhower & Kay Summersby
  - ❖ Thomas Jefferson & Sally Hemings
  - ❖ FDR & Lucy Mercer
  - ❖ James Garfield & Lucia Calhoun
  - ❖ John Tyler & The Majority of His Slaves
  - ❖ George H.W. Bush & Jennifer Fitzgerald
  - ❖ LBJ & Alice Glass
  - ❖ JFK & Angie Dickinson
  - ❖ Marion Barry, D.C. Mayor
  - ❖ Cory Booker, Newark Mayor
  - ❖ Rev. Ben Chavis, NAACP
  - ❖ Henry Cisneros, HUD Director
  - ❖ Eliot Spitzer, N.Y. Governor
  - ❖ Anthony Weiner, N.Y. State Rep

  - ❖ The Richest Women in the World
  - ❖ The Grown Man as "Child"

- RISE OF THE "CHICKEN HEADS": EVEN UGLY WOMEN CAN GET "LAID AND PAID"

  - ❖ The Reality of Alimony: Ka-Ching!
  - ❖ Child Support Payments: Ka-Ching!

    - ❖ Little Bow-Wow
    - ❖ Jermaine DuPri
    - ❖ Chief Keef
    - ❖ Allen Iverson
    - ❖ Terrell Owens
    - ❖ Evander Holyfield
    - ❖ Bobby Brown

> ❖ Dennis Rodman
> ❖ Flavor Flav
> ❖ Shawty Lo

- DON'T HATE THE PLAYA OR THE GAME: HATE THE SYSTEM THAT PRODUCED AND ENDORSES BOTH!

> ❖ The Side Chick

CONCLUSION
REFERENCES

Newsweek's "The Secret Lives of Wives": An Africentric Analysis

The Myth of the "Pretty Girl's Curse"
Executive Summary
Introduction
Creation of a Slut: An Evolutionary Observation

- Go Big Red(necks)! (Nov. 27, 1998)
- Sluttification of Teenaged Girls (Part I)
- Sluttification of Teenaged Girls (Part II)
- Sluttification III: The Search for More Condoms
- Wayward Wives 101: A Partial History

White Women, the American Dream and "New Gomorrah:"

> A Response to "The Secret Lives of Wives"
- "Suppressed Promiscuity:" The Movies, White/Black Women and Adultery

> > ❖ Double Indemnity
> > ❖ The Postman Always Rings Twice
> > ❖ Sex, Lies and Videotape
> > ❖ Consenting Adults
> > ❖ Indecent Proposal
> > ❖ Damage
> > ❖ Woman's Guide to Adultery
> > ❖ The Affair
> > ❖ Caught

Introduction

Women have been pimping men for a long time. Even when the female was the one being dubbed a "prostitute," she was still in control. In order to understand this most interesting thesis, let's examine exactly what a pimp is.

According to the Merriam-Webster Dictionary, criminal who is associated with, usually exerts control over, and lives off the earnings of one or more prostitutes." As a verb, the Free Dictionary informs us that a pimp, "criminal who is associated with, usually exerts control over, and lives off the earnings of one or more prostitutes." Take note that both definitions refer to a pimp as a "criminal." But nothing could be further from the truth, because pimping is as old as this country and as acceptable, on so many levels and in so many ways, as apple pie.

Even when women were at the bottom of the socioeconomic ladder – which they claim they still are – they were the ones in control and no matter what the economic system – be it tribal, agrarian or industrial – the woman is the foundation of that system. Though her work may be menial, it is nevertheless ultra-important in the long-term maintenance. In the tribe you may be related by blood, in the agrarian system you may be dealing with plants and animals for survival and food and in the industrial you begin to depend on machines and technology (where the female began to experience more "independence" because less of her work was dependent on brute strength), but the woman was the one in control.

The one who was physically strongest was presumed to be the male because of the tendency to wage war and engage in conflicts. But the real power was giving birth and providing food to energize the male in his daily quests for survival. Because I am not an expert in world history, let us confine my thesis to American society because it is a capitalist society, an economic system that feeds directly into the pimp-prostitute paradigm that I am discussing in this book.

Do you know how much strength and intestinal fortitude it takes to remain silent, to play mum while you see the male continue to make an ass out of himself? Do you know how much discipline it takes to raise children to perpetuate a system that you know is rooted in misogyny and racism? That is what took place during America's embryonic beginnings and what is taking place to this very day.

There are other examples of the "power" that the female had while all the while playing the role of the docile little female waiting around for a man to talk her out of her panties. She had to teach her daughters the tricks of the trade, how to apply makeup when the time was right, how to handle that "time of the month" which even the white man's Bible refers to in some of the most derogatory terms possible. All this is stacked against her: institutions including banks, legal institutions controlling land, the military which banned her, the health care system that destroyed and used her body, and others including, as I say, religion – an institution that assigned her to a category of inferiority.

And still she rose.

On July 27, 2016 Democratic Presidential nominee Hillary Clinton became the first woman to ever get the nomination of a major political party. After it was announced, she said, by satellite, "I can't believe we just put the biggest crack in that glass ceiling yet!" That glass ceiling should have never been there in the first place because women have been running shit all the time, but were just forced to keep it under wraps because men are so bitch-like and thin-skinned. And the "crack" that these women used to gain power was the one between their legs. Historically, women have been able to "get laid and paid." This book provides evidence and examples.

In the 1960 movie "The Facts of Life," two married people are having an affair. They have not yet agreed to tell the people they are married to, but the woman (Kitty, played by Lucille Ball) has brought it upon herself to leave her husband by good-bye note. Later, as she and her lover Larry Gilbert are headed for their hideaway cabin for a three-day weekend, she tells Larry about it. In the 1996 movie, "A Strange Affair," Judith Light says at one point to her daughter: "Every wife has to invent her own life." These two examples of two ways that white people have created a "new normal" and in doing so, despite the male façade, have handed the power, the money and the family over to the female. Although he is all for it, that is not really the issue.

The issue is for you to see how many women have always and continue, to make major decisions based on what they want and how they figure things and then impose it on the male. Kitty did it twice: once to her husband with the letter and then to Larry. Now he's in a "no choice" situation; she imposed her will on him and did what she felt was "best for them both."

This new-found confidence is long overdue and is perhaps best summed up in the lyrics from Alicia Keys' 2008 hit, "Superwoman." In part, it goes something like this:

Everywhere I'm turning
Nothing seems complete
I stand up and I'm searching
For the better part of me
I hang my head from sorrow
State of humanity
I wear it on my shoulders
Gotta find the strength in me

I am a Superwoman
Yes I am
Yes she is
Even when I'm a mess
I still put on a vest
With an S on my chest
Oh yes
I'm a Superwoman

For all the mothers fighting
For better days to come
And all my women, all my women sitting here trying
To come home before the sun
And all my sisters
Coming together
Say yes I will
Yes I can
I am a Superwoman
Yes I am
Yes she is

… When I'm breaking down
And I can't be found

> And I start to get weak
> Cause no one knows
> Me underneath these clothes
> But I can fly
> We can fly, ooh
> I am a Superwoman …

But there's another side. In the same movie mentioned earlier, the goodbye note that she left for her husband. She flies back home to take it back but he's already there. He comes in and he's having a drink. The child is crying in the other room but before she goes to see about it, she asks her husband, who has the envelope with the note in it still sealed, to toss it in the fireplace. She goes into the other room to check on the child and this trick does just that: he doesn't open it to see what it says, he just blindly tosses it on the fire.

Superwoman. Gettin' laid and getting' paid. And with all that power and influence can still whine, cry and lie with the best of them.

So just as women manipulate situations and dominate without being "dominative," men are childlike thralls and, for the sake of pussy, do just about anything to get themselves a "girlfriend," "a woman," "a fiancée" and then of course the final scam, "a wife.

This philosophic scenario fits women and their roles in setting up, maintaining and controlling relationships, by way of getting "laid and paid," like a glove.

Not a few people have heard the maxim, "When life gives you lemons, make lemonade." This is supposed to encourage people to be optimistic and have a "go get 'em attitude" about whatever it is they are pursuing. This saying is the perfect way to describe the philosophies of most women when it comes to "getting laid and getting paid." And I'm going to explain to you how I arrived at this conclusion.

Take the concept of lemons and use the word "sperm" instead. In this book I will discuss the sexual tango that goes on between men and women but for the most part the aim and intention of "dating" and this kind of thing is to have sex. Women view sex differently than men do. In my view they view a potential mate as being more than just a sex partner; they are looking for some kind of financial assistance. That's why they ask you where you work, who you work for, and other questions related to your financial situation. Most, not all of them do this by the time you've gone on your second "date."

A woman who is young and just out for orgasms is one thing. But when they get older they begin to understand how serious relationships are supposed to be as it relates to how their friends and family will view them and also in regard to their future. So now we go back to the adage: when life provides you with a man (or men) who want to screw you, and you find one that has economic potential, then "make lemonade." Translate that sperm into a pregnancy. In many cases she makes the right decision – for her. And once that decision is made, she will figure out a way to impose it on YOU.

By the time most men realize the historical tendency of women getting laid and paid and how, even though held back with gender bias, glass ceilings and sex role socialization, women have seized control of the relationship. They do it with their vaginas, with the mythology and social pressure that surrounds family and sexual relationships, and with the uncanny ability to take over and control family budgets. They have even so mastered the system that they have pussy whipped their white male partners into passing legislation that gives them half of your shit during a divorce and in some cases, entitles them to it even if you are not married to them.

Getting laid and getting paid.

How do little girls learn how to suck dick, trick men into giving them money, take it up the ass when necessary and of course, master the straight fuck? From their mothers, where else? Many learn in the streets of course. But the curiosity is raised by what they see at home. In the day and age of the single mother, young girls grow up seeing their mothers looking and smelling good and then going out on dates. They see men come into the house for long and not-so-long periods of time as the 'boyfriend.'

These are the only logical ways to figure how it is, from one generation to the next, women continue to get over on men one way or another. There is however, yet one more constant variable in this formula regarding how women get laid and paid. And that is the "social psychology" of the dating process, the game playing that goes on, and how easy it is to trap men, get them to pay for almost anything and then use that power to determine what role you want him (or them) to play in your life.

Generally speaking women learn about male desperation, gullibility and peer pressure. Here's how it works. And what they learn they pass on to their children, both boys and girls. But the fact is, there are two different sets of lessons that are imparted. And these divergent lessons come together as the child gets older and grows into adulthood, and at the end of those crossroads is one beneficiary: the female. It might not seem that way because of all the sexist articles in her way, but in the final analysis, no woman in her right mind would ever want to be a man (outside of the workplace, that is).

To begin with, boys learn from their mothers about what a "good woman" is. As part of this programming they are told that you never "hit" a woman, but very little is taught about what to do if a woman hits you. You're just supposed to take it. And you aren't supposed to let her pay for the dinner or the date and so on. The mother hands these tips down to her sons while she is teaching her daughters how to fight, exploit and take full advantage of any "sucker" that comes along. The more soft-spoken, dainty and submissive the boy is, the more the mother likes it.

Using their spoil-happy mothers as a model, the boys seek to find that type of treatment from and that type of person in person in a girl. Grown-ass men are often heard telling women, "that ain't how my mama would do it" and similarly infantile statements. That is one reason why the wife and the mother oftentimes bump heads: each sees the other as competition for this man who is being treated like a little boy by both of them.

Desperation begins to increase as increasing number of their male "buddies" have girlfriends, go on dates and start getting "hooked up." Then they learn how to compare stories and experiences, including the truth, some small lies and of course, the infamous "cock claiming" where they claim they fucked girls that they haven't. That reality is what leads to a number of conflicts, guy on guy and girl on guy. And it is as old as cockhounding itself.

In simpler terms, the peer pressure increases after the first piece of pussy and comparisons are made. Women know about it because they talk amongst themselves and their sisters, classmates and others talk about men and what it took to land one. Women share notes on men and as they get older, begin to see something universal among us: men are crude assholes who can be easily seduced by something that women carry around all the time: pussy.

Women grow not to respect us, although many of them will pretend as if they do, claiming for instance that they want "somebody like my daddy." Realizing that their father wasn't shit either (which is why they never saw him), they nevertheless have to have something to fall back on, lest their mother be deemed or perceived as a slut. So each generation protects the other one. And both have one thing in common: the low regard for the male species that, for some reason, seem to crave and obsess over this thing called "pussy."

After all, what's all this fuss about something that smells, something surrounded by hair, and something that serves no real use other than to get the man off, a factor that is negated by the fact that this same human hole is responsible for impregnation which tends to tie a man down for no less than eighteen years? That's right: because of desperation and peer pressure, the man seeks out the very thing that is going to trap him and change his entire life. And then there's the issue of gullibility.

It is clear that men are gullible because we fall for the same old shit. We screw a girl and she tells us we are the greatest lover she ever had, that our dick is huge and that she can't resist us. After that she begins luring us into these public displays of affection which is the modern day version of the "brand." By brand I refer to the ways that farmers mark their cattle and other animals. They took a hot poker with initials or a design and tattooed it onto the animal's flesh. That then, was your "brand."

Today and in this case, there are several other types of "brands."

The first of these is what I call "The first love tat." This is a tattoo that girls of today get on their arms, breasts, backsides and inner thighs in most cases, with the name of the boy who they "love" emblazoned across their skin. These dumb bitches think and act as if this is the "real deal" just because this guy might have claimed that he "loved" them. Now having had sex with him, they think he'll be around forever, but little do they know: he might not even remember her name the next day.

The second form of brand is where women literally "mark their territory" the way gang members (and dogs) tend to do. One way women do it is through public displays of affection: walking up to you when you're with your pals and kissing you, walking down the hall holding hands, flashing the engagement ring you so foolishly purchased so you could get the pussy and so on. Despite their sister-like behavior toward one another, women do not trust each other when it comes to "their man."

By the time we realize that maybe she's not the one, it's too late. She's spread the necessary news and rumors to trap you. And it's about that time that you spot two, maybe three other girls who you would love to screw. But they already know about you and your "girlfriend." Many won't give a shit and will fuck you anyway. But remember this: when the dyad (a group of two) becomes a triad (a group of three) power relationships shift and there is always a tendency for danger on some level. You see it all the time, but on no more show displayed most vividly than the TV program "Snapped." And if you haven't seen it, I strongly suggest you watch it. You might learn something.

Let me close by saying this: I wrote this book to serve as a basis for discussion between men and women and whomever else. You cannot arrive at sane conclusions without someone being able to offer up some sane variables. *This emotion-laden screaming match type bullshit will no longer suffice.* This is a capitalist society, and what is capitalism? It is the ceaseless pursuit of profit. Not just money, not just a paycheck or a stipend, but PROFIT. And in my view women have been paying a huge price for the "profits" they've acquired over the years. We have hurt them emotionally, socially, culturally, physically and intellectually. All the while they were getting paid.

The bleeding has therefore been reciprocal.

<u>Introduction</u>

You took my kisses and you took my love
You taught me how to care
Am I to be just the remnant of a one-sided love affair?
All you took, I gladly gave
There's nothing left for me to save
All of me why not take all of me
Can't you see I'm no good without you
Take my lips I want to lose them
Take my arms I'll never use them
Your good bye left me with eyes that cry
How can I go on dear without you
You took the part that once was my heart
So why not take all of me.

"All of Me"
-   Ruth Etting, 1931

All of me. Although it was performed by a woman, two Jews – Seymour Simons and Gerald Marks – wrote the words and the music. This song should be re-named something like "The Trick's National Anthem" or "Confessions of a Turned Out John." All of me? For pussy? Come on, y'all. You know that for decades men have been begging for pussy as if it was lined with gold and women, seeing how desperate we were and how low we were willing to stoop just to get some "stank," decided to comply. But that is, after we pay for it with dates, flowers, candy, hotel rooms, trips and cruises, rent payments, car payments, a house and in many cases, a diamond ring that commits us to marrying her. Then and only then, are we promised to get all the pussy we want. But ask any married man: once you're married, you're lucky if you even SEE it once a month, let alone actually get it (that is, unless she's setting you up with a kid).

The fact is, men have been paying for sex and women have been selling it throughout recorded history. For the most part, these activities have been viewed and written about negatively, but it is fair to say that these negative views were put out there by men who were talking out of both sides of their mouths. On the one hand the talk is about morals and about not coveting other people's wives, while in real life, pussy was being purchased using everything from the bartering system and the offer of status to outright monetary exchanges.

How have women been able to get "laid and paid" all these years while appearing to be the victims of male chauvinism? First off, make no bones about it: they were victims. But much like a wolf that swallows a cobra, the results are going to be disastrous even though the wolf's belly is full. He's going to end up fuuuuuuucked up! And so it has come to pass with the male-dominated, chauvinistic, misogynistic society that we all call the United States of America.

The "state" of the female America is "united" when it comes to refusing to continue taking shit off of men. And men are just now beginning to pay for it.

But pay we will. And we will pay big time. Let me show you how by outlining what women "want in a man" based on a survey. The survey results and my analyses, follow.

<u>What is a "Mitch"</u>

What is up with the title of this book? That is an understandable question and one that can best be answered with straight up facts and attribution.

One of my favorite movies is "Trading Places" and it is a flick where Eddie Murphy was at his comedic best. There is a prison scene in that movie where Eddie is confronted by two large inmates after boasting about all the women he had. In that scene Eddie, in the role of Billy Ray Valentine, is trying to talk his way out of an ass-kicking by the two huge men as a smaller inmate sits on the side witnessing the entire scenario. Here is that dialogue:

> **Billy Ray Valentine**: [Billy Ray is in jail] I wish my bitches would get here. I ain't got time to be sitting in this cell with you.
> **Even Bigger Black Guy**: Where are your bitches, Mr. Big-Time Pimp?
> **Big Black Guy**: Yeah!
> **Billy Ray Valentine**: [to cellmate #2] Didn't I tell you that the phone in my limousine is busted, and I can't get in contact with my bitches?
> **Cellmate #2**: [to the Big Black Guy] Yeah! The phone in the limo was busted. What is ya, ignorant?"

This scene refers to the imaginary women that Billy Ray is pimping as "bitches." For the most part a "mitch" is a male bitch, and the term was created by Kevin Hart in the BET series, "Real Husbands of Hollywood."

In simple terms the title of this book is what today's women might say since, in my view, they are the real pimps. And today's males, appearing to be more effeminate than masculine in far too many instances, are today's "mitches," points I began to lay out in the earlier section of this book.

The next layer of the theory regarding this entire scenario is an outline of the present-day way that the sex roles were formally flipped. I have already offered that the female has always been in control although it may not have been in a formal setting. In my theory of "the transformers," the sex roles are crystal clear and the female is in charge because the white male has abandoned his role as the male figure and has elevated himself to the level of meta-human or demi-god. Explanations follow.

The "Transformers": The "Flipping" of Sex/Gender Roles

You've seen those women clad in black leather, maybe a mask and carrying a whip. You've seen men groveling at their feet waiting to get their ass literally whipped as a form of sexual release. Now translate this picture into a more figurative dimension: woman in charge willing to inflict pain, man on his knees taking a beating just so he can get a nut. And that, my friends, is the male-female relationship in America, in terms of power. And I'm talking about the white man and woman but there are "negroes" who copy everything they see their former slavemaster doing.

American society has undergone a series of "transformations" that come in five forms: The white man is the new demi-god. The white woman is the new white man. The black man is the new gay. The black woman is the new black man (A combination of machismo and lesbianism). The gay is the new "nigga." This is what I see and this book will explain it to you and provide evidence. Sex roles and perceptions are changing and as a result, so are power relationships.

The question is, what is all this shit about being afraid of women and doing things when they are not present that you wouldn't do if they were there? It's a changing of the guard and men, because of the laws and because of her independence, have become afraid of women. But in my view there is more taking place than meets the eye. There's a "transformation" taking place and it's about time somebody did more than just laugh about the possibility of what is taking place.

Roles are changing and shifting, and not just in terms of endogamy, exogamy, hypogamy or hypergamy. The roles I am talking about are incredibly significant because they transcend sex role socialization, but are about essential sex roles themselves and the sociopolitical roles and obligations that come with them: in sum, the white woman is the new white man, the black woman is the new white woman, the black man is the new "gay" man, the homosexual is the new "nigga", and the white man is, indeed, the new deity (demi-god). But this book is about that white woman and her new "masculinized through feminization-type" role that she's assumed.

She's formerly the societal Barbie Doll, the woman who is pursued and being kissed on by every man on earth. Because of the pervasiveness of this mythology, even the ugliest white bitch believes that the world is her oyster because she has been programmed to think in utopian terms. And this bitch is angry. The lyrics from the song "Fight Song" by Rachel Platten may well sum it up:

This is my fight song
Take back my life song
Prove I'm alright song
My power's turned on
Starting right now I'll be strong
I'll play my fight song
And I don't really care if nobody else believes
'Cause I've still got a lot of fight left in me

Does it sound like this bitch is bullshittin'?

And there may be yet another reason for this rise in what could be called "feminine mannishness:" on October 23, 2015 Gloria Steinem was a guest on the "CBS Morning Show." She stated at that time that because of the growing militarization of the world over the decades, for the first time, there are more males than females on earth.

Could there be a concerted effort at "accidentally bombing" and otherwise killing females during war and other crises? And what about the proliferation of both heart disease and breast cancer with men claiming to care so much that they are sporting the color pink, even during football games? Perhaps there is. But knowing this, we can now better explain and understand this change in "sex roles" and why increasing numbers of women have decided to "go it alone" when it comes to associating with or marrying the male of the species.

For the most part, the white woman has been brainwashed to believe that her whiteness, aided in a number of ways by numerous man-made "tools" are intended or designed to make her appear as something that she is not. Following are just a few of what I perceive as being the white woman's "tricks of the trade." While exerting herself politically, socially, educationally and all over the realm of popular culture, she still falls prey to and utilizes cosmetically adapted manifestations of reality.

There are tons of cosmetics ranging from Maybelline, Revlon, Estee Lauder, Cover Girl, Avon and Mary Kay to Alberto-Culver, Clinique, Helene Curtis and Max Factor. All aimed at helping her to paint her face, patch holes in her skin, lighten or darken her hair, enhance her eyes and so on. It's the demi-god's way of telling her that he's not satisfied with the way she looks and by complying, it's her way of telling him that she'll purchase the goods and use them, but she's doing it so that she can eventually seduce him, take control of his family, and then take over his role as someone who wants to rule the world.

She takes care of herself physically for the most part. Even now there is a product being advertised called SeroVital, which is nothing short of a human growth hormone, an "amino acid complex." A blonde white woman named Kym Davis, claiming to be a "beauty expert," (and claims to be 56 years old) sings the praises of this product, and women can get it through the mail. It will help her reduce body fat, reduce the appearance of wrinkles and enhance energy. It boosts your HGH "naturally" and sells for $99 in stores. They shoot it up and it gives them energy and "restores vitality." This white woman, despite being a woMAN, is not cutting short her role as seductress.

And there's something for the hair. Daisy Fuentes, an Anglo looking Latina, promotes a product called SecretExtensions gives "even more volume" to the hair and makes it appear longer than it really is. Made of a keratin conditioned fiber that enables you to wave it around – like the white girls do. You can wash, trim and straighten your SecretExtensions. Now, in vintage white girl fashion, these women can flip their hair, flash it when they turn their heads and so on. Black women, white women and Latinas are going crazy over this style and the hair extensions business is a billion dollar a year industry.

Then there are the numerous types of brassiers, from the U-Plunge, the convertible bra and the full cup to the srapless, the push up and the under wire – all geared toward doing something to her breasts. He also has training bras for the young girls so, at an early age, they can get trained in the purchase of these "aids" that will comply with what he has established as "female norms."

There's the panty shield and panty liners, underalls (to give the appearance that she has an ass) and he even has an operation called a labioplasty, where he can remove the skin covering the clitoris and entrance to the vagina. It's for women who experience pain when they are having sex. I refer to this operation as a "pussy lip adjustment." Speaking of lips, the set on her face are also under cosmetic control (in terms of manufacturing and sales) by the demi-god. Not only has he trained women to wear that lip stick like a badge of honor, but he's developed this shit called Revita-Lift Volume Filler that, like spackle, helps this bitch improve the flaws on her pale face.

Then there are the eyes. There are colored contact lenses (in September of 2015 Air Optix aired a commercial for colored contact lenses promising, "create a beautiful look that works for you …it looks natural"), and even dark women are seeking to walk around with blue, green and hazel eyes. And let us not forget the numerous forms of plastic/cosmetic surgery: Botox, the face lift, the breast augmentation, the beast reduction, the tummy tuck, the buttock lift, the breast life and the Jewish female favorite (usually at the age of 16 as a "gift"), the rhinoplasty (nose job). In many cases cosmetic surgery will get her the man of her dreams (translation: a rich one) and she can live that white picket fence (or gated community) lifestyle that will, in turn, make her the envy of her siblings and the apple of mommy and daddy's eye.

And to make sure that she dresses the part of a slut, male-run companies are making a killing: there's the Wonder Bra, Spanx, Frederick's of Hollywood and Victoria Secret. All this for men who jump on her and get a nut in about 45 seconds. But it's the thought – and the bank book – that count. And the more skin she shows the more she can seduce the male of the species into providing free social outlets called "dates" (actually, its more like "turning a trick"). The shorter the dress, the more breasts she can reveal from the top of her deep-V blouse, the better.

And don't forget the new wave where the mini-skirt is no longer enough: now with the advent of the thong, the skirts are shorter and can even include a slit up the front or side. Add to this the 8-inch stiletto heels and the blouses where huge revealing holes reveal the elbows, lower back and the hips, and you have a socially sanctioned strip tease masquerading as fashion.

And another point that people don't seem to notice is her cartoon-like voice. Have you ever heard them talk? It seems like the more intelligent they are, the more like children they sound. There are articles about blondes and one of the things they describe are their narrow noses and their almost childlike thought patterns. Could this be true? Based on my observations from intelligent blondes like Hillary Clinton, Meryl Streep, Greta van Sustrun, Barbara Stanwyk, to the sheer idiocy of Paris Hilton, Heidi Klum, Marilyn Monroe, Cheryl Tiegs, Joy Behar, the Bush twins, and so many more, they sound like wind-up robotic dolls. But they don't have to be blonde to have that silly voice: what about Sarah Palin, Tina Fey, Fran Drescher, and almost every white female news anchor.

In spite of all these physical attributes that lend themselves to a "false femininity, it does indeed appear that image has changed in recent years, and this sex kitten has become more assertive, more confrontative, more crass and in doing so, has become the new white man. But don't get it twisted: even marginal looking white women like Gwyneth Paltrow are deemed "beautiful" by the white man's standards. And far too many so-called "black" men.

A case in point is this bitch Kendra Wilkinson-Baskett and her reality show, "Kendra On Top." She's married to this guy who looks black named Hank Baskett. They've got three little kids together and this bitch acts like she's single. She talks to him like he's a bitch (translation: "mitch"), she texts other guys, got caught kissing another guy and it was all over the internet. Lives in this mansion, and this guy doesn't seem to get the hint. "Even just a 'hey' from another guy from my past turns me the fuck on," she said during one episode. In another segment she said, "This whole traditional thing bores the shit out of me." In short, this blonde, blue-eyed skank "has it all" and this is the prototype. Her marriage is in trouble and she doesn't give a fuck.

Show after show this bitch wines, cries and spills her guts to her white friends. When she doesn't have makeup on, she looks like shit. She talks about being bored and wonders why she laughs about serious things. She laughs right in her husband's face. She explains that when she was in London she felt free and had a gun. And when she got back to the States, the times got "dark." This bitch is a party girl who intentionally set this well-to-do brutha up with three kids. She has a nanny and claims to love the kids. Now she's seeing a psychiatrist, Dr. Shahbaznia. He had an affair back in the day and she hasn't forgotten it. She claims her intentions are not to hurt Hank, but she keeps doing it.

Why? Because she has a reality show and the more conflict, the higher the ratings. This is one side of the new white bitch: open marriage and open legs.

On the flip side of this control freak we find the more aggressive and physically confrontative style. For instance, what else would make a martial arts fighter like Rhonda Rousey talk about fighting boxing champion Floyd "Money" Mayweather?

> To MMA enthusiasts, there's no doubt Floyd Mayweather would get dumped on his head by any of the male UFC champions. But what would happen if the greatest boxer in the world stepped into the cage with Ronda Rousey? The UFC women's bantamweight champ is the alpha female in a sport that encompasses much more than a punching contest. Kicks, knees, takedowns and submissions—these are all aspects of fighting in MMA in which Mayweather hasn't trained. This would explain why Rousey, an Olympic bronze medalist in judo, nonchalantly told Power 106 FM that she could beat Mayweather in an MMA fight (McElroy, 2014).

Oh, a point of clarification. All that hoopla and female bravado about beating a black male boxer and guess what took place when Rousey stepped in the ring with another white female in November of 2015:

> Ronda Rousey is no longer the undefeated UFC champion: She fell to Holly Holm in a Melbourne match on Saturday night, going down by knockout after Holm struck her in the head. Holm and Rousey shared a tense moment ahead of the fight, which was broken up by security. "You're getting your ass kicked tomorrow, and I'm really going to enjoy the beating I give you," Rousey wrote on Instagram ahead of the fight. She was the heavy favorite and Holm's win is one of the most unexpected upsets in UFC history. Rousey, now 12-1, fell in

the second round after a left head kick. Holm, a boxing champion before her UFC career, went in for another punch and the referee intervened. (Mosendz, 2015).

But the white woman's attacks are not just physical. Even the woof tickets that Rousey was selling were more psychological than physical. Remember when the white man brought in a giant to fight Jack Johnson. Johnson kicked his ass. Remember when the white man brought in Gerry Cooney to fight Larry Holmes? Holmes kicked his ass. Remember when much bigger Donny LaLonde fought Sugar Ray Leonard? It was called "for all the gold," and took place in November of 1988. LaLonde was much taller and Leonard was coming out of retirement for a third time and moving up in weight. Leonard destroyed him.

Why else would these white women be given all these super-aggressive television and movie roles where not only do they out-duel men, but they show that they don't need them? Most recently we have "Atomic Blonde," "Laura Croft," "La Femme Nikita," "Wonder Woman" and many others where these white women are outright kicking the white man all up in his ass.

Why else would lesbian behavior like women-on-women kissing and sex be getting more and more popular? The white woMAN is taking over the role formerly occupied by the white male, as he moves up to the status of "demi-god."

Even now in summer of 2015 commercials are being aired for Contenelle toilet paper, convincing white women to "go commando." This means walk around with no draws on (as if pussy, even with panty shields and douche, didn't already have odor-related issues). Even now they're selling lingerie on television through a website called AdoreMe.com, where these women can order bras and panty sets. All designed to promote the façade of femininity when, in reality, they are really women.

Anyway, they call it "girl power" as they break records and accomplish various "firsts," but I don't see these bitches as "girls." I don't see them as traditional women either. They know what they're doing, they have game, they don't have much respect for males and they're out for themselves. Hence, my new term for her: woMAN.

Not only is she the new Black woman in spirit (certainly not in soul), she tans her skin, has makeup to make sure that she stays brown, has Underalls to simulate having an ass, has pushup bras galore, gets her lips injected with collagen so she can have the perpetual "pouty mouth," steals urban language so she can sound hip, and practices all she can so that she can convince people she can dance.

The fact is, she has always been the (procreative) key to the oppressive system, but in the past her actions may have been more covert. But who was sitting there during slavery? Who was staring out the front door as enslaved blacks worked from "can't see in the morning 'til can't sleep at night" on the plantation? Who was standing there with whitey to block the school house doors and make sure niggas didn't get in? She's always been there to send the boys off to war, and that includes the war against niggas.

Don't get me wrong: she's still white politically, ideologically and culturally. A recent spate of reports on CNN titled, "Trump and Women Voters" proves that some 60% of those polled liked the remarks Trump was making, including the insults aimed at women. These white bitches who want to be black in spirit and skin color, are the new white man with female bodies. No, they are not transgender; they are simply more committed to their whiteness than they are to any "ism."

The white woMAN (spelling intended) is an oppressor in her own right and in many cases, has the law on her side. She's a female physically speaking, but in every other way she has become a vindictive male-oriented oppressor that is serving notice on everyone else in the world. Just as he had James Bond and other womanizers using "dick power" to seduce and control women and get information from them, she has replaced him with "pussy power" and is now doing the same thing to gain power, access to power and information. The white woman is the new white man in temperament, purpose and direction.

In fact, she's being treated as such. As CNN reported on August 19, 2015, women can now be Navy Seals if they meet the requirements. On the same day it was announced that two women had made it through the strenuous Ranger School. Who, but the white woman would dare to be a part of the system where men not only outnumber her, but will harass her and if they think they can get away with it, rape her? She is the new white man in terms of mentality and it's only a matter of time that she matches him in physicality.

Already, she's challenging men in more ways than one. On March 5, 2014, the following challenge was issued by Rhonda Rousey, a white female Mixed Martial Arts champion. Check it out:

Need I say more? These white women are slowly but surely integrating themselves into the jock straps of what was at one time a male domain! And it's not only in the military and sports.

A "female Viagra" pill was approved in August of 2015. This "pink pill" is designed to help improve sexual desire in women, and check this out: unlike Viagra that works on boners and nutsacks, this pink pill works on the woman's "brain" and addresses sexual disorders and dysfunction. Women don't need any pills, man; even the most pathetic of losers among them can gap their legs and engage in sex whenever they want to! But that's not enough; in August of 2015 they started airing commercials to get more men to buy Viagra. The commercial begins with women claiming that they want to "cuddle," but that's not Viagra is for! They want to get you on that couch, get your dick hard and then make sure you bust a nut in them so they can set you up with a pregnancy! The result? Eighteen years of child support, marriage or not!

The fact is, the white woman – the new white man – is paving the way for the "transformation" that I allege exists. And her force and influence, like her options in life and her legs in many cases, are opening wider on a daily basis.

It's about control on all levels. For instance, during a September 24th edition of "CBS This Morning," author Jill Schlesinger stated that women make three-fourths of all household purchasing decisions. She quipped at the end of her interview that, "my mother used to say [in reference to the household division of money] 'what's mine is mine and what's his is mine'. That's the way most women, including black women, have felt about household finances for centuries.

Even now there's a commercial by Experian that shows a blonde plopping her feet on a bank officer's desk (while her husband looks sheepishly on) and informs the bank official that she already knows what her credit score is. The bank officer is amazed at her knowledge, and he agrees to her terms. Then, as she walks out of the building, husband in tow, the narrator continues kissing her ass.

On September 14, 2014, Sen. Kirsten Gillibrand appeared on CBS' "Face the Nation" to talk about her new book, *Off the Sidelines*. What she said and what the book contains buttresses my belief that the white woman is the new white man.

What is she talking about? The white man talks about issues the way he sees them and rarely ever included the white female. Now that he's moved on to "demi-god" status and left the role of white male to her, she's doing the same thing. All of a sudden the struggle is about "women" (and when they say women they mean white women) and how to get more power, be heard, protest and so on. And what is it for? There ain't no black women on their agenda: it's about white women getting more than they've already got. They appear to be just as power hungry as their man is. In both cases they believe that they speak for everyone when they say "we," "us" or "women."

It was at one time referred to as "the old boys network," those fuddy duddies who sat there making decisions that influenced millions of lives. Now he's elevated his status to the level of "demi-god,' and the "old boys network" has become "the white girl's network" because it transcends age. White women from all backgrounds benefit from the fact that they lack skin color (white privilege) and have marketed it into a key to their power. She's the new white man and is not afraid to make it plain: back are the skin bleaching creams that promise to " make your skin clear" while deeming anything dark on your skin as a "blotch," and back are the stockings, bras and undergarments whose color is called "nude" or "flesh" – as if everyone's skin color is the pinkish color of hers. The white man may have created it, but she's marketing and benefiting from it.

In simpler terms, the white woman is calling the shots. For instance, the same lust the white man had for women of color she now has for men of color. Well, she's always had it but because of social conventions, had to keep it to herself. But now, under the guise of being "independent" and "liberated," she can suck all the black dick she wants, give birth to all the mulatto kids she chooses to, and date and flaunt whatever black man suits her fancy. You might call this the "Kim Kardashian Syndrome." She will have no problem picking one up: black men seem to find white women, no matter how ugly, simply irresistible. In simpler terms she can have free sexual choice just like the white man had during slavery. She is, indeed, the new white man.

She no longer needs him for babies. They've got sperm banks all over the place, and she can do whatever she wants to do with those embryos. She has enough financial wherewithal to adopt any child she wants, and in many cases it is a child of color. Perhaps she knows that little white boys grow up to be racist white men and she doesn't want anyone to threaten her power, and she doesn't want to cope with all that excess baggage when little Johnny comes home having gotten his ass kicked for calling someone a "nigger" or a "spic."

At one time such audacity would be viewed as "sassy" or "uppity." At one time she would have gotten her ass kicked for some of the things she's doing – and thinking - today. Go back a few centuries and she would have been lynched or burned at the sake. But social progress has been to her advantage, and the white man, pussy whipped as he used to be, has stood by why she's racked up college degrees, gone to work and earned her own money, and etched out a philosophy of "fuck you" when she feels like it (that is after she puts into motion her "where do you work" approach).

Although the traditional male role included rape and sexual abuse of women, the white woman accomplishes these things without the use of physical force because there are different types of "force" or coercion: there is economic coercion, social coercion, political coercion and ideological coercion. The later serves as the basis for this role she has assumed and for the power, both latent and manifest, that she now exudes and exhibits.

Look at Hillary Clinton. Do you think this pants suit-wearing bitch is going to be any different than her husband was, or for that matter when it comes to black people, much different than either of the Bush's? She talks all that shit about caring about the poor and about "Black Lives Matter," but that's the same shit her husband did. Once he got in office, he apologized for slavery – something he didn't have the power to do, and then proceeded to lock up more black males than anyone before him with that minimum Federal Guidelines shit. Just recently, in June of 2015, he said he was sorry for having voted for that legislation.

According to the August 5, 2014 edition of the "PBS News Hour," half of all advanced business degrees are now going to women. What does that say for the changing of the guard, impact on economy and the action-oriented/man-like superwoman who is white? Two decades ago I charged that the white woman was simply saying scoot over and let me oppress people with you. She wanted to be the white man's assistant in global domination.

But since that time his maltreatment of her, the gap in the pay scale between white men and white women, his on-going trivialization of her prospects and potential have turned her against him. She not only wants to "wear the pants," but she wants to burn the pair he has on – with him in 'em! And remember: those old white bastards who run corporate America are married to white women. Who do you think takes over and inherits the power if she wants to? Who do you think he tells all his secrets do at night while they're in bed? Who gives him children to train to become new racists? "The hand that rocks that cradle rules the throne."

The July 12, 2004 issue of *Newsweek* is one that has generated controversy because of the manner in which the authors dealt with their topic, "The Secret Lives of Wives." According to their bold faced thesis situated above the article after the preface, "Why They Stray," the statement posits that, *"With the workplace and the Internet, overscheduled lives and inattentive husbands – it's no wonder more American women are looking for comfort in the arms of another man."* This "breakthrough" is nothing that men of color haven't known for some time about white women – who are, after all, the numerical majority in this country.

Therefore, I am in full agreement with Darlene Clark Hine when she wrote,

> At no time in our history have we been in greater need of the wisdom, courage and determination of our Black foremothers. Many black communities today exist in a state of chaos, crisis, and conflict. There is no progress without survival, and our survival is currently precarious. However, at the risk of sounding sanguine, I believe there is power in history. To tap the hidden reservoirs of power, we must listen to the voices and look into the lives of the women who have brought us this far. In order to ensure that a new American history includes us all, it is imperative that we look at the face of our past (Hine, 2000: B100).

Maybe the words of the great civil rights activist Fannie Lou Hamer is a good way to end this section of my analysis for all concerned. She once said, "The only thing you have to do that's important in life … is just go on being your own normal, black, beautiful selves as women, as human beings." Because of the conditions we live under, and the precarious situation of most black families. It may well be too late. These black women are imitating the white woman, from the fake hair and the makeup to the fucked up "man-hater" attitudes.

In simpler terms, the white woman cometh ...

Politics

What I refer to as "The politics of "tears and the law" is a weapon that women have come into in recent years. Time was you could slap the shit out of one of them and that was that. But now, with this white woman using her pussy power and expanding it into the political arena, you can't even touch a woman and expect not to go to jail. In fact, they've taken it a step further: find a man they don't like, and then set him up to violate a restraining order or, for that matter, to simply enter the house. And if that house is in her name, she can just let out a scream and when the cops come, point at you and charge assault. And off you go. This is politics in its purest form: having the system at your beckon call.

If fact, many states, including Texas, have a law that if there is a call for a domestic issue, "somebody is going to have to go to jail." Even if the man is the victim, in many cases he will go to jail if it is proven that by protecting himself, he pushed her to keep her away. And now they've come up with a new law, which was described on a September 6, 2015 segment of "Dateline on ID" (the Investigation Discovery channel). It's called, "rape by deception." Women can now claim that they were not forcibly assaulted by were taken advantage of if a man pretends to be someone he's not. That makes all men guilty, in my book! But this is what happens when you concoct a bullshit myth of "the weaker sex" to use as a tool to control a female. She comes back, via the legal system, with a vengeance. "Hell hath no fury like love, to hate, turned."

On another level you can see what happens to the few white women who manage to get elected into the system – they are as callous and cold as their white male counterparts. The likes of Michelle Bachman and Sara Palin, and not to be outdone are Nancy Pelosi, Diane Feinstein and Hillary Clinton. For the most part, hawks draped in doves clothing. That is why I refer to them as "woMEN."

In August and September of 2014 there was a big controversy about "sexism in Congress." This might sound like the white women being feminine and being hurt. But no. It's about a masculinized person who wants a bigger piece of the rock. She's not telling her newly deified mate to slow down; she wants more power and she wants to share it. And it's getting to the point where she wants a larger and larger slice of the white supremacy pie. She wants to be recognized and not treated the way she and her white male mate used to treat black people.

The controversy started with one white Congresswoman charging that there is "sexism in the gym." The gym?? Sexism in the Senate? Kirsten Gillibrand in her book, *Off the Sidelines* documents sexist comments from members of the House. One white man told a white woman, "You're even pretty when you're fat." Another said, "Don't lose too much weight – I like my girls chubby" as this particular member of the Senate squeezed her waist. No woman whose been around there is shocked that it is taking place, according to Gillibrand. On "Meet the Press" the same week the discussion was that the sexism in Congress, is generational. What do these women expect?

So this "MeToo" bullshit did not spring up overnight. White folks envy black people and mimic almost everything they do. They advantage they have is that they are pale and can therefore be automatically "credited" with that which they rip off or co-opt. The "MeToo movement" is a white female attempt at what a black woman actually started and then tweaked to make it appear as if it is a civil rights issue. They get attention because so many of them are voters and are married to white men who make decisions. And they took full advantage of it and are now turning it on their pale mate.

At the root of these political antics is the fact that the white woman has come to the realization that when all is said and done, all women need men for is their sperm; impregnate them and the job is done. Many are even refusing child support because, according to these newly "masculinized" white women, men are simply a pain in the ass. And they make a valid point.

The white woman is in control even when the white man trips all over his demi-god status. Take the case of the handling of the Ray Rice case by the National Football League. Rice was suspended "indefinitely," but that was after the league initially only suspended Rice for two games prior to that. Women (read: white women) were appalled and threatened to boycott the League. Roger Goodell, the commissioner of the NFL crumbled and put the male bastion at risk. This demi-god immediately patronized the "new white woMAN" by appointing four white women (read: new white men) to help lead some kind of bullshit commission on "social responsibility." Again: "the hand that rocks the cradle rules the throne" and when it comes to women and their impact on the demi-god's purse strings, "the hand that shakes the pom-pom has the final say."

What about the "politics" of police work?

A woman named Connie Fletcher wrote a book called *What Cops Know: Today's Police Tell the Inside Story of Their Work on America's Streets.* I reviewed it a decade ago (my review was over 250 pages) and following is what Fletcher described based on her interviews with Chicago cops and my interpretation of those findings and how this all relates to the "transformation" that I allege has taken place when it comes to the white woman.

As I wrote, "Moving to the issue of sexism – a twin to the racism that most cops practice, belief in, and work to hide from the white public. Sexism permeates the thinking of every man on earth, but the white man is the one who has institutionalized the degradation of women even in the workplace. That includes criminal justice. Check out what one cop says about his female counterparts:"

> You gotta know when to turn it on and when not to turn it on.
> If you turn it on alt the WRONG time –and there are police
> officers who do that – it escalates things. That's the problem
> with some women police, you know, they want to come on
> and be the hard-ass all the time, they're Jane Wayne, they're
> Dirty Harriet; they think they got something to prove, and it
> ends up just escalating things. It's not good (p. 17).

White women are white first and female second. This may sound harsh, but I make this statement based on their actions. As women first, would they not despise the white man's acts as much as people of color do? As women first would they not expose some of the dirt that he brings home and tells her about? No, she's white first and her job is to work next to "her man" (demi-god) to ensure and maintain white supremacy. She's white first and female second and that's why I alleged that she is the new white man: her "femaleness" is physical only. Read what the cop said in the previous paragraph. Mentally, she is as racist as he has ever been and that's why her children grow up to be racists. Again, "The hand that rocks the cradle rules the throne."

As it relates to the "politics of policing" as I call it, these women are imitating what they see on the street and in the locker room; they imitate what they hear during roll call and it is clear that the more "hard" you are, the more distant you are, the more hate you can show toward "those other people," the more respect you get from the white male. They may have had a father, uncle or brother who was or is a police officer. They feel they must prove themselves and that means being as much like the white male officer as possible.

Besides, most of the female cops are white and they are just as racist as their man is; they cling to the same myths and stereotypes as the white male. The only difference is gender. And some of these women even incorporate the sexist beliefs that the white man has circulated about them (in the same way that some black people suffer from what Dr. Roderick W. Pugh called "adaptive inferiority").

One female cop told Connie Fletcher in Fletcher's 1990 book, *What Cops Know:*

> Women have limitations. I'd be the first to admit it. We're
> not as strong as men. But—as a woman you can do things. I

remember we were driving through Lincoln Park one night, and I was sitting on the lap of one of the guys I work with. We were laughing, but we were working. We sat there like a couple watching someone break into a car. And he knew we were right there; didn't pay any attention to us. I'm sitting in my partner's lap. I have my arm around him, and I'm talking into the police radio I' m holding behind his head … and they moved on the guy. He just thought we were a couple sitting there, necking (pp. 30-31).

The only "limitations" women have are the ones that the white man (demi-god) places on them. This thing about strength has long since been offset by the coming of technology (and you can add to that her trickery, shrewdness, and "fuck anybody to get what you want" attitude). The white man knows this. So he works on the self-worth of the woman at all levels.

In the case of the female cop quoted earlier, this is but a metaphor as far as I'm concerned. If the white woman wants to be a cop, it begins with the classes she takes where she must study male theories, deal with male teachers and be programmed to believe that justice, whiteness and "maleness" are synonymous.

By the time she reaches the police academy she's in a nearly all-male domain and is treated like a pariah. If she makes it through, she's usually paired with a guy who is trying to fuck her during every minute of down time that they get.

That TV shit where the white man and woman are partners and he goes through this "I don't really notice your tits" bullshit is just that: bullshit. In real life, "Law and Order: SVU"'s Elliott Stabler would have screwed the shit out of his partner, Olivia Benson on "Law and Order: SVU"; Rick Hunter would have bedded Dee Dee McCall on the regular during the seven seasons that "Hunter" ran; Rick Castle, the writer who is teamed with detective/cop Kate Beckett would have fucked her much earlier were it real life (as of the writing of this book they are engaged to be married).

Again, the cop/cadet scenario is but a metaphor for the manner in which the white woman has transformed her pink playmate into a "mitch": *with gifts, gams and ideological game.* A similar method of operation and value system can be found in any system or institution where the white man is in the majority or in charge. And she doesn't complain about it because she wants to share the power.

<u>Popular Culture</u>

The white man's mythology is permeated with machismo and the suppression of the female. So when you see her begin to boss him around, insult his masculinity – even in the realm of his super heroes – you know that she has now assumed a role that dominates what was at one time the white male domain. And she's got a slew of role models paving the way for her. Her image, like her role politically, culturally, socially and intellectually, has been *masculinized.*

There was an old TV show called "Remington Steele." The show was about a woman who wanted to start a private detection agency, but was not being taken seriously because of the fact that she was female. So she found an office space (luxurious of course – money is never an object) and created an illusory character named "Remington Steele." She found just the "type" and hired him. They got plenty of clients because most customers felt that the place was headed by a man. This is much the same as the image and basis for the white family; everyone thinks the man is the head (and their Holy Bible backs this bullshit) when, in reality, she uses pussy politics on a number of levels to wield the *real* control

This, in essence is the gist of the white woman as action oriented superwoMAN; in essence, the new white male. She takes charge of him and orders him around to the point where he has relinquished his male-oriented role and tasks to assume the higher role of demi-god (see elsewhere in this book). She is now a "man" in the traditional sense of the word, although she still retains female body parts and power hungry attitude.

Back in the day on TV there was Barbara Stanwyck, a beauty who got many roles as a leading lady but was a dyke in real life. But the role that set the stage for the white woman as the new white man were two, in my view: first, as the seductive woman who duped Fred MacMurray into killing her husband in "Double Indemnity" (1944), and then 21 years later (1965) with her role as Victoria Barkley on "The Big Valley."

The reality is now beginning to manifest itself more regularly in the popular culture, especially the movies. Led by Angelina Jolie and her action roles in movies like, "Salt," "Wanted," and "Mr. and Mrs. Smith," she's paving the "I don't need no man" path for others to emulate, the polar opposite of the 1940s and 1950s when "Donna Reed" and "Ozzie and Harriet" set the stage for female passivity. Not only is this white woMAN the new white man, she's even more vicious than he is: not only does she have the power to "sic" him on whomever she hates, but she has her own secret feminine weapons that enable her to do the crime without really doing any real time.

That's right: like their cowardly white male counterparts the white woman has now taken his place in the realm of being assassins and snipers. An upcoming flick called "Cleaners" features not one, but two female assassins. Let us not forget the aforementioned "Salt," "Lucy," and we cannot forget the hit ABC show from a few years back, "Alias," which starred Jennifer Garner. Along similar lines is

"Covert Affairs," which features this blonde named Annie who goes all over the world fucking up men in the name of the U.S. government (art imitating life).

The popular culture projection as the white woMAN as the new white man continues on. How about the CBS program, "The Good Wife," where this woman has all the power and week after week, does what she wants to do no matter what it is. She is no "wife" – she is an intrepid iconoclast that doesn't give a shit about any man, let alone a husband! Even now her power grows as, by October of 2014, she is about to embark on a bid for political office! Today, in a more politically powerful role, CBS is coming out with "Madam Secretary," a show starring Tea Leoni as a secretary of state "with an attitude." During a promo for the show that was aired in August, she's in bed with some guy and she's telling him, "I'm here to make change in the world."

In another promo for "Madam Secretary," as she sashays through her office flipping her blonde hair, one caption reads, "It isn't politics as usual," and a yet another adds, "Defend the nation – by any means necessary." On yet another bravado oriented promo she tells another member of the Cabinet, "I've never met a situation where I don't have a choice in the matter." Finally, while walking down the hall with another official, September 5, 2014 promo for the show has her uttering, "You may have picked up on this, but I'm not big on protocol." Just what this country needs: tits, a short skirt, blonde hair, a menstrual cycle, an attitude and access to the most powerful military in the world!

Now remember that just a few years earlier in 1995) this same woman – Tea Leoni - made a movie with Will Smith and Martin Lawrence called "Bad Boys" where she wore a skimpy hot pants outfit in the entire movie and spent the entire films dick teasing both Will and Martin. Hence, "transformers" - she wants her man's power but she has the dual threat ability to get that power through the legal system, through seduction or by political means ("gifts, gams or ideological game," as I theorized earlier).

By November of 2015 the Sunday lineup on CBS, following "60 Minutes" was, as follows: "Madame Secretary," "The Good Wife," and the new "CSI: Cyber," the latter starring Patricia Arquette. Three white women, all aggressive slut-like power brokers.

Not to be outdone, NBC aired "State of Affairs" featuring another ultra-powerful blonde, Kathryn Heigl. A promo for an upcoming Marvel comic book spin-of (an eight part series), ABCs "Agent Carter," includes the statement, "Sometimes the best man for a job is a woman." See what I'm saying? She's mastered all the masculine and androgynous behaviors, she clearly wants nothing to do with her white mate, and for the most part, he thinks he's too good for her. The white woMAN is the new white man, plain and simple.

When it comes to popular culture it's not just about the white woman exerting themselves in the political arena. It's also about pussy politics combined with the power that comes with it (ala the Biblical Delilah or history's Mata Hari and Cleopatra). In white America TV shows like "Mistresses," "Scandal" and "Revenge" immediately come to mind. And don't forget the secret agent recruit played by Angelina Jolie in the movie "Wanted," the rich ghoul she also played in the movies, "Tomb Raider" (which is now being re-made with a new white women, Alicia Vikander (with the promo poster including her picture in f ront of the huge word "Survive.") Or how about the international assassin Black Widow of the "Avengers" super hero movie?

Then the popular culture invokes the power of these white women (new white men) as cops. There's a show on the Oprah Winfrey Network (OWN) called, "Police Women of Dallas." Now I lived in Dallas for six years and there's two things about the cops: (1) they're stupid and (2) they don't play around. So I don't know what makes these women so special that they have a show based on their gender, but I know that they can't be much different from the white males because they, like their real male counterparts, seem to have a license to kill, one that they are more than happy to use, especially when it comes to Latinos and Blacks.

All these new wave crime fighting bitches have a "don't take any shit" attitude. The woMAN on the show "Stalkers" is hard core and doesn't give her partner the time of day. We already touched on the female on "Law and Order: SVU" who has risen through the ranks and now with her original partner, Elliott (Chris Melroni) gone, Mariska Hargitay's character Olivia Benson, is large and in charge. The first few years some viewers thought she was a dyke because she was so hard core, but now she's been allowed to adopt a child named Moses (don't worry – he's white) and they've humanized her. But she still has an "I don't take no shit" attitude. The new white male personified.

White women, *the new white men,* are being inspired by popular culture to embark on power trips and killing sprees and have the same ends and goals as their man used to before his status was self-elevated to the level of "demi-God." Joanna Coles, editor of *Cosmopolitan* magazine, is taking the magazine into the political realm just in time for the upcoming election. On the September 5, 2014 interview on "CBS This Morning," she claimed that, "Sixty two percent of college intake is young women."

Back in the old days you'd see a white woman slap her man and he'd take it like a punk (except for Humphrey Bogart and James Cagney). She would slap anyone knowing that she was getting her point across because such action was presumed to be her "acting out of character" and as a result, you knew she was angry. Not only has this drastically changed where now she will slap the shit out of anyone, but she is now hitting men with her closed fist and kicking him in the balls. It's becoming so common that it's being deemed as "funny." I don't see anything funny about such action in the face of the society myth that "a man should never hit a woman." If a woman hits me, she's gonna get the shit knocked out of her, plain and simple.

In the movie "Thor: The Dark World ," the so-called demi-god is once again united with the woman he loves (a scrawny earth woman played by Natalie Portman). Upon his return to Earth, he locates her and she's supposed to be happy because he's been gone back to his home, Asgard, for a while. After having expressed the fact that she missed him, she turns around and slaps the living shit out of him, not once but twice. He does nothing about it. He even goes so far as to take her back to Asgard with him and she proceeds to be the basis for its near destruction and the death of his (Thor's) mother (she was defending the earth woman when she got killed). Does Thor hold his earth ho responsible? No.

In the movie "Young Guns II," Billy the Kid and his gang are trapped in a building by an evil land baron and the cavalry. As the situation grows more dire, a man who is a supporter of the Kid tells his wife to leave the house and forces her out for her own good. This red-headed white bitch leaves the house and walks up to the leader of the cavalry. She proceeds to slap the living shit out of him and calls him an "animal." He has her taken away, to where we do not know. But I do know this: there was no counter-slap by this man who was a killer (in the name of the United States) which means that the "never hit a woman" message was alive and well on several levels.

In the movie "Wyatt Earp," the Earps have just finished a shootout with the Clanton gang at the OK corral. They're rehabbing in a room with the Earp wives after one of the Earp brothers has been shot. This particular Earp brother's wife turns to Wyatt Earp (the ringleader and deputy) and says, "I wanted him to leave here but he wanted to stay here with you." Then she slaps the shit out of him. Wyatt Earp has just finished gunning down a group of men, he's got a rifle in one hand and his handy six-shooter strapped to his waist. And this bitch slaps him. If that's not "balls," then I don't know what is.

During a September 9, 2014 episode of "The Young and the Restless," this ex-GI green beret type guy named "Stitch" is sitting at the table with Victoria Newman discussing the baby she's carrying – which might be his. As he's talking Victoria's younger sister, Abbie, walks up behind him and cuffs him upside the head – hard. Not one of those staged soap opera slaps, but an actual cuff, the kind that snaps when you do it right. She had just hired him for a job and was "angry" because he was talking to her sister – who represents a competing fragrance company. What did he do? He didn't do shit but stand up and start arguing with her.

These bitches know who to slap and who to hit. There is no way that a real black man is going to take that shit from her or her mate. But then again, she's white and can get away with almost anything she chooses. After all, she has the white man behind her, submissive as ever, as her willing thrall.

In short, *the white woman has no fear of the white man and has taken his place as the oppressor of all she surveys.* I saw one white woman slap the shit out of Bruce Banner, who she knew could turn into The Hulk at any time. Another one is Mystique of "X-Men" fame. She's a shape-shifting villainess who can transform, even assuming male figures, which is probably the ultimate for these new empowered white women: look like a women but when you need to, assume a male appearance in order to dupe the public. Men have been doing it for years: you can hardly name a white male star of any merit who has not gone "drag" in some movie or TV role. And the white man has been getting black men to do it as well; David Chapelle walked off the set when these peckerwoods tried to get him to put on a dress for a skit. What's wrong with these homoerotic white boys?

In July-August of 2014 Scarlett Johannsen assumed the movie role of "Lucy," some woman that could use almost 100% of her brain (scientists claim that the average human can only use about 10%), and she was wreaking havoc on the scientists that were manipulating her and any other man that stood in her way. Women know they have power, but the white man, who is more committed to and concerned about maintaining control over the world, doesn't give a shit. She rules human beings - he (the white man) rules the planet itself and let him tell it, all of the "known universe."

In September of 2015, a promotion for a new show proves the status of this white woMAN and her new role. The NBC show is called, "Blindspot" and the lead actor, a white woman known only as "Jane Doe" - is billed as "the female Jason Bourne." As part of the promo she is deemed by one of the male officials as "the best chance" for America or something along those lines. Another promo tells us that she cannot remember who she is but then cut to the line where she demands, "I want to see someone in charge!" The perfect white woman: blank slate of a brain, power hungry, aggressive and loaded town with tattoos.

Not to be outdone, ABC is airing "Quantico," about some FBI bitch who is out to look for a snitch inside of the organization. The white woMAN lives! In addition to that little number they have another slated called "Blood and Oil," which pits two white bitches – one who loves her family and another who craves power, both blonde – against one another.

Finally, another example in popular culture and it has to do with the world of sport.

Women learned long ago that men like football and they enjoy watching it. So they boned up on their lingo and learned the game. It was then used as another "tool" to go where the boys are, become one of the gang, and hang around until they can find one who will fuck them. Women are the majority in America so professional sports teams have to tow the line.

The hypocrisy of white folks knows no bounds. So as part of their commitment to "character," sports teams are now concerned about losing fans. So they are passing rules that if you are involved in any domestic violence issues, you (the athlete) will be suspended without pay - meaning loss of hundreds of thousands of dollars -- in some cases, millions. These sports decision makers are also talking about when it comes to drafting players out of college, meaning that if any player has any incidents of domestic violence, then pass him up come draft day because they don't want the female fans on their ass (they spend money on games, too).

Since most of the athletes being drafted are Black males, and since most of them have girlfriends, wives or some kind of significant other, the "deal" that is made, the contract that is extended, has everything to do with how he treats that female -or how she CLAIMS she's treated - and whether or not he's going to make the professional ranks. In most cases she's latched onto him while in college, sucked his dick on a regular basis and put up with his shit – all in preparation for him to turn pro.

If she likes him, has him under control and is in a good mood, then he'll make it. But if he fucks up or she has reported him in the past, right or wrong, if he gets out of line, then he's screwed. In other words these women control the fate and future of the blue chip athlete – during college, during the draft and after he signs the contract. If they so choose, they can *ruin* him.

Does this not mean that the woman is in control? In a sexist society where the man is presumed to be in control of his own life, doesn't this show that SHE is the one in charge? And in fact, based on the way the law is written, hasn't this bitch ALWAYS been in control? Black women – the new white women – have copied the white female's looks and fucked up attitude, but they can't access any real power because of their skin color. But they can roar as if they rule when it comes to the faggotized Black male. And what white women do to the world and to American society, the Black female (the new white woman) does to the black man, every chance she gets.

Under the false veneer of caring about this new and improved white woMAN, professional sports leagues are taking it out on the male athlete. These bitches know what they're doing. They can't whip a man's ass physically, but they sure in the hell will try. Then it court they use their documented evidence that they were simply acting in "self-defense" and that they feared for their lives.

The woman who ran up on Ray Rice knew she couldn't beat him up. What was on this woman's mind? "I'm gonna knock Ray the fuck out?" So she gets her ass kicked (knocked out) and now Rice is fucked and out of a job forever. After the incident he went so far as marry the bitch (why, I don't know), and the white male (demi-god) still didn't cut him any slack. Pretending to give a fuck about women's rights, white boys canned Rice's Black ass. Lucky for Rice the woman was also Black - had it been one of those white bitches, he might have gotten life with no chance of parole!

As in the case of Joe Mixon. Remember him? Here is how the Washington Post's Rick Meese partially reported it in 2017:

> The surveillance camera footage shows Mixon, then a powerful teenage football player, unleash a ferocious punch, sending a young woman to the ground, shattering her face. That's what Mixon did. This is what Mixon now says: that he wishes he could take it all back, and he's thought about that night every day since — what it did to the young woman, what it meant to his school and this community, how it nearly derailed his college career, and how it now casts a cloud over his football future.

But before he fired the white girl up, she walked up on Mixon – who everybody knew was going to turn professional (and he eventually did) pushed him, and tried to take a punch. He responded and this is what happens. This is but an extension of the "sacred white womanhood" that has led to race riots and destruction of entire black towns, not to mention the hundreds (if not thousands) of lynchings of black men.) And what Mixon did followed him on into the pros and there were those white women in the stands with signs and overlooking the fact that the white woman "drew first blood."

If any one of these women, realizing the pro potential (read: millionaire) status of one of these men, and decides to "get' this guy because they found out that he has another woman on the side, or might have prematurely ejaculated on the pussy one time too many, these women can wreck that man's future. They can have him on his knees begging, "oh please, baby please!" so he won't lose his job, his money and his status. She now has that kind of power. And don't think these bitches are beyond blackmail or bribery: they've been setting men up for centuries with that "you got me pregnant" and "the baby is yours" bullshit. A recent on line article written by a professional prostitute said that up to 25% of married NBA players have been blackmailed at one time or another. So engaging in the actions I just outlined is not beyond their moral compass.

The white woman is taking over, replacing the white man as the world's dominant oppressor. Television cop/detective shows like "Castle" and "Bones" (and more recently "Law and Order: SVU") show the white woman large and in charge and, while falling for the white man, still dominates not only her profession, but also the home life. She is independent and there is never any leeching for bill money and every time they go out, he pays. He has become her ho, her bitch, her willing thrall -- whether he wants to admit it or not. And this brings me to my closing point.

This bitch is taking over with HIS help. There are a number of examples, but let me give you one that I've noticed. In my book, these dating websites and all that shit – it's just an economic engine that this bitch can use to hook this pussy-whipped asshole into financing her future, getting into debt and then when she feels like it, divorce his ass and get half his shit.

Check out how lonely these white men (and their negro lackeys) must be, busily pursuing the woMAN. They've got E-Harmony, Zoosk, and Match.com, just to name the most popular ones. And basically what is it: white men and negroes searching the web for pussy. Some of the sites claim that they are about long-term relationships, but once again, that depends on how good the pussy is. These women can lie and fake orgasms all day long and trick any man into believing that "she's the one." But what is a date in America? For the most part it's the man taking this bitch anywhere she wants to go, and the more expensive, the better. He pays because in America, it's the "gentlemanly thing to do."

And all the while this over-rated, egotistical bitch is thinking of herself. A national commercial aired on TBS is for a new perfume called, "Si." As you know "si" means yes in Spanish. This white bitch tells viewers, "si to life, si to freedom, si to seduction, si to us, si to love" and now, get this: *si to myself.* And after all when it comes to women in general and these Barbie dolls in particular, isn't this what it's all about?

So he's hunting for pussy, she knows it and she makes him grovel for it. It takes more than one date (one website tells you, "Like comes before love") because in that way she can find out if he has the financial wherewithal to be considered for the long term. If this woman just wants a casual relationship, does this mean that she will pay? Hell no! Oh, some of them will go through the motions and talk that "let's go dutch" shit, but it's a front. The more they pretend that they don't want that man's money the more likely they are to get it.

I include sick negroes on this list as well because there are some left who aren't fags. They do whatever whitey tells them and I would have to say many (most?) of them are cruising the internet looking for white bitches. The word is out that she's weak minded and easy to fuck (most will suck your dick before they'll shake your hand), but that has nothing to do with physical attraction or finding a "match." It has to do with pacification and placation. As long as you pay, that's more money they'll have to stockpile and save it for a rainy day. That's the key to power: long-term thinking. Men are after pussy and power, she's after power, period. Besides, many of them are sucking more pussy than any man could ever hope to. They just keep it on the downlow.

The Pimp/Prostitute Relationship Re-Defined

In the previous chapter I outlined numerous popular culture examples of the white woman, on television and in film, being able to slap the living shit out of her man and never fear retaliation. This is a metaphor for what she has been doing in her perpetual exploitation of the "never hit a woman" ethic that men, for some reason, have elevated to the level of a social norm and a second belief that she is "the weaker sex." Nothing could be further from the truth.

Research enables one to light a flame that can lead to enhanced knowledge. Such was the case when I came across an article in the New York Times titled, "Stockholm Syndrome in the Pimp-Victim Relationship." A light came on as I had been writing about the Stockholm Syndrome as an explanation as to why black people are so forgiving of the people who enslaved them for over 350 years. But this article went to the heart of this book, "I Got to Get in Touch With My Mitches" because as the new person in charge, the white woman is truly involved in a set of relations that smack of "the Stockholm syndrome."

Hence, the "re-definition" of both the pimp-prostitute relationship as it relates to the American scenario and also a look at the Stockholm Syndrome where victims end up falling in love with or admiring their former abductors. Following is the text of that article with my analyses, applications and metaphorical explanations being interjected as it relates to the white female's control and why she stays in contact with her "mitches."

Before we get into the gist of the article, let me provide you a little background on the Stockholm Syndrome, why it is so named, and what took place inside of that bank back in 1973:

> [In 1973] … Jan-Erik Olsson, a convict on parole, took four employees of the bank (three women and one man) hostage during a failed bank robbery in Kreditbanken, one of the largest banks in Stockholm, Sweden. He negotiated the release from prison of his friend Clark Olofsson to assist him. They held the hostages captive for six days (August 23–28) in one of the bank's vaults while torturing them with nooses and dynamite. When they were released none of them would testify against either captor in court; instead they began raising money for their defense … (Adorjan, et. al., 2016).

In case you haven't recognized it yet, it is clear that this is what we call "some white folks' shit." There is no way that Black people are going to be subjected to that kind of degradation and not do something about. Although a poor example, you see how we kicked the white man all up in his ass once we got out of enslavement! At any rate, identification with the oppressor is a common excuse by these white people. A white woman, Patty Hearst, also used it when she got "freed" after being "kidnapped" by the Symbionese Liberation Army. Again, as someone in the Bay Area at the time it was clear that Cinque and those bruthas turned this bitch out, had her robbing a bank, got caught with a machine gun in her hand inside of the bank, and still came out looking like some kind of vestal virgin.

So that's what it is. And that is why the pimp-prostitute relationship, in so many instances, is comparable. And that is why I chose the article that follows as an example of how the white woman has flipped that relationship and is now using it in her own image and interests.

The article by Kitroeff (2012) begins, thusly:

> If you want to understand why girls who are sex-trafficked don't run straight to the police, Withelma Ortiz, known as T, could tell you a thing or two. The 22-year-old has a pretty good grasp on the issue — having been first sold for sex at age 10. (Kitroeff, 2012).

Now, as a metaphor we now have the beginning of the pity party. Sure, the girl is young, but she has an active brain stem. There is no doubt that she knows what she's doing and she has a plan. Sheh has a good grasp on the issue now that it's over, but it is my position that she had a more than adequate "grasp" on the issue when she decided to hang out with a grown ass man when she was but ten years of age. The saga continues:

> T was 10 years old when she met a man who said he could change her life. She had told him that she'd essentially been in foster care since birth, living with families that sexually and psychologically abused her. He was appalled. He said he wanted to take care of her. He would feed her, clothe her, take care of her when she was sick. "He basically told me that I could survive," T recalled. "You know, when nobody cared what happened to me, nobody cared what was going on with me, I could survive." T's biological father was in jail, and her biological mother was nowhere to be found. She was not about to turn down the first person who ever tried to make that kind of connection with her. (Kitroeff, 2012).

After the pity party come the specifics: in this case she's been raised in the foster care system which in my view is a haven for perpetuation of deviant behavior. The foster families in far too many cases are taking kids in for the money and the treat them like shit. The kids know a good thing when the see it and, like the white woman, they flip the script. They turn the foster parents in and claim that they were "abused." And the cycle continues and the kids continue to get over like a fat rat on a piece of cheese.

Furthermore, because her parents were not available, she had to adopt a survival strategy. And foster care was it. She was being taken care of. She didn't have to hang out with some grown man. But he was slick and probably told her she could make a bunch of money and that's all she cared about. This is another metaphor for the white female: as long as she's being taken care of and is made to feel secure, she could care less what happens to the people that her "protector," the white male, screws over. She's right there with him, gaining his confidence and doing what has to be done, no matter how degrading, to keep getting paid. The pimp-prostitute has been born: selling ass one hand and controlling the "man in charge" on the other.

Moving on:

> In a way, the man was right: He did change her life. He began selling T for sex across the West Coast. It turned out that her youthful "tween" body was a major selling point, and he demanded that she meet a quota of a thousand dollars a night. "The chains around the mind, the captivity of the mind, it started there," she said. "But it got to a place in which my physical life was threatened." Her pimp would beat her mercilessly — but then would beg for her forgiveness. This was unusual for T. She was used to caretakers beating her, but no one had ever been sorry for it. "Somebody finally beats the crap out of you and then comes back and kisses it and says, 'I want to make it better.' " To a 10-year-old T, this was love. (Kitroeff, 2012).

The metaphor continues as "T" talks about the chains around her mind and the captivity of it. She knew what she was doing and it didn't take much. Men prematurely ejaculate on her, she gives up some head, and walks out with big bucks. How is this any different from the American housewife and the "norms" that they accept and practice every single day that they're married?

Now, the point that pimp supposedly "beat her mercilessly." Again, the metaphor rings true. These house wives have been taking ass whippings for centuries. In fact, there are three Biblical sayings that come to mind. First, Ephesians 5:22-24 where it states, "Wives, submit to your husbands as to the Lord. For the husband is the head of the wife as Christ is the head of the church, his body, of which he is the Savior. Now as the church submits to Christ, so also wives should submit to their husbands in everything." Second, Exodus 21, verses 20-21: "If a man beats his male or female slave with a rod and the slave dies as a direct result, he must be punished, but he is not to be punished if the slave gets up after a day or two, since the slave is his property. And finally, check out 1 Peter, 2:13: "If a man beats his male or female slave with a rod and the slave dies as a direct result, he must be punished, but he is not to be punished if the slave gets up after a day or two, since the slave is his property."

To this day these ministers promote this bullshit and the Black churches across the nation are 65% women. They listen to and believe this shit. That is prostitute related thinking, but they know that when they get home they will immediately adopt the role of pimp. They know that in the church is where they can meet a man (or so they think) who is moral and that means he can be controlled. So the prostitute is once again the pimp.

Back to the story of "T":

> After five years of this abuse, her pimp was arrested on sex-trafficking charges. But it took T years to realize that he could no longer hurt her. And when he was put on trial, she refused to testify against him. She regrets that decision deeply, but is very clear about why she made it: "One word," she told me bluntly. "Stockholm syndrome." (Kitroeff, 2012).

So all this abuse and she refuses to testify against him. What she's not saying is that she was probably threatened by some of the other women in the stable or perhaps some of the pimp's male acquaintances. Whatever the reason she didn't say anything and in the mind of the courts, "silence is consent."

Metaphorically the white woman only testifies against her man if the time has come to enter the next phase of pimpdom. She can't do it the first couple of times because he will seen "payback" and it might jeopardize any future access she might have to the bank account. So she has to be mellow, keep quiet, and act as if she believes him when he says, "It won't happen again" or "look what you made me do."

Now comes the pseudo-intellectual "rationale" for T's behavior.

> The psychological manipulation involved in T's relationship with her pimp seems to be a common feature of sexual exploitation in America. Pimps prey on vulnerable girls and women, using a cunning mix of violence and tenderness to alternately degrade and then elevate them. The result is that these girls and women become psychologically attached to their pimps, and do not turn against them out of a dependency that is equal parts fear and misplaced affection. (Kitroeff, 2012).

Metaphorically, what you just read can be compared with the feminist argument against men, in general. You can see versions of the "vulnerable girls"/bullying men" argument used in courtrooms all over the nation, In some cases these arguments are used after the woman has killed the man, who she paints as the bane of her existence.

Kitroeff claims that the responses to the pimp is a matter of "equal parts fear and misplaced affection." That is bullshit. It's like the white coed who goes to college and starts dating black athletes and giving black men head. Using the tricks that we taught her, she can then use them on white men, turn them out, graduate and get married and then move into a gated community across town from "those niggers." I've seen it time and time again in California's Bay Area, in Milwaukee, in Dallas and in Omaha. There is no "fear" after they get away, but there may be some residual affection because, as they say, "once you go black, you never go back." Not all the way, that is.

The reason for this white woman's on-going attraction to the black man may be in the theory offered by Calvin C. Herton in his book *Sex and Racism in America.* His shakey theory is that the dominant class is the white male, alone. Then in the "semi-oppressed class" the black man and white women share. At the bottom is the black woman. He thinks that the sharing of that "semi-oppressed class" status creates an attraction between white women and black men.

But in the world of the new white male – where the white woman is in charge – bruthas can forget that shit. Sperm is the last thing the white woman has time for in her climb to the top and her arduous task to stay there. She knows that sex is a leisure activity and there is no time foreplay – not if she wants to pick up the crown of the oppressor formerly held by her white mate.

Skipping past the slave trafficking stuff, let's go to the end of the article where again, we can make a metaphorical juxtaposition:

> T's story has a happier ending. When I first met her in New York
> City, she gave me a bright pink business card. Just under her name in
> small print, it reads: "Advocate/Activist/Go-Getter." T is an
> ambitious woman with an undeniable will to survive, and those
> descriptors fit her perfectly. After seven years of being sold to men,
> she managed to escape that life, and even get her high school
> diploma. (Kitroeff, 2012).

And that's how it ends: mass marketing translating into empowerment through some type of nonprofit grant funded program. She'll go out on the lecture circuit and share her story and even if she doesn't influence anyone, she'll still get paid. See? Now who's the pimp? Now who's in it for the money? Now who's using the gift of gab to generate a revenue stream? The prostitute morphs into the pimp and vice-versa. And it gets better:

> Now her eyes are set on college. T's dream is to get a degree in mass communication, and perhaps even spend a semester studying abroad in Puerto Rico, where her father's family still lives. She has even started a campaign – T Goes to College 2013 – to raise funds to cover tuition. (Kitroeff, 2012).

The perfect metaphorical ending for the former prostitute-pimp, akin to the scenario I pained earlier regarding the white college coed. The black man and "the streets" give them enough game to obtain "unique" status among their white peers. These white women can then be looked up to by their fellow race members and as T shows above, achieve whatever they want to. Once they do, they are then in a position where they can be independent enough to exercise the option of being a pimp (which they already are because they're pimping the system) or a prostitute, another word for housewife.

In sum,

> When I asked her what she wanted to do after college, T said she would always continue her advocacy work for sex-trafficking victims and foster children. But she didn't want to commit to a career just yet. "I don't want to limit myself," she explained. And that, you can be sure, she won't. (Kitroeff, 2012).

The key words: "I don't want to limit myself." But who gave her the experience and the options to arrive at that conclusion? The person who she tried to say treated her so badly who she then would not testify against. It is clear that not all of those experiences were harmful or bad and the fact that she is around to move on with her life proves her intestinal fortitude.

And that is a characteristic all women have: guts and courage. You cannot carry life around for nine months or give birth to a child and not be a very strong creature. Even if you don't have children you are raised in a society where you are viewed as a second class citizens. Even if you're a white woman you are forced to find a white man to "adopt" you. And that is where they begin the pimp-prostitute transformation; once they get "adopted" in some capacity – even if it's by the streets the way "T" was – they have one foot in the door.

As the children's poem goes, "First comes love/then comes marriage/then comes the white woman with the baby carriage." And that is what we are going to delve into next? Procreation and the role it plays in the new way that women "get in touch with their mitches."

Birth Control and the Paradigm of "Sex for Sex's Sake"

Since it is a fact of no meagre importance that "the hand that rocks the cradle rules the throne," then it only follows that pregnancy manipulation and the power to decide when a birth will take place only makes that power over life and death even more intense and powerful.

To begin with know that men are very insecure and in my view, I believe we are jealous of the female's power to bear children. The closest we can come is planting the seed and as a result you still see men beaming and boasting about "being pregnant" meaning that they have a child on the way. This overriding sense of pride of ushering a child into the world is at the base of the white man's fear of being genetically annihilated. Dr. Frances Cress Welsing made this point rather emphatically when she charged that the white man suffered from a sense of not only genetic inferiority (he cannot produce a child of color unless it is with a person of color) but also from what she called "a sense of numerical inadequacy." Here is how Dr. Welsing put it in her incredible essay, "The Cress Theory of Color Confrontation":

> The Color-Confrontation theory further postulates that whites are vulnerable to their sense of numerical inadequacy. This inadequacy is apparent in their drive to divide the vast majority of non-whites into fractional, as well as frictional, *minorities*. This is viewed as a fundamental behavioral response of whites to their own minority status. The white "race" has structured and manipulated their own thought processes and conceptual patterns, as well a those of the entire non-white world majority, so that the real numerical minority (whites) illusionally feels and represents itself as the world's majority, while the true numerical majority (non-whites) illusionarlly feels and views itself as the minority (Welsing, 1974 – emphasis original).

Long ago white people were aware that their numbers were dwarfed by people of color, especially from Asia and Africa. In 1968 Dr. Paul Erlich published a book called *The Population Bomb*. He was a biologist but his concerns were racist in my view: basically what he said was that "niggas are going to eat up all the food"! Before him there was Thomas Malthus, whose 1798 book, *An Essay on the Principles of Population* said the same thing. Now these two books were almost two centuries apart, were "concerned" about the same thing.

My point is that if they had an idea about the numbers, then they had the racial breakdowns as Dr. Welsing surmised. And they saw it as a threat to the white race. They knew they were genetically inferior and as a result, they had to have more white kids while at the same time, impacting negatively on the birth rates of kids of color. Do you think they are "saddened" when white kids are born out of wedlock? Of course not. Even their terminology about "rosy cheeks" and the like is a white nationalist indicator. But they have been able to do something about controlling the birth rates of children of color.

So in addition to my claim of "sex for sex's sake" is the simultaneous genocidal attempts against people of color. Who has America been bombing and fighting against in its most recent wars? Nations of color, brown people for the most part. Whose very language denotes a negative vibe against anything that is not white? Black cats bring bad luck, blackmail is a crime, a blackheart is a bad person and at the same time, blondes have more fun, angel's food cake is white and a "white lie" (as was a recent claim by Trump publicist Hope Hicks) is only an innocent or tiny one. Language is a reflection of thought and if you are afraid of color, then it's going to be reflected in your art, your culture, your literature and so on.

When the white woman sat by as her man continued to show his "bitch-like" ways – from the powdered wigs in European courts to his popular culture tendency to want to dress up like women and impose this foolishness on black men as well (as David Chapelle revealed), he shows what he is. He's been jealous of her from the outset and is even now working to replace her in his science labs so he can produce life without her presence. So the concept of "sex for sex's sake" is being slowly changed to "procreation at all costs."

When I taught sociology at the University of Nebraska-Lincoln, one of the areas that we delved into late in the semester was a discussion of the role of technology on human interaction. One of the topics covered was the "technological fix." As examples the text used the birth control pill. According to the authors (Donald Keller & Suzanne Light), the 'free love' movement of the 1960s made men and women more relaxed when it came to "free sex" and there was a population boom. As a result the birth control pill was created and once women began taking it, there was more relaxation but the pill was not 100% effective. The boom continued until white women went to Congress to protest its oral use.

Long story short: the more talk about birth control there was, the more stable the continued birth of children became. White women knew this because they were probably among the first to play games with the pill: pretending to take it when they really didn't, telling their men they were "safe" and then set them up for more pregnancies.

So from "sex for sex's sake social controls were put in place where the birth population could be somewhat limited to whites only. Women of color continued to have children but look at the risks: the highest infant mortality rates of all racial groupings and I charge that this is by design. The more impoverished you are the more likely your child is to be negatively impacted. White people have a history of eugenics campaigns and sterilization of women and men of color, so this is not some far-fetched notion.

The white woman was in the driver's seat. Her needs were taken care of by a society that enabled her and provided resources. Women of color have to live in fear not only for becoming pregnant, but they have to worry about their daughters and sons every time they walk out that door and head down the street. The police are no protection – they are a part of the problem. Look at the prisons where far too many black men and boys are being "housed." And look at the black fashions of the 21st century: blurred lines by young boys in skinny jeans, earrings and video game obsessions. The black girl is fending for herself, so if she gets pregnant, her child is more likely than not going to be another poverty statistic.

Why am I writing this words and making these allegations? The real question to ask is why the people who know are not and have not already made them! These peckerwoods know a basic fact: white people, in general, do not like black people, in general. Sure, they will steal our cultural art forms and admire us on the dance floor and athletic field, but those are categories that we've been "allowed" to excel in because the white man controls the purse strings at the end of these ventures! Who controls the distribution of the music? Who controls Hollywood? Who owns the stadiums and mega-auditoriums on college campuses and in the professional ranks? Who has the power to make an example of incredible athletes like Colin Kaepernick and banish him from the sport he excelled in?

The white boy, that's who.

The reason why Trump is hated by the so-called liberal establishment and the progressives is because he is bringing into fruition and stating the anti-black sentiments that most of them believe but are too gutless to make public! They are angry not because he's promoting the white supremacist agenda, but because he's running the risk of pissing off all these niggas and fomenting and inciting a racial revolt!

The "mitchification" of men has been very successful. In my book *The Black Athlete as House Negro* (Amazon.com), I outline how the most visible and powerful black men, the potential sowers of the seed of life, are really nothing more than uniformed clowns "performing" like court jesters for the entertainment of white families. The white man will even allow his woman to sit in the stands and applaud the actions of black men doing things the white man could never do. That is because he knows and she knows that all of those touchdowns, slam dunks and world record sprinting records are all being controlled by the white race in general and the United States of America, in particular.

In the past children were the key to contributing strong backs and arms to the tribe and its development. That has since evolved with the advent of technology, but the need is still there. The white race is disappearing and the one who carries life for that race – the white woman – is well aware of that. Therefore it is both a racial and cultural imperative that she snatch the reins from her effeminate mate and show him how it's done, a form of "a kinder and more subtle oppression."

And it is for this reason, among others, that she "needs to get in touch with her 'mitches'."

How Women Get Laid and Paid: A Socio-Historical and Political Analysis

<u>Preface</u>

On July 27, 2016 Democratic Presidential nominee Hillary Clinton became the first woman to ever get the nomination of a major political party. After it was announced, she said, by satellite, "I can't believe we just put the biggest crack in that glass ceiling yet!" That glass ceiling should have never been there in the first place because women have been running shit all the time, but were just forced to keep it under wraps because men are so bitch-like and thin-skinned. And the "crack" that these women used to gain power was the one between their legs. Historically, women have been able to "get laid and paid." Following are but a few examples of the "laid and paid" motif in popular culture.

In the 1944 flick "Double Indemnity, " Barbara Stanwyk (a dyke in real life) seduces an insurance salesman because she wishes her husband was dead. She talks the salesman into helping her kill the man so she can collect. The concept of "double indemnity" refers to refers to a clause in certain life insurance policies that doubles the payout in rare cases when death is caused accidentally, such as while riding a railway." And that is how they killed him, but the salesman is blamed and kills her for setting him up.

Fast forward sixteen (16) years. In the 1960 movie "The Facts of Life," two married people are having an affair. They have not yet agreed to tell the people they are married to, but the woman (Kitty, played by Lucille Ball) has brought it upon herself to leave her husband by good-bye note. Later, as she and her lover Larry Gilbert are headed for their hideaway cabin for a three-day weekend, she tells Larry about it. Remember, this movie was made almost six decades ago.

In the 1996 movie, "A Strange Affair," Judith Light says at one point to her daughter: "Every wife has to invent her own life." These two examples of two ways that white people have created a "new normal" and in doing so, despite the male façade, have handed the power, the money and the family over to the female. Although he is all for it, that is not really the issue.

The issue is for you to see how many women have always and continue, to make major decisions based on what they want and how they figure things and then impose it on the male. Kitty did it twice: once to her husband with the letter and then to Larry. Now he's in a "no choice" situation; she imposed her will on him and did what she felt was "best for them both." These women have been using their knowledge (that they kept hidden from their male associates) and have been getting laid and paid, on one form or another, long before the first movie about it was ever made.

Some peckerwood knew about it as far back as so-called Biblical times. They put the weakening of Samson on Delilah because she is rumored to have cut his hair, which was the source of his power. But that part of the myth is bullshit. She summoned barbers to do the actual cutting, which is still a form of ultimate seduction and manipulation on her part. But even in those days the female was given the benefit of being clever, conniving and visionary.

This new-found confidence is long overdue and is perhaps best summed up in the lyrics from Alicia Keys' 2008 hit, "Superwoman." In part, it goes something like this:

Everywhere I'm turning
Nothing seems complete
I stand up and I'm searching
For the better part of me
I hang my head from sorrow
State of humanity
I wear it on my shoulders
Gotta find the strength in me

I am a Superwoman
Yes I am
Yes she is
Even when I'm a mess
I still put on a vest
With an S on my chest
Oh yes
I'm a Superwoman

For all the mothers fighting
For better days to come

And all my women, all my women sitting here trying
To come home before the sun
And all my sisters
Coming together
Say yes I will
Yes I can
I am a Superwoman
Yes I am
Yes she is

… When I'm breaking down
And I can't be found
And I start to get weak
Cause no one knows
Me underneath these clothes
But I can fly
We can fly, ooh
I am a Superwoman …

But there's another side. In the same movie mentioned earlier, the goodbye note that she left for her husband. She flies back home to take it back but he's already there. He comes in and he's having a drink. The child is crying in the other room but before she goes to see about it, she asks her husband, who has the envelope with the note in it still sealed, to toss it in the fireplace. She goes into the other room to check on the child and this trick does just that: he doesn't open it to see what it says, he just blindly tosses it on the fire.

Superwoman. *Gettin' laid and getting' paid.* And as I've made clear in this book, with all that power and influence she can still whine, cry and lie with the best of them.

So just as women manipulate situations and dominate without being "dominative," men are childlike thralls and, for the sake of pussy, do just about anything to get themselves a "girlfriend," "a woman," "a fiancée" and then of course the final scam, "a wife.

This philosophic scenario fits women and their roles in setting up, maintaining and controlling relationships, by way of getting "laid and paid," like a glove.

Not a few people have heard the maxim, "When life gives you lemons, make lemonade." This is supposed to encourage people to be optimistic and have a "go get 'em attitude" about whatever it is they are pursuing. This saying is the perfect way to describe the philosophies of most women when it comes to "getting laid and getting paid." And I'm going to explain to you how I arrived at this conclusion.

Take the concept of lemons and use the word "sperm" instead. In this book I will discuss the sexual tango that goes on between men and women but for the most part the aim and intention of "dating" and this kind of thing is to have sex. Women view sex differently than men do. In my view they view a potential mate as being more than just a sex partner; they are looking for some kind of financial assistance. That's why they ask you where you work, who you work for, and other questions related to your financial situation. Most, not all of them do this by the time you've gone on your second "date."

A woman who is young and just out for orgasms is one thing. But when they get older they begin to understand how serious relationships are supposed to be as it relates to how their friends and family will view them and also in regard to their future. So now we go back to the adage: when life provides you with a man (or men) who want to screw you, and you find one that has economic potential, then "make lemonade." Translate that sperm into a pregnancy. In many cases she makes the right decision – for her. And once that decision is made, she will figure out a way to impose it on YOU.

By the time most men realize the historical tendency of women getting laid and paid and how, even though held back with gender bias, glass ceilings and sex role socialization, women have seized control of the relationship. They do it with their vaginas, with the mythology and social pressure that surrounds family and sexual relationships, and with the uncanny ability to take over and control family budgets. They have even so mastered the system that they have pussy whipped their white male partners into passing legislation that gives them half of your shit during a divorce and in some cases, entitles them to it even if you are not married to them.

Getting laid and getting paid.

How do little girls learn how to suck dick, trick men into giving them money, take it up the ass when necessary and of course, master the straight fuck? From their mothers, where else? Many learn in the streets of course. But the curiosity is raised by what they see at home. In the day and age of the single mother, young girls grow up seeing their mothers looking and smelling good and then going out on dates. They see men come into the house for long and not-so-long periods of time as the 'boyfriend.'

These are the only logical ways to figure how it is, from one generation to the next, women continue to get over on men one way or another. There is however, yet one more constant variable in this formula regarding how women get laid and paid. And that is the "social psychology" of the dating process, the game playing that goes on, and how easy it is to trap men, get them to pay for almost anything and then use that power to determine what role you want him (or them) to play in your life.

Generally speaking women learn about male desperation, gullibility and peer pressure. Here's how it works. And what they learn they pass on to their children, both boys and girls. But the fact is, there are two different sets of lessons that are imparted. And these divergent lessons come together as the child gets older and grows into adulthood, and at the end of those crossroads is one beneficiary: the female. It might not seem that way because of all the sexist articles in her way, but in the final analysis, no woman in her right mind would ever want to be a man (outside of the workplace, that is).

To begin with, boys learn from their mothers about what a "good woman" is. As part of this programming they are told that you never "hit" a woman, but very little is taught about what to do if a woman hits you. You're just supposed to take it. And you aren't supposed to let her pay for the dinner or the date and so on. The mother hands these tips down to her sons while she is teaching her daughters how to fight, exploit and take full advantage of any "sucker" that comes along. The more soft-spoken, dainty and submissive the boy is, the more the mother likes it.

Using their spoil-happy mothers as a model, the boys seek to find that type of treatment from and that type of person in person in a girl. Grown-ass men are often heard telling women, "that ain't how my mama would do it" and similarly infantile statements. That is one reason why the wife and the mother oftentimes bump heads: each sees the other as competition for this man who is being treated like a little boy by both of them.

Desperation begins to increase as increasing number of their male "buddies" have girl friends, go on dates and start getting "hooked up." Then they learn how to compare stories and experiences, including the truth, some small lies and of course, the infamous "cock claiming" where they claim they fucked girls that they haven't. That reality is what leads to a number of conflicts, guy on guy and girl on guy. And it is as old as cockhounding itself.

In simpler terms, the peer pressure increases after the first piece of pussy and comparisons are made. Women know about it because they talk amongst themselves and their sisters, classmates and others talk about men and what it took to land one. Women share notes on men and as they get older, begin to see something universal among us: men are crude assholes who can be easily seduced by something that women carry around all the time: pussy.

Women grow not to respect us, although many of them will pretend as if they do, claiming for instance that they want "somebody like my daddy." Realizing that their father wasn't shit either (which is why they never saw him), they nevertheless have to have something to fall back on, lest their mother be deemed or perceived as a slut. So each generation protects the other one. And both have one thing in common: the low regard for the male species that, for some reason, seem to crave and obsess over this thing called "pussy."

After all, what's all this fuss about something that smells, something surrounded by hair, and something that serves no real use other than to get the man off, a factor that is negated by the fact that this same human hole is responsible for impregnation which tends to tie a man down for no less than eighteen years? That's right: because of desperation and peer pressure, the man seeks out the very thing that is going to trap him and change his entire life. And then there's the issue of gullibility.

It is clear that men are gullible because we fall for the same old shit. We screw a girl and she tells us we are the greatest lover she ever had, that our dick is huge and that she can't resist us. After that she begins luring us into these public displays of affection which is the modern day version of the "brand." By brand I refer to the ways that farmers mark their cattle and other animals. They took a hot poker with initials or a design and tattooed it onto the animal's flesh. That then, was your "brand."

Today and in this case, there are several other types of "brands."

The first of these is what I call "The first love tat." This is a tattoo that girls of today get on their arms, breasts, backsides and inner thighs in most cases, with the name of the boy who they "love" emblazoned across their skin. These dumb bitches think and act as if this is the "real deal" just because this guy might have claimed that he "loved" them. Now having had sex with him, they think he'll be around forever, but little do they know: he might not even remember her name the next day.

The second form of brand is where women literally "mark their territory" the way gang members (and dogs) tend to do. One way women do it is through public displays of affection: walking up to you when you're with your pals and kissing you, walking down the hall holding hands, flashing the engagement ring you so foolishly purchased so you could get the pussy and so on. Despite their sister-like behavior toward one another, women do not trust each other when it comes to "their man."

By the time we realize that maybe she's not the one, it's too late. She's spread the necessary news and rumors to trap you. And it's about that time that you spot two, maybe three other girls who you would love to screw. But they already know about you and your "girlfriend." Many won't give a shit and will fuck you anyway. But remember this: when the dyad (a group of two) becomes a triad (a group of three) power relationships shift and there is always a tendency for danger on some level. You see it all the time, but on no more show displayed most vividly than the TV program "Snapped." And if you haven't seen it, I strongly suggest you watch it. You might learn something.

Let me close by saying this: I wrote this book to serve as a basis for discussion between men and women and whomever else. You cannot arrive at sane conclusions without someone being able to offer up some sane variables. *This emotion-laden screaming match type bullshit will no longer suffice.* This is a capitalist society, and what is capitalism? It is the ceaseless pursuit of profit. Not just money, not just a paycheck or a stipend, but PROFIT. And in my view women have been paying a huge price for the "profits" they've acquired over the years. We have hurt them emotionally, socially, culturally, physically and intellectually. All the while they were getting paid.

The bleeding has therefore been reciprocal, and it begins at a young age. The white woman is not playing around but male chauvinism and societally-wide misogyny blind far too many from seeing what is taking place. So let's take a stroll down "mammory lane" and share my observations.

Recall the lyrics from the song "All of Me" that I used earlier in this book. Now refer back to them for a moment.

All of me. Although it was performed by a woman, two Jews – Seymour Simons and Gerald Marks – wrote the words and the music. This song should be re-named something like "The Trick's National Anthem" or "Confessions of a Turned Out John." All of me? For pussy? Come on, y'all. You know that for decades men have been begging for pussy as if it was lined with gold and women, seeing how desperate we were and how low we were willing to stoop just to get some "stank," decided to comply. But that is, after we pay for it with dates, flowers, candy, hotel rooms, trips and cruises, rent payments, car payments, a house and in many cases, a diamond ring that commits us to marrying her. Then and only then, are we promised to get all the pussy we want. But ask any married man: once you're married, you're lucky if you even SEE it once a month, let alone actually get it (that is, unless she's setting you up with a kid).

The fact is, men have been paying for sex and women have been selling it throughout recorded history. For the most part, these activities have been viewed and written about negatively, but it is fair to say that these negative views were put out there by men who were talking out of both sides of their mouths. On the one hand the talk is about morals and about not coveting other people's wives, while in real life, pussy was being purchased using everything from the bartering system and the offer of status to outright monetary exchanges.

How have women been able to get "laid and paid" all these years while appearing to be the victims of male chauvinism? First off, make no bones about it: they were victims. But much like a wolf that swallows a cobra, the results are going to be disastrous even though the wolf's belly is full. He's going to end up fuuuuuuucked up! And so it has come to pass with the male-dominated, chauvinistic, misogynistic society that we all call the United States of America. The "state" of the female America is "united" when it comes to refusing to continue taking shit off of men. And men are just now beginning to pay for it.

But pay we will. And we will pay big time. Let me show you how by outlining what women "want in a man" based on a survey. The survey results and my analyses, follow.

<u>The Myth of the "Pretty Girl's Curse"</u>

The myth on the streets is that pretty girls lose out because they are so pretty that guys don't approach them because the assumption is that they are going to be vain or that they already have a man. This sounds logical but it's bullshit. This society is based on women and their overall physicality and as I point out later in this book on ugly women, any woman in America can get laid any time she wants to, no matter how she looks. But it is the image of "the pretty girl," popularized by television, film and magazines, that has so many young females feeling depressed and fucked up.

One of the biggest musical hits of all time was Roy Orbison's, "Pretty Woman." This 1964 hit described a man who was longing for this bitch, from beginning of the song to the end. His whole worldview was about trying to get this good looking woman to give him a chance. Following are the lyrics:

Pretty woman walkin' down the street
Pretty woman, the kind I like to meet
Pretty woman, I don't believe you
You're not the truth
No one could look as good as you
Mercy
Pretty woman, won't you pardon me
Pretty woman, I couldn't help but see
Pretty woman, and you look lovely as can be
Are you lonely just like me
Pretty woman, stop a while
Pretty woman, talk a while
Pretty woman, give your smile to me
Pretty woman, yeah, yeah, yeah
Pretty woman, look my way
Pretty woman, say you'll stay with me
Cause I need you
I'll treat you right
Come with me baby
Be mine tonight
Pretty woman, don't walk on by
Pretty woman, don't make me cry

> Pretty woman, don't walk away
> OK
> If that's the way it must be, OK
> I guess I'll go on home, it's late
> There'll be tomorrow night
> But wait, what do I see?
> Is she walking back to me?
> Yeah, she's walking back to me
> O-Oh
> Pretty woman

Pretty girl's "curse"? This hunk of bullshit is defined as a good looking woman not being able to get a lot of suitors because she is so fine that most men will assume that she has someone already and will bypass her for a woman who looks closer to "ordinary" or "attainable."

This myth says more about the people doing the pursuing than it does about the actual woman. To begin with, women know if they're fine or not. In fact, even ugly bitches think that if they slather on enough makeup, put on some false eyelashes, perhaps some contact lenses that make their eyes green, a wig or extensions. Some underalls and a panty liner, a pushup bra, a super short micro skirt, and some "fuck me" pumps, they can land a man. And because men are so fucked up, in most cases they can do just that. It has nothing to do with "pretty" or "beauty" because beauty is in the eye of the beholder.

But remember: so is "booty."

And that is what men pay for: pussy, not looks. Sure, looks help and the call girls that cater to a wealthy clientele look good as far as their faces are concerned. But white men are closet homoerotic assholes and they want their women's features to be tiny: small nose, no lips, flat asses, small breasts and so on. In that way they can pretend that they're having sex with a young girl. So it's the sexual desires of the men that enables women to get "laid and paid," not much else. Perhaps blonde hair doesn't hurt, but there are so many bitches dying their hair today there is no doubt in my mind that Clairol, Vidal Sassoon, L'Oreal, and Revlon – to name but a few – are making a virtual killing.

Where did the concept of a "pretty girl's curse" originate, one wonders? Who knows. More likely than not some loser – or a group of them – were having a hard time getting some pussy. So they came up with an excuse akin to that of the fox and the grapes. Remember that Aesop's fable? In case you don't, let me briefly recap:

> ONE hot summer's day a Fox was strolling through an orchard till
> he came to a bunch of Grapes just ripening on a vine which had

been trained over a lofty branch. "Just the things to quench my thirst," quoth he. Drawing back a few paces, he took a run and a jump, and just missed the bunch. Turning round again with a One, Two, Three, he jumped up, but with no greater success. Again and again he tried after the tempting morsel, but at last had to give it up, and walked away with his nose in the air, saying: "I am sure they are sour." (Aesop, 2001).

In other words, since he couldn't reach them he had to convince himself that something must have been wrong with the grapes – instead of something being wrong with his abilities to reach them. So I believe this kind of failure created the "pretty girl's curse." And I only mention this because in this book on women "getting laid and paid," one might be led to believe that only the fine ones are benefiting. Let me tell you something.

Over the millennia, pussy is the only thing that never loses value. Women learned that a long time ago, even before capitalism was created. They also knew that men weren't about shit and were only good for physical labor, getting them pregnant, and menial chores. In the meantime, they (women) sat at home on their pussies and prepared food, cleaned the house and thought about just how stupid men, who seemed happiest when engaged in wars, bar room fights and other macho struggles, really were. And they waited and planned and have been getting "laid and paid" even before recorded history.

And this is taking place whether the woman is "pretty" or not.

The Top 20 Traits Women Want in a Man: A Survey Analysis

A March 11, 2016 article on MSN.com carried an article titled, "The Top 20 Traits Women Want in a Man." These "traits" as they called them (what they really meant was "characteristics" – only animals have "traits") are just the kinds of tendencies that enable women to control and further enhance their abilities to get "laid and paid."

These "traits" are rated by percentages based on how important they are as stated by the women themselves. I will address each of these, include the statements that were provided in the original article and then analyze those statements with my own evidence of the control mechanisms that truly show how women control men and in doing so, control their bank accounts of overall financial wherewithal.

These traits are broken down into four areas: character traits, personality traits, practical skills and physical characteristics. There are twenty (20) traits altogether and we are to gather that these traits, based on a survey, are what women want. Now I will break each down and show you the link between money, sex and female security. They all overlap but in American society we refer to this as "love" or "family life." Read and learn.

Top Character Traits: 1. Faithfulness 84%

More than 8 out of 10 women rated "faithful to me" in the top 10 attributes they find sexy in a man. A woman's tendency toward attachment is a biological imperative, a matter of raising offspring right. Reassure her (often) that you're not going anywhere.

This is been the way to ensure a long-term trick with money to take care of "the family," which translates to mean HER. The white man's system is so fucked up that he created sex role socialization where the man "goes out and does the work" and the woman "takes care of the home and the children." Little did this asshole know that while she was at home she was thinking and planning. And as technology became more sophisticated and accessible, she could learn new ways to stockpile money in the name of the children, have a bank account on the side, and lay guilt trips on his sorry ass when he loses his job or starts coming up short with her "allowance."

In order for any of this to have any impact on her wallet, the concept of being "faithful" must be widely circulated and accepted. But not because she gives a shit: it's because if he's out there fucking around, that means that HER money is going into some other woman's purse or pocketbook. She can never allow that. Women are close in a lot of things, but they don't trust other women around "their" men. A man who is unfaithful is a man who is unpredictable and in being un predictable, he is more difficult to control.

Top Character Traits: 2. Dependability 75%

Three out of four women say they look for a man who makes commitments and follows through. Being responsible—even if it's just remembering to pick up salad dressing on your way over to her place—sends a positive signal that someday you might commit.

Dependability is really tied with "faithfulness" in my book. In order for her to keep getting paid she has to be able to count on the man to come up with the money. That is why pussy whipping him is so important. She makes it look like he's talking her out of the pussy or that there's something about him that just turns her on, but these bitches know what they're doing: they know that as men, we are some simple muthafuckas. All she has to do is give us some pussy or some head and we lose our minds. The more and better she does it, the more spoiled we become. The more spoiled we become the easier it is for her to control us. And that control mandates that "dependability" means falling in line with the "men's responsibilities" which means "taking care of and supporting your family" which means taking care of HER.

Top Character Traits: 3. Kindness 67%

> Young women may still fall for the bad-boy type, but more-mature women are turned on by kindness, because kindness inspires confidence. In other words, if you treat the waitress well, your date figures you'll treat her well, too.

Kindness? That's a very general term that could mean anything. If the woman wants to get knocked around during sex and the man wants her, he will comply. Is this therefore an act of kindness? Of course not – by most standards. But when these women in this survey were talking about kindness, pay close attention to the defining statement: if you treat your waitress well, your date figures you'll treat her well too. Notice that in the example money is exchanging hands, which means that what I am alleging is valid: marriage and dating are about prostitution. By tipping the waitress you are showing that you are willing to "pay for good service." Not only that, but she's checking out HOW you tip: do you have an attitude, do you complain, do you count every penny? Or do you flash a wad of green or an American Express card. These bitches are checking out every little gesture, movement and nuance and that's why and how they get "laid and paid."

Top Character Traits: 4. Moral Integrity 66%

> Having the guts to tell the truth means to a woman that you have the guts to be a good, caring, decent partner over the long haul. White lies are okay; just avoid any that are tinged with gray.

Moral integrity? How can a bitch who wants to find a guy to take care of her have the gall to be concerned about moral integrity? The fact is that she is lacking in it, so she makes sure he has it. Why? Because that means he'll have bought into that whole "man take care of woman" bullshit that she is fishing for. If he's moral he'll buy into a number of other bullshit myths: "a man should never hit a woman," "a man pays for the dinner," "a man opens the woman's door," "a man lets the woman go first" and so on. The higher the moral integrity of the man, the better a trick he makes. Women know this. That's why preachers and ministers get over on so many bitches: women think these guys believe in the religion, but in reality they're pimps using the pulpit as their foundation.

According to the caption above you have to have the guts to tell the truth. That is bullshit. Women hate the truth. They want to be lied to if that lie jibes with what they are looking for. Tell them they look good when they look like shit; tell them that you'll take care of them no matter what – and so on.

And the racism implied about the "white lie" is just the white man's way of making it appear as if it's alright: a white lie is better than a black lie in Euroamerican culture. But a fabrication of the truth hurts no matter what it is. As the old saying teaches, "Dress a liar as you will, a liar is a liar, still."

Top Character Traits: 5. Fatherliness 51%

> Being a good dad (or having the potential to become one) is about being a good role model—and about being patient and caring, qualities women like in a partner. If you're not a father, then tell her about your favorite niece or nephew, or the employee you're mentoring at work.

This is one of those "after the fact" traits where she's already set you up – you know – "accidentally" getting pregnant. This can happen before or during marriage but when she decides it's going to happen, trust me – she'll make it happen. And she sizes up the guys that she wants to be the fathers and "fatherliness" is only a minor consideration. You have to have a good job, not have any other children and be a sucka for that "one big happy family" bullshit.

Being a good role model for your child? She only uses that when she's pissed or she thinks you're going to leave her. Then if and when you leave, she will spend years dogging you out behind your back, making sure that the kids hate your fuckin' guts. The kids never ask "what in the fuck did you do to make him want to leave us"? You don't believe it? Turn on a pro game and listen to LeBron James, Kevin Durant, Dwyane Wade, and all those professional athlete whine about how their mother made them the men that they are.

And where did this woman learn about the importance of fatherliness? From her mother. And what did her mother tell her? She told her that men ain't shit and to be careful of them. When she brings you home to meet her family, watch how her mother looks at you as you shake her hand. First, she's measuring dick length, then your eyes to see if you might be a playa. After that she's making sure that she helps get you on board the "we are family" bandwagon, which makes you a trick for the whole family to game on and enjoy.

Top 5 Personality Traits: 6. Sense of Humor 77%

> Being able to laugh at the stresses of this world is a must, according to the women on our panel. You get bonus points if you can make them laugh. Humor tells a woman that you can laugh at—read, handle easily—the many difficulties that life throws at you.

Yeah – being able to laugh will help you offset the reaction you get as you watch the bank account decrease little by little; or watch her continue to buy dresses and shoes that she saves for church or some other bullshit event; or as she continues to complain that you don't "touch her the way you used to" despite the fact that the bitch has gained 60 pounds and has TB – two bellies.

Sense of humor? Laughing at difficulties doesn't provide solutions to them. Cracking up at problems doesn't diminish their impact. Smiling, skinning and grinning don't stop her from doing what she wants to do if she has made up her mind to do it. And when she files for divorce and gets half your shit, all the jokes and wise cracks in the world ain't gonna get your snaps back.

Top 5 Personality Traits: 7. Intelligence 55%

A worldly, interesting man is a man she likes to show off. Men who are take-charge problem solvers make women feel secure, and men who are always improving are never boring.

This is bullshit. She wants an intelligent man to show off so that she can look good for her friends. Her friends will think that since he's so smart and he's with her, she must be a good catch. Other than that, the smarter you are the bigger the threat you are to her goal of getting laid and paid, more the latter than the former.

No matter how intelligent a man is the woman always has the advantage. And do you know why? She knows that no matter how many degrees you have, how high your IQ is or how accomplished you are, you must not be worth a shit or else you wouldn't be with her! She knows that with all that intelligence, for some reason she has something you need – or think you need. And it is that advantage that enables her to maintain the power in the relationship.

Top 5 Personality Traits: 8. Passion 46%

Why have women always melted for musicians? Because rock stars are passionate in public. Women like displays of passion because they're not accustomed to seeing them from men. Get passionate about something: kayaking, impressionistic art, barbecuing, or Habitat for Humanity. It's proof that you care for and about something beyond yourself.

Passion is the key to maintaining control – for HER. Your passion is going to be taken, twisted and shoved right up your ass. Oh sure you used to be a great musician. Oh sure, you used to be able to dunk backwards. Yeah, you used to be able to sit down and write an essay with the best of them. But her very presence and her goals of getting laid and paid are going to take that passion and twist it so that it works in HER image and interests.

The previous description says that being passionate about something is "proof that you care for and about something beyond yourself." And that is the target for her: reversing that trend so that the passion is not about the things you have interest in: it's about taking your interests and re-directing them at HER.

Top 5 Personality Traits: 9. Confidence 41%

A man who feels secure in his own skin makes the woman he's with feel secure. By showing you can handle unfamiliar people or situations, you tell the woman in your life that she need not fear, either.

This one is debatable. Women will answer any kind of way to make it appear as if they see men as human beings and respect them as such. Nothing could be further from the truth. Women see men the same way men see women: as commodities. This is a commodity society, one rooted in the market and in capitalism. You are one of two things: a tangible asset or a crippling liability. Women view men as both, and seek to turn them more into the former than the latter.

When it comes to a man with confidence, this works against the "laid and paid" ethic. A man with confidence won't fall for the bullshit lies, the fake orgasms and the "you sure have a big dick" falsehoods that we have been programmed to fall prey to. A man with confidence will first of all understand a key point that most men miss: anything worth having is worth studying first and foremost. You can understand what you want and what you are after once you understand the nature and essence of that "thing."

Women are not "things" but remember that we live in a commodity society which has men treating women as such in the same way that women treat men that way. Therefore you have to study and know yourself and work to enhance your skill set in the bedroom and socially. Once you do that, and you know what you can do, no one can come along and "flatter you" out of your bank account, money and life. A man who is truly confident is first of all confident in the fact that he knows things. If you know about women, this society, and the tendencies I am outlining in this book, then you can afford to be confident in the correct way.

What was described above in terms of confidence can be misconstrued. For instance, it states that, "By showing you can handle unfamiliar people or situations, you tell the woman in your life that she need not fear, either." Confidence is much more than what was just hinted at. It starts within and emanates outward, not the reverse. Women want to see if you can handle unfamiliar people and situations so that you can protect HER. It's a selfish definition for a woman to view men in this manner. We are more than bodyguards and off-duty cops; and any woman worth her salt is going to know how to protect herself in various situations. If not she's only setting herself up for dependency and abuse.

Top 5 Personality Traits: 10. Generosity 38%

This is more important to women over 35 than it is to those under that age. Generosity, however, doesn't just mean springing for dinner at a four-star. Your willingness to give your time and lend your ear is what women crave.

If this survey was real, this one would be ranked first. The old street saying teaches, "Catch a fool, bump his head." And men have been getting their heads "bumped" for centuries. A smile here, a batted over there, an "oops-I-didn't-mean-to-show-you-my-panties" curtsy and voila! We become their willing thralls.

An age-old maxim teaches, ""Generosity consists not the sum given, but the manner in which it is bestowed." But when it comes to women getting laid and paid the sum is more important than the manner. You've heard it time and time again: women, married or not, taking ass whippings and psychological abuse because the man buys them nice things, is paying the rent or the car note. The sum is very important in a capitalist society because it's when the elites are excluded and it comes down to male-female relationships, what you have left is a "zero-sum game." There simply are no real winners other than those at the top who are defining the game.

Generosity, in fact, is defined as, "the quality of being kind, understanding, and not selfish," and the "willingness to give money and other valuable things to others." If you do not view self as the basis of nation, then you are going to always be someone's stooge. The greatest number is number one and number one should be you. That's what makes you want to help people because as the Bible teaches, ""To those whom much is given, much is expected." So you believe in yourself and you use your skills and gifts to help other people – not allow them to help themselves TO you.

And here's the key to the definition provided above when it comes to male generosity: "Your willingness to give your time and lend your ear is what women crave." Giving your time and lending your ear are the keys to the female assessing or evaluating just how gullible you are and how many resources you have. The more time you give the more money you spend – on HER. The more you listen, the more lies she is set to tell, usually a sob story or some myth about how she "hasn't been with anyone for years." All setting you up to let down your guard and to place your common sense on the back burner. Before you know it you're having sex with her and she's paving the way for finding out how generous you are in bed. But even if you're not, if you are willing to spend and invest money and time, she's got you hooked.

Top 5 Practical Skills: 11. Listening 53%

Pay attention. A woman feels safe and secure when she knows her man will put down his BlackBerry and listen to her. Magic words: "I'm here. Tell me everything."

This one is an extension of the "generosity" principle that I just described. This is the key to the game plan: the more you listen the more you learn. But the fact is, what you may be learning could be bullshit. But the bullshit is based on the stereotypical views that you may already have and hold about women.

Listening is an art. There is regular listening – which is what far too many of us males do and that's how we end up getting bamboozled. But then there is "mindful listening," like the kind that I do. Some people say that I am "too analytical," but in my view, there can be no such thing. This is my life and if I'm going to let anyone else in, I'll decide who it will be. This goes back to what I said earlier about the importance of study. I try to teach my children the same thing. As an adult who went through what most kids go through, what I've learned is that you look at what people produce, not what they say. People will say anything, and that is why mindful listening is so important. But if they produce something, it is an indicator of what they are about, what they believe and what they have the ability to do.

This seems to be the way women think. They want a man who is industrious, and that means willing to bring home a paycheck. That's why women accept a man who is an idiot, works a menial job or degrades himself at work. In the case of black people, that's why so many intelligent and conscious sistahs marry some of the biggest sellouts and Uncle Toms there are: the money is more important than the consciousness or character of the man they married. They don't care what he is producing on the outside – even if he produces nothing – as long as he brings home a paycheck and takes care of her needs and wants. It's called marriage – deal with it.

If you're smart, you'll do some serious listening. Women run their mouths all the time, and the more secure they feel about the amount of control they think they have over you, the more they are bound and prone to talk. This is not to say that they don't have secrets: every single one of them does. And on earth, there's at least one other bitch who knows that secret. Therefore if you listen closely enough not only will she run her mouth, but when she gets angry, that's when the REAL truth comes forward. Some of them have discipline and can control their mouth because they learned, from their mothers, that "loose lips sink ships." But for the most part when a woman wants someone to "listen," it's a key to the control mechanism: she wants you to know something for a financial reason. And even if the reason is a personal or intimate one, in the final analysis it comes down to money. Because if it didn't, she wouldn't be trusting you and telling you in the first place!

Top 5 Practical Skills: 12. Romancing 48%

Romance appeals to a woman's right-brained, less-logical side. Every woman fantasizes about being swept off her feet. Romance is bold because you're displaying your desire for a woman and revealing a softer, more vulnerable side that women find irresistible.

We live in America so I'm going to deal with this "romantic" bullshit that has been promoted throughout American popular culture. Even now the white man and his negro lackeys are having what are called "play dates" for their young sons and daughters, having them play together and go out on fun time dates. This paves the way for the "romance scam" that translates into major income for American businesses.

"Romance" is defined by the Merriam-Webster dictionary as, "Ardent emotional attachment or involvement between people; love." In my dictionary of life I define it as, "the process of spending a lot of money on the person you hope to fuck." That's what it boils down to and it's done through another concept known as "the date."

What is a date? It's turning a trick. If you're a guy, you're spending money on a woman hoping to get in her panties. If you're a woman, you're looking for a guy to take you to concerts, dinner, or to otherwise spend money to expand your social horizons. In 2016 America when you say "I used to date him/her," what that means is that you used to FUCK them. You went out and when the time was deemed right, you got the pussy or the dick (in America, it could be both). Therefore as I view it, "Romancing" the woman is paying for her attention and then based upon her assessments and evaluations, taking her to bed. She will determine how much "romancing" it will take to move beyond the initial sex act.

The previous explanation about "romance" makes the claim that, "Romance is bold because you're displaying your desire for a woman and revealing a softer, more vulnerable side that women find irresistible." Bold? Romance, if anything, is the prelude to what I call "the sucker assessment." You show attention and she decides if you can move on from there. On the streets it's called "choosing." Any man who thinks he "chose" the woman he's with is a damn idiot. They choose the time, the place and the person. They decide when you'll fuck them, how you'll do it, how much money you'll spend before you fuck them and if and when you get to fuck them again. Welcome to America.

When the definition says that romancing reveals a "softer, more vulnerable side that women find irresistible," what they should be saying is that romance shows the degree of how weak-minded you are and how big of a sucka you will be. Romancing in America is linked to spending money, plain and simple. If you're a cheapskate or don't flash that cash, most women won't give you the time of day no matter how "cute" you might be or how big your dick is. Back in the day there may not have been such business-oriented tendencies. But that was during a time when there were a lot more black men around. Today, when you subtract the ones who are locked up, dead, dying from some disease, taking it up the ass (homosexuality) or who are on the downlow, that translates to mean "slim pickin's" for the sistahs. So they have to roll the dice and put family and personal security over good looks and a dick. "Romance," in such a context, is nothing more than icing on the cake of "financial security" that most women seek and crave.

<u>Top 5 Practical Skills: 13. Being Good in Bed 35%</u>

A woman knows that a man who takes care of her in bed will take care of her out of bed. Your enthusiasm for her body is more important than your sexual prowess.

This is one of the keys to the colors of how women get "laid and paid." The bedroom is the arena that you step into once you've passed some of the "tests" that I've outlined in this short book. Let me explain.

Being "good in bed" is something that men are going to have to master even before they get pussy. You are going to have to study the female body, study social customers and learn how to apply them to your concrete needs. You are going to have to find out something about that woman, even if it means studying her astrology sign. I don't subscribe to spookism but astrology does have some accuracy and gives you a basic foundation on learning the characteristics of a person born during a certain time of the year. I'm going to tell you: it's worked for me in as much as it let me know what kind of woman I was dealing with. Sometimes I was wrong; many times, I was right.

If you've learned what I just suggested, it doesn't matter who the woman is. They're all built the same. The only difference is the previous experiences they may have had. And let me tell you something: most of the ones out there are damaged goods because of US. That's right: show me a cute woman who is available and I'll show you somebody who had a boyfriend early in life, got dogged and dismissed and it bitter as hell. And you are going to inherit that bitterness because to her, all men are the same. This is where being good in bed comes in.

Most women know that men crave pussy. Therefore they spend a lot of time dolling themselves up and showing you just enough to let you want to see more. That's why the hems are going up, that's why the thong bikini draws are the rage, and that's why many of them have their breasts hanging out. The want to get dicked. But first come the wine-and-dine rituals that I outlined earlier. But once you get her to give up the pussy, you have to be prepared to do to her what her previous man may not have done: you have to give her an orgasm.

Back in the old days women didn't seem to give a shit. They wanted dick and that was about it. But in today's America, these bitches will take it up the ass, give up head and lick your balls just to "turn you out" and make you the kind of man that they can use. If they don't cum, they'll either fake it or act as if it doesn't matter. If you've gotten to the point where you've shown them a good time on a date or where they see you as a marketable commodity (read: someone who has or will get a good job) then they'll tolerate you fucking up in the bed.

Two points about the previous definition. The first is where it makes the claim that, "A woman knows that a man who takes care of her in bed will take care of her out of bed." It is up to the woman to determine if she's been "take care of in the bed" or not. Some of them are cum freaks and want to have as many orgasms as they can because they don't plan on seeing you again or they don't plan on you getting the pussy any time soon. Some of them just open their legs, act as sperm spittoons, and then let you get off so that they (the woman) can get on about the business of figuring out what role you'll play in the days ahead.

The fact of the matter is a woman who thinks a man that takes care of her in bed will take care of her out of bed is falling prey to the scam run by most playas and pimps. Those of us who have learned the art and science of mastering a woman's body know how to deal with it in the bed just like we can talk a woman into the bed by saying the right words. We have been doing it for centuries, and while they may fall for it when they're young, once we've gotten what we want, the next guy who comes along is going to pay a huge price. At any rate, compliments in bed should never be confused with achievements in life.

The second point lies in the claim that, "Your enthusiasm for her body is more important than your sexual prowess." Wrong, again. All enthusiasm leads to is premature ejaculation, let's face it. And as for "sexual prowess," unless you're an athlete, by the time you turn 55 that shit has diminished (as has your interest in her for the most part). Enthusiasm that leads to sex is like buying a new car: once you drive it off the lot the value decreases by fifty percent! In like manner, once you get the pussy, the thrill is gone in many cases. Don't get me wrong: you might want to get it again. *But after that first time, all the time, energy and money that was spent on getting it weighs in on how you view having gotten it and whether or not you think it's worth hanging around for after that first time.*

Top 5 Practical Skills: 14. Cooking, Cleaning, etc. 23%

> Self-sufficiency means you're not going to expect her to be like your mother. Learn how to make one or two killer breakfasts or dinners, and you'll win her heart.

This is a good practical skill, one that I tried to inculcate into the minds of my sons. But be careful: one woman's "practical man" is another woman's reason to be a lazy bitch. The fact is women have been programmed by their mothers (especially black woman whose mothers actually worked) to keep a clean house, know how to cook and know how to be "a good housewife." In many circles this thinking still exists today, especially in the South. And many of today's men, as gluttonous as ever, continue to look for a woman who is "like my mamma."

Unfortunately for single black mothers, too many of them have raised these effeminate ass boys, known today as "mitches." These muthafuckas act just like bitches, from wearing two earrings and having their "hair did" to skinny jeans. These kids of dudes aren't looking for someone who is going to motivate them to be independent men; these "guys" are a new breed and as such, if they do any cooking and cleaning it's going to be in their bachelor pads as they play the field with women as well as men. The art and science men knowing how to sew, cook, and clean is a thing of the past. Many of them know how to braid but that's only because a lot of them have been locked up and learned how to do that to earn money and keep Bubba's dick out of their ass.

Top 5 Practical Skills: 15. Earning Potential 21%

> One in five women surveyed said a man's successfulness in his career contributes to his sexiness. If you've demonstrated talent, goal achievement, and follow-through, you give women confidence that you will be a good provider.

Whoomp! There it is! Earning potential is an essential key to how these women get laid and paid. Their concerns? "Where you work at?" "How much you make?" "Who you work for"? "You gon' buy me a drink or what?" "What kinda car you got?" "You married?" Of course I'm talking about the sistahs because that's what I know. But white bitches, though the vernacular may be different, put their white men through the same "paces."

Now let's get to the "commodification" of human beings that I talked about earlier.

The previous quote claims that, "One in five women surveyed said a man's successfulness in his career contributes to his sexiness." This statements speaks volumes. How can a career contribute to a man's "sexiness" unless that career is generating enough money to take this woman wherever it is she wants to guy, feed her and otherwise give her a lifestyle that she feels like she deserves? If he does all that, then he can prematurely ejaculate all he wants to! The fact is, it is the "career" and that hard work the contributes to men's sexual dysfunction as they get older, and she knows that. But as the jewelry and status increases, so do the lies about how "great" he is in the bed, whether it's true or not. And in fact, a growing number of these "happy women" sleep in separate beds and in many cases separate bedrooms.

As Simmel wrote in his book *The Philosophy of Money*, "money is the ultimate confounding of things." What he means is that money can make the puny look large, the weak look strong, the ugly look attractive and so on. Now add that to the definition that was supplied above: "If you've demonstrated talent, goal achievement, and follow-through, you give women confidence that you will be a good provider." The key word is "provider" – one who provides what? Not dick. Not pussy licking. These are just the ersatz manifestations. She wants a house, a car that will make her neighbors jealous, and kids that she can use to set you up at a later date and a nice bank account that she has access to.

This then, is what "earning potential" has come to mean when it comes to men and women in America.

Top 5 Physical Attributes: 16. Sense of Style 30%

The way you dress reflects on the woman you're with, and she knows it. The man who knows how to match a patterned shirt and tie will notice when she's dressed well, too. (And maybe he'll pay for the Blahniks.) Keep your tailor and your dry cleaner busy, and spring for posh, touchable fabrics like cashmere, suede, pima cotton, and brushed corduroy.

This is some of that "clothes make the man" bullshit that white boys, mainly Jews (who control the garment industry) helped to promote back in the day and it still holds as a constant belief in 2016. The only problem with the belief is that it is only partially true.

As I see it, the way the man is perceived is what makes him and as a result, it doesn't matter if he has on a Hart Schaffner and Marx double-breasted suit or a pair of jeans and a t-shirt. Black men in America are the sharpest dressers on the planet and what has it gotten them? Very little other than token jobs, prison and a few white bitches. One of the richest men in the world is Warren Buffett and he is also one of the slouchiest. Do you think that when he walks in a room with that undeserved "Oracle of Omaha" moniker that people give a shit what brand of suit he's wearing?

And one more thing: numerous millions of women have been duped by sharp-dressing men who weren't worth a shit. Look at these black ministers – they wear nice suits and they are nothing more than pimps in the pulpit. Look at drug dealers: brand name clothes up and down, jewelry and the like – and most of them are no-talent wannabes who may also be borderline faggots. Clothing is one way that men have been able to dupe women, just like an average woman with a mini-skirt, some pumps and some fishnets can land just about any man. Clothing is external and subjective.

If style were power, black men in America would be running the world. But it is not – it is a pacification tool that benefits those who make the clothes (and we know who that is). Being clean is one thing, but donning an expensive suit so that you can impress some woman is not a good idea: she grows to expect this all the time which means you have to keep on doing it. Now you're spending money to impress her and that's in addition to the money you're spending on trying to get her.

I've learned that real style is mental. If you have personality and charm, people will remember you no matter what you have on. Keep that in mind.

<u>Top 5 Physical Attributes: 17. Handsome Face 26%</u>

The science of attraction, which has been studied ad infinitum, says it's all about symmetry. Imagine you have a dotted red line (Nip/Tuck style) vertically through the center of your face, down your nose. Are your features similar in form and arrangement on both sides of the line? Do your eyes and ears match up? The closer one side mirrors the other, the more attractive you are. Women in cross-cultural studies have also ranked men with broad chins, high cheekbones, and large eyes as the most attractive. Best way to improve your looks: Smile more, and make certain your sideburns are even.

Handsome face? This makes some sense. I've read a number of studies that show that physically attractive people fare better in life and at the workplace than those who just look average or who are downright physically unattractive. But my concern here are the descriptors that were just provided, so let's break them down, interject the variable of race, and then see how the shoe fits.

According to the previous paragraph, "Women in cross-cultural studies have also ranked men with broad chins, high cheekbones, and large eyes as the most attractive." According to my research, although the sources are dubious at best, I found that South Asians, Indians (from India), Pakitsanis, Arabs and Armenians, south Europeans (meaning Italians and Greeks) and Sub-Saharan Africans) (Yahoo Answers, 2016). None of these groups are the "typical" white folks in America which, as we know, are mixed up with some of everything.

Here's some evidence based on what I've heard: white women have a saying that they want their men to be tall, DARK and handsome. Why is "dark" in there and what do they mean? Do they mean olive skinned like a lot of Italians of Middle Eastern guys? Or do they mean black men? Judging from the way they clamor for black men, from the rich black guys to the young black men who many of them cruise the ghetto for (while their husbands are at work), one has to wonder.

And here's one more thing: take note that while a quarter of the women sampled rated "handsome face" as a top priority, this doesn't mean anything in capitalist America. Look at all the ugly muthafuckas that have fine women: look at all the beat up old white boys who have fine younger women. Case in point: Donald Trump, Michael Douglas, Phil Jackson, George Bush and so on. They make it a point to attract women who look fairly good to take attention off of their own ugliness. But one thing they all have in common: money and power, and that's all the average bitch cares about. After all, she can always "rent" a cabana boy on the side if she needs to, right?

Top 5 Physical Attributes: 18. Height 15%

Tall, dark, and handsome isn't the be-all and end-all. Women say they like feeling smaller than their men, but height doesn't necessarily mean might. They will feel comfortable as long as they aren't towering over you.

The average male height in the United States is 5'9". Some women have a height requirement because many of them link height to dick length. I don't know if this is accurate enough. Some say it's the size of a man's hands or the length of his fingers. But one thing is for sure: if you're tall and broke, you can hang it up.

Based on the previous definition there is a point that I want to fine-tune; that is where it is written that, ". Women say they like feeling smaller than their men, but height doesn't necessarily mean might." Women aren't dumb – despite the century long attempts by a male dominated society to make them think that they are. They know that if a man is tall he is going to let his guards down once he sees that the woman is shorter. I believe that a lot of these guys that you see on television on shows like "Snapped", the ones lying in caskets, were white boys who were taller than their woman but who let their guard down, started acting real macho and got a cap busted in their ass.

And one last point: no matter how much a man "towers" over a woman vertically, he should remember that a pussy can stretch enough to produce a small human being larger than a good sized watermelon. So all this "I got a big dick" shit falls deaf on the ears of the woman who knows better. Towering over her when you're standing up is immediately nullified when you lie down with her and see how easy it is for your dick to slip in. Feel me?

Top 5 Physical Attributes: 19. Muscular Build 13%

Spend more time with the bathroom mirror and less time with the gym mirror. Nearly three times as many women value a clean-shaven face over the clean and jerk. Muscles help ward off rivals and assure a woman that you won't drop her during a dip, but your overall appearance is more important than the size of your biceps.

As is the case with height, all those muscles don't mean shit to the woman who knows what she's doing.

Take for example, those assholes who take steroids and get testosterone injections. Their balls swell up the size of peas. They might have huge thighs, large chests and great abs, but when it comes to fuckin' they just don't measure up. Women know this shit. When men are young they have fairly muscular builds, but the thing that gets them over on women is the woman's naivete. But once she starts getting dicked and begins to incorporate the strategies and tactics that she learned from her mama and her girlfriends, those male muscles are only good for two things: lifting groceries and toting them to the kitchen and showing off to her girlfriends to make them jealous.

Top 5 Physical Attributes: 20. Fitness 12%

Women recognize a good body as indicative of a man of discipline and self-control. It tells a woman you can keep up with her, in bed and out.

Being physically fit may or may not have anything to do with muscular build when it comes to men and women. Being in shape translates to mean that you can fuck for a long time. It means that your blood vessels are in good shape and the blood can get directly to your dick or your pussy. I know: the commercials try to make it look like it's more than that but I'm telling you the facts. All those white boys and negroes on the movies doing all this hour long fuckin' is bullshit, and they know it.

Look at what the definition says: "Women recognize a good body as indicative of a man of discipline and self-control. It tells a woman you can keep up with her, in bed and out." But that works two ways. If they see someone who has an average body, many women know he can be controlled. A growing number of women don't even like getting fucked for a long time or, for that matter, don't want big dicks stuck in them. Maybe this is the way it always was, but in our youth culture, we measured sexual pleasure by what we were able to do and what we wanted when we were in our teens and our twenties. I'm not really sure.

But what I *am* sure of is that recognizing a body as a sign of discipline or self-control may not be what you think. If a woman sees a man with what she sees as a good body, she may be targeting him for a pregnancy set up. All women want healthy children and if you're in shape, then you attract someone of the same type. Fat bitches know they can't get muscular dudes, although large numbers of them move on skinny guys. In that way the child will average out to be normal in size. I'm just sharing with you what I've observed among the men and women I've seen in the cities I've lived in.

Keeping up with her in bed is important. According to one website, the recent spate of white men working out, jogging, going to the gym and so on may be at attempt to compensate for lack of dick length. Chancellorfiles (2006) makes the following claim:

> Blacks have larger penises than whites, and whites have larger penises than oriental Asians. All of the other racial groups' and ethnic groups' penis sizes fall on the same level as whites. On one extreme blacks of African descent and black Africans have the largest penises in the world, and on the other extreme oriental Asians have the smallest penises. Whites and all other non-white racial groups have medium size penises thus putting them in the middle between Blacks and Asians (Chancellorfiles, 2006).

There are one billion Asians on the planet meaning that dick length ain't got shit to do with potency. It's about diet and effort, and apparently they have plenty of that. The bruthas with the big dicks are sticking them in each other's ass or so it appears and they learn that from prison and from their mother's spoiling them and turning them into "mitches" when they're young. Their fathers aren't around because too many of them are on the downlow or out chasing some white bitch.

There you have it. How bitches get "laid and paid" based on the words that come out of their mouths. But there's more. Let us now look at *motive and psychological intent*, which I believe lies in the concept of "misandry" – the hatred of men, which is a response to the fucked up way that male dominated societies have mistreated women over the centuries.

<u>Signs That a Man Is Bad-in-Bed</u>

Women have always known the difference between what they want, what they need and what they can tolerate. If they have to fake orgasms or tell an idiot that he has a big dick, they'll do it. Why? Because they have a goal in mind, and that goal involves long-term stability on some level. Even if they don't plan on keeping this particular guy around, he'll make do for now until a better one (read: more money) comes along.

In a 2014 article titled, "The Male Bad in Bed List," Coeli Carr offered up some signs that a man is bad in bed. I am going to share those with you and then analyze them based on how they relate to women "getting laid and getting paid.

LARGE WAIST

In other words, fat. Medically speaking, a man who is fat usually has health problems. According to the article,

> **Large waist**
> Bigger is not always better. "By consensus, men with a 40-inch or larger waist size are generally defined as having metabolic syndrome," says Irwin Goldstein, MD, director of sexual medicine at Alvarado Hospital in San Diego, and clinical professor of surgery at University of California, San Diego. "Metabolic syndrome increases the risk for morbidity, diabetes, high cholesterol, hypertension, vascular disease -- and also erectile dysfunction … (Carr, 2014)

You who I blame: black men. Sure, these women we marry believe that if they feed us well, they'll keep us. Their mothers told them that, "The way to a man's heart is through his stomach." That was bullshit. The way to HER heart is through HER stomach, which is why these bitches are always "sampling" what they cook: take a little bite of this, and a bite of that. What was once an hour glass figure transforms into a hefty bag in no time flat. And the same thing goes for us.

For the hardworking man, even we have been fat at times. We might work in a foundry where the heat is mover 100 degrees, construction or the railroad, but when we get home, there's those muthafuckin' chitlins staring at us: beans and rice, gumbo over rice, big chunks of steak and pork chops. So we get fat and we sleep a lot. She's already landed what she wanted: a husband with a job. So she's satisfied.

How could so many men have diabetes unless we got it from these bitches? Of course, as I say, you can't force someone to do something if they don't want to do it. But these women can get us to do anything with the threat of pussy hanging in the air. If they said, "eat healthy or no more pussy," black men would look the way we looked back in the 1960s when we got together and played pickup basketball and flag football, rain or shine. The white man saw that, imitated it, poisoned us with drugs and then opened up "health spas" that he makes sure we can't afford to get into.

Also in regard to the waist, the author writes that,

> "The connection between a man's large girth and erectile dysfunction is low testosterone, says Goldstein. "If a man has enough testosterone, then stem cells, which are present in all the organs, can be converted into muscle," he says. "If his testosterone level is low, stem cells will convert into fat. "The most synergistic remedy is typically lifestyle change, along with testosterone administration, if indicated, says Goldstein. (Carr, 2014)
> '

Unless that "lifestyle change" also includes dietary changes, you can forget it. As for that testosterone, that's what fucked us up in the first place. The craving for pussy is what made us susceptible to the lies that these women tell us. Feeding our ego about how "good" we look or perform in bed. And we start spending that money and to make it look good, she might spend a few bucks as well. But with her, any expenditures are a long term investment in HER future. After that comes the, "guess what honey? I'm pregnant." Now you're hooked for 18 years. And as she gets bigger, she makes sure you do, too. In Biblical terms, "fatback begats fat, jack."

Next is something called a "claw hand." Check it out:

CLAW HAND

What does a claw hand have to do with being able to fuck? Well, according to this article by Carr, the following is the explanation:

> Claw hand
> Can't high five? "Men who can't flatten their fingers and spread them may also have problems with excessive scarring in the wall of the erection chambers of their penis, which results in curvature of the erection," says Goldstein. "These men are often incapable of shaking hands or grasping objects." (Carr, 2014).

This is why I have issues with these white people and their "sexual analyses." Take note that the author writes that people who can't flatten their fingers and spread them "MAY also have problems with excessive scarring in the wall of the erection chambers of their penis." How? Prove it. If it is a fact, then instead of saying that it "may" be the case, it should be WILL be the case.

At any rate, an attempt at an explanation by the author follows:

> Goldstein says that the conditions, called Dupytren's contracture,
> are often seen in men with Peyronie's disease. "Both are metabolic
> disorders of connective tissue -- there's difficulty in stretching the
> thick tendons in the hands or penis" … Because claw hand is a
> systemic condition, both hands are typically affected, says
> Goldstein. "Fortunately, pending FDA approval, there's a remedy
> in the wings: Collagenase, an enzyme which can digest excess
> collagen and can be injected into the erection chamber's thickened
> walls to decrease penile curvature." (Carr, 2014).

I have issues with Jews when it comes to anything medical. It seems to me, having researched what they do as a group, there is a tendency to promote anything that directs people toward purchasing medications or getting operations of some kind. It is already a fact that the Israelis have worked out a way to manipulate the genetic codes so that DNA can be distorted or "altered," and now we have this. The claim is that "connective tissue" is the key and the question I have is this: does this apply to ALL humans or just the white folks that these people tend to use in their theoretical constructs? I have already proven over the years that medicine is "racialized" and that indeed, we are NOT all the same under the skin.

So if that is the case, then who is Goldstein talking about? Other Jews? White folks? How could it pertain to everybody when diet and surroundings impact one's physicality? Are Asians impacted the same way? And then he has a "remedy" already in mind even though most of his concepts are theoretical: "hey, just by some of this and you'll get a boner." I say don't trust any doctors any further than you can throw them. They get paid to promote certain medications to their patients, and we all know the history of Jews and their orientation toward "profit at any expense." Their "clawed hand" seems to always be draped around the cash register button or a wad of bills.

SHORT ARMS

Short arms? Again, this Jewish doctor seems to be engaging in what real social researchers refer to as an "ecological fallacy." If you think the "clawed hand" was weird sounding, check out his explanation of being good in bed and having short arms:

> Men whose long-sleeved shirts fall way past their fingers may be
> in for a shock. "Longer measurements from men's underarms to
> the tips of their middle fingers are statistically associated with
> long-sized penile erections," says Goldstein, editor-in-chief of The
> Journal of Sexual Medicine and co-author of When Sex Hurts,

Generally, he says, an erect penis is about five-and-a-quarter
inches long. When it is longer than that, the arms will be longer,
too. Unfortunately, the opposite is also true, he says, noting,
however, that for many partners, size is not the most important
issue. (Carr, 2014).

His measurements of the length of an erect penis is collected by taking averages of the dick lengths of the majority of men in this country who are, after all, white. Just the fact that you've got people measuring other men's dicks is in itself fucked up; but now they want everybody to think that they have shrunken dicks just because the white man's is. By the white man's own mythology and social statements, black men's penises are larger. So if we can establish that the statistics on dick length are skewed toward white men, then why shouldn't we further conclude that the findings in the "Journal of Sexual Medicine" and the findings in Goldstein's book, When Sex Hurts, are equally as biased? In fact, the reason why sex probably hurts is because the white man realizes that he has a shrunken dick! Ever think about that?

LOW-HANGING GUT

Low hanging gut? What about these bitches? The new "thing" appears to be for women with pot guts to wear tight blouses, expose their tits, wiggle their way into a pair of skinny jeans, put on some pumps and waddle their fat asses down the street. What's that about?

According to Carr (2014), "Most men would love to make their guts vanish. But when it comes to sex, men should ask what part of the anatomy their low-hanging guts make disappear. Turns out, it's the penis. "Statistically, a small penis is associated with a pear-shaped gut, also known as the pannus." says Goldstein. "Because the pannus extends out several inches -- and the shaft of the penis is also several inches -- the pannus can obscure the penis. The medical profession often refers to this condition as 'buried penis ….'" (Carr, 2014).

The fact of the matter is that if you look around, most of the men who have power have these guts. That is because they have sedentary lifestyles because they are rich – they call the shots. These hard bodies that you see on TV and in movies may appear virile, but they work FOR these fat assholes. In your view, the hard bodies – who you call "celebrities" are rich. But the fat boys are wealthy. The rich men and women receive the checks – the guys with the low-hanging guts SIGN those checks.

In a capitalist society, it doesn't matter what you look like because money, as George Simmel points out in his work The Color of Money, is the ultimate confounding of things. It makes the ugly appear beautiful, the small appear large, and the low-hanging gut types – when wealthy – appear most attractive. And guess who finds these fat boys attractive: the women who get laid and paid. Do you think the average bitch gives a fuck if you've got a fat gut if she's on your yacht or riding in your private jet?

So once put in the proper perspective, all this shit about what women like or dislike in bed is bullshit. Even young women will fall for an out of shape guy if he has money. If she has enough game she can always get some dick on the side. But what she wants and is attracted to is power and money.

FINGER RATIO

Growing up I had a lot of bitches tell me I had long fingers and nice hands. And that is when I started hearing shit about you can tell the size of a man's dick by his hands. I immediately bought into it and as part of some of my approaches to women, I'd often say, "see these hands?" and they would automatically know what I meant. So I guess the belief in the fingers and the hands is a widely known belief.

Now here's what Carr (2014) has to say:

> A man's fingers can reveal a lot about libido, if you know where to look. "Studies have shown a correlation between the length of the index and ring fingers and behavioral traits based on testosterone," says Goldstein. In what's known as the "2D:4D Digit Ratio," he says, there's less libido when the index finger (2D) is longer than the ring finger (4D), which indicates that the man was exposed to more androgen while in the womb. There's more libido – -- a sign that a man was exposed to high levels of testosterone during gestation – -- when his ring finger is longer than his index finger. Heredity has everything to do with these ratios. "A mother will pass on her own high or low testosterone levels to the fetus," he says.

This one sounds like bullshit, although a number of women do go by that "big hands big dick" philosophy. So it stands to reason that if you have long fingers, then these same female types would view it as a reflection of dick length. Valid? I don't know and to tell you the truth, I don't give a fuck. Why? Because women are liars and will shout and scream about how big your dick is when you haven't even put it in yet! So how can you rely on finger length when most of them have pussies so deep you could stick your leg in it and barely touch the sides!

TUBERCLE PROMINENCE

More weird sounding shit is to follow, this one having to do with the lips –
no, not the pussy lips – the ones surrounding her mouth! Check it out:

> The tubercle -- the slightly plump protrusion found at the bottom-
> center area of the upper lip -- has a surprising connection with
> pleasurable sex. In 2011, a study published in The Journal of
> Sexual Medicine cited that the greater the prominence of a female's
> tubercle, the more likely she is to experience a vaginal orgasm.
> (Carr, 2014).

What? Now let's try to figure this out logically. This information was
gleaned from The Journal of Sexual Medicine. Sexually speaking, who are the
most fucked up folks on the planet? White people. Now, since they only care about
themselves, who would this "journal" be aimed at? Their fellow white folks. So,
when we start talking about lips, who most closely lacks lip texture and has lips
closest to those of chimps? White people. Knowing all this, how could a plump
spot on the lips of women who are lacking in lips determine their likelihood of
having an orgasm? Lets delve a little deeper:

> "This relationship between tubercle and orgasm has been studied
> primarily in women, but it may also exist in men, pending further
> research," says Goldstein. "In the sexual medicine field, what
> happens in women usually happens in men, and vice versa." (Carr,
> 2014).

But the question is, who created this journal and for what purpose? Do you
actually expect me to believe that they are concerned about the sexual health of
blacks? The fact is, they have been working to destroy our sexual vitality for
centuries! That is what castration and pseudo-science were all about! No, it's about
the white woman who is lacking in lips (hence the rise of botox) and her man, who
is equally lipless. That may be why they lust to kiss one of us, the full-lipped black
man and woman and once they do, they apparently can't get enough. Now study
THAT, peckerwoods!

MAN BOOBS

This is nothing but an extension of the fact that if you get fat it's going to
impact on your sexuality. If you've got a fat gut then there's an effect. Now we
find that if you have fat around your tits – as many men do – then it's going to
have an effect. What if you have "man boobs" but a big dick? What then, white
boys? At any rate, check out their theory:

> Man boobs, which occur when excess fat is deposited in the chest
> area, are no laughing matter. "The condition is caused by excess
> estradiol -- an estrogen hormone -- and insufficient testosterone,"
> says Darius A. Paduch, MD and Ph.D., director of sexual medicine
> in the department of urology at New York Presbyterian
> Hospital/Weill Cornell Medical College. Not surprisingly, man
> boobs appear in overweight men whose bodies convert testosterone
> to estradiol. "In addition to having feminine-appearing breasts, a
> man will also lose his libido and have difficulty sustaining an
> erection because of the decrease in testosterone and his high levels
> of estradiol." (Carr, 2014)

This makes sense until you interject the variable of race. A black man who is overweight can still be physically fit because our people usually work blue collar jobs. Those fat bruthas you see in the bar who are dressed to the nines used to be janitors, bricklayers, foundry workers and the like. They just got fat because they ate a lot of red meat, and eating greedily is an after effect of being born poor and not having a lot of food. So when you grow up and get a job, you tend to over-do it. This behavior can lead to the formation of man boobs in later years.

But again I have to ask, is the previous conclusion based on a study of a white male sample? That is what they tend to do and then they try to "generalize" their bullshit findings and apply them to other races of men. Now I don't think a Sumo wrestler has enough dick to compensate for his fat tits and gut. But we're black men and there's plenty of white bitches who will testify to the fact that they black man's "man boobs" don't stop him from shoving boocoo dick up her pussy (and ass, if she swings that way). Look at these black and white linemen in the National Football League: many of them have manboobs, but they are still in shape.

I think that this area might need to expand and so a cross racial study. But wait: there's more!

> Paduch advises men with this condition to lose weight, which will
> help reduce testosterone conversion, and to cut down on the
> consumption of soy products, which contain phytoestrogens. (Carr,
> 2014)

How about this: grow a dick! In that way, no matter how fat you get, you can still get enough of a boner to have sex with your woman. How about that? Testosterone is important and white boys are injecting it every day. And it's not just them: black men have found out about testosterone and human growth hormone and are over dosing on the shit (just like we did when we found out about the effects of cocaine, marijuana and crystal meth!). So man boobs may be a hazard, but up to this point in our history, these bruthas have produced a lot of kids and even though they might die early, they die with a smile on their faces.

SNORING

Snoring means you're overweight and therefore may have a problem breathing. But Carr is only discussing physicality: if I'm bored with this woman lying next to me, I'm doing to take my ass to sleep. So boring is a symptom of being bored shitless in this case – it's not the origin of it! Here is what Carr claims:

> Snoring, which in men is associated with obesity and low testosterone, often indicates the sleep disorder called sleep apnea, says Paduch, associate professor of urology and reproductive medicine at Weill Cornell Medical College. "Sleep apnea causes grogginess on awakening," he says. "When you combine an already low testosterone level with the chronic fatigue that results from sleep deprivation over time -- which further lowers testosterone -- there's little or no energy for sex." (Carr, 2014).

And what would make a man allow himself to get this fucked up? First of all, if he's married or in a relationship, his woman is loading him down with carbs in the name of "good cooking." I believe this to be especially true of black women and Latinas. People of color have been programmed to "feed their man" and that "the way to a man's heart is through his stomach." But since most of these bitches are the ones with TB (two bellies), it appears that the way to HER heart is also through her stomach.

Not only that, but low testosterone levels are inevitable. If your relationship is totally reliant on sex, then you don't have one and she has all the advantages. Even after menopause, all she has to do is gap her legs and she can have sex. Not so for the male. So sleep apnea is the result because you allowed yourself to get fat. And you got fat because you got comfortable. If bad sex is the result, then all you have to do is condemn your physical state with the introduction and establishment of its opposite: in other words, stop eatin' so much, muthafucka! But seriously, even if you do eat a lot, if you exercise regularly you can steal keep from getting a pot gut, belly overhang and snoring. I know one sistah who is 66 years old and has the body of a 36 year old. How? She works out. She eats like a dog and is still svelte. Why? Because she cares about how she looks. Now don't get me wrong: she's batty as a bed bug, but her body is in great shape.

Moving on, the writer adds that, "Paduch advises men with this condition to lose weight and get treatment for sleep apnea to restore healthy sleep patterns." (Carr, 2014). There is another alternative: stop fuckin'! When you eat you will get fatigued unless you're in shape. Don't each after 8pm and maybe you can force a boner so you can stick it in this bitch so she'll stop running her fuckin' mouth about how you don't "love her" any more. You can buy that bitch all the flowers, candy and presents you want to, but if you ain't sticking it to her, the automatic conclusion is going to be you don't want to love her – or that you're "giving it" to someone else.

This is the perfect lead-in for the next issue addressed by Carr:

DEPRESSION

According to an article that appeared in the May 25, 2011edition of the Huffington Post, **Nineteen percent** of Americans will suffer from depression at some time during their lives. Sadly, depression hits the young and old alike. Fifty percent of children and adolescents and 20 percent of adults report some symptoms of depression." As you can see this information is over five years old so the numbers have increased without a doubt. If we are to buy into Carr's claim of depression and its impact on sex, is there any wonder why the birth rate among white people (no doubt the primary people who were tested) is on the decline.

This is not to equate sexuality with pregnancy, but it can be an indicator. Carr's article makes the following observation:

> To have good sex, you need to focus. "Unfortunately, men who are depressed, despite their best efforts at sex, have too many other things on their mind," says Paduch. In some cases, he says, their depression is associated with anhedonia, a condition that makes it difficult or impossible to experience pleasure, even when having sex. (Carr, 2014)

This is but the tip of the iceberg. Good sex is partially linked to mystery. As a major player in the sex game, I know that the quest is as important as the conquest. If a woman has a dress on so short you can smell her pussy and tits pushed up under her chin, where is the mystery? That plays a role I am sure. As for depression, who wouldn't be depressed as one's consciousness and awareness grows when it comes to male-female relationships. You begin to realize that it amounts to the male being a "trick" and the female selling pussy to the highest bidder. This is known as prostitution folks, despite the fact that it is referred to as "dating" in the American lexicon.

Continuing:

> Paduch notes that men who've gotten into a "not-in-the-mood" groove need to distinguish between what might be their temporary

moratorium on sex -- because of illness or after certain disruptive
events -- and long-term avoidance. Trusting your sexual partner is
critical, he says. And, adds Paduch, antidepressants should not be a
permanent solution. "Many anti-depression drugs, especially
SSRIs, have significant sexual side effects." (Carr, 2014)

And that includes Viagra, Cialis and Levitra, despite their claims. The white man doesn't give a shit about side effects. He wouldn't even be printing or broadcasting warnings about side effects if he hadn't been forced to by law. For decades these quacks have "prescribing" this and "recommending" that and people have been dying. If you take a pill to deal with this ailment you might end up paralyzed; if you take medication it doesn't cure anything – it just brings about temporary relief.

STIFF WALK

White men know it. Their scholars watch black men and have named what we do and have tried to emulate it, with no success. Eliott Liebow wrote about *Tally's Corner* and how black men carried themselves and then there was *Cool Pose,* written by Richard Majors about the young brothers and how they act on the streets. Everybody sees the walking style of black men (except the trained Uncle Toms, who still do it but not around their white bosses). They admire the hell out of it as do women, black and white alike. For instance, Steven Seagal has attempted to mimic black style but has failed miserably in his attempts. Ditto for Robert "Baretta" Blake and a host of others.

Carr writes that, "An easy rhythmic walk is a good indicator of how well you'll perform in bed. When the pelvis lacks total mobility, there's less chance of having a good orgasm, says Paduch, and an inflexible spine may be associated with nerve impingement." I believe that the same can be said of activity on the dance floor. White women are watching as black men gyrate and other try to imitate those moves. White women move madly on the dance floor in an attempt to display some sense of eroticism, but it's like a young baby who keeps beat with the music and adults consider it "dancing." As Karenga (1967) once wrote, "Whites can imitate or copy soul, but they cannot create out of that context."

Carr continues:

When it comes to sexual response, the nerve signal goes from the
brain to the spinal cord, where nerves travel through the vertebrae
to tell arteries in the penis to open," says Paduch. "This results in
increased blood flow and an erection." But, he says, if the vertebral
openings are squeezed because the spinal column lacks flexibility,
those signals won't get through to the penis. To improve

> flexibility, Paduch suggests a combination of exercise, yoga,
> muscle-relaxing practices, and acupuncture. (Carr, 2014)

There you have it. Back in the day, black youth played basketball religiously on the courts. White men drove by and saw it. Black people, until recently, were always in good physical shape. The best way to offset that is by impacting on the diet, so here comes inferior quality food stuffs at markets that serve a black clientele. Here comes an overload of malt liquor, usually not even sold in suburban siores. Here comes crack cocaine and on-going sabotage of the black family's life chances. Here comes mass incarceration of black males and prisons just recently snatching weights and other exercise equipment out of the prisons for fear that black males, who can already kick their ass, will just get stronger and stronger, and increasingly "buff."

Want proof? A book I reviewed and analyzed, *What Cops Know: Today's Police Tell the Inside Story of Their Work on America's Streets*. was a lengthy interview with Chicago police officers, and they spilled their guts to the author, Connie Fletcher. One part of it deals with this issue of black men and their walking style and physique, and here is an excerpt from those statements and my analysis:

> You can tell if somebody's just out of prison just by looking at
> them. They've got what we call a "joint body." They do the prison
> strut when they walk down the street. Say you're a young fellow,
> you're five-ten, weigh only 160 pounds. You go into prison.
> You're fresh meat, baby. You're gonna be breakfast for these cons.
> The first thing you do – you start pumping iron to have strength to
> survive in the joint. You get a big chest, huge arm muscles. It's an
> attitude you want to give off to people; it says, get outta my way,
> don't mess with me. These guys get out of the joint, they come at
> you down the street, they look like gorillas. They swing their
> torsos when they walk; they look menacing. You see somebody
> like that walking toward you, you get out of his way, right? He's
> got the joint body, the prison strut. You can spot an ex-con in a
> second that way (Fletcher, 1990, p. 25).

See? White men – including cops -- have always envied the bodies of black men. Black men have different muscle structure, much of it coming from hard, menial work. Since slavery, this white man has admired the black physique. These cops suffer from that same thing; even young black males who haven't done time have a "cut" physique, and white boys know it.

Calling that look a "joint" body is the white man's way of dealing with his sour grapes. There are white boys who go to prison and come out fat, overweight and sloppy looking. Even when they lift iron, they seldom have the cut of the black physique. Ask any body builder what the standard is.

As for that "prison strut," black men have always had a certain stride, a certain gait, if you will. The old school brothers used to call it "percolating." The white man is well aware of the walking patterns of blacks because he all too often admires us from a distance. It's part of the black cultural style. We call it "the pimp walk." The white man calls it the "prison strut" because, once again, he wants to take that which he craves and can never obtain, and consign it to a category of negativity. By calling it the prison strut, he can explain why he lacks the rhythm to do it: "I've never been to prison."

Don't get it twisted. Women don't care about any of this shit because being good in bed doesn't bring home the "bread," if you know what I'm saying. In capitalist America if you are a "good provider" and can make her feel comfortable, she'll overlook your shortcomings. Don't believe it? Ask Jewish men.

At any rate, the reasons why men may be "bad in bed" are probably just a few of the inner workings of some random female mind. But they are good to know because these reasons are part of the reason why the prostitution industry is multi-billion dollar industry. Men who ain't shit can still get pussy: they can prematurely ejaculate or not even be able to get a boner, but if they can pay, they can find a woman who takes the money and will say what he wants to hear, pose the way he wants her to pose and do what he wants her to do. And being a housewife is a more socially acceptable form of the same prostitution that you see on the streets and in the suites. And as a result, women continue to "get laid and paid."

The Foundation: Disguised "Misandry"

Many people have heard the term "misogyny" in reference to a lot of what's going on and being said today by white men, including Donald Trump. It translates to mean "the hatred of women," but it's far older than trump. In fact, one of the first movie shorts ever made by the Three Stooges was a 21-minute piece consisting of a long rhyme. The movie was called "The Woman Haters Club" and that was back in 1934. Here we are today some 83 years later and the issue is still a reality.

The Woman Hater's Club

This was in 1934 when television was still in its embryonic beginnings. And even back then white men – specifically Jewish white men – were pawning off sexist mistreatment and commentary off as "laughs." They even had women in audiences laughing at themselves.

In "Woman Haters," the Three Stooges – Moe and Curly Joe – join the "Woman Haters Club" and take a pledge to never have anything to do with women. In the meantime, Larry gets married anyway and tries to hide it from his buddies. But they take a train trip and Moe and Curly end up finding out.

I actually saw this one several times, and in my view it is one of the most misogynistic movies ever made. These guys HATE women and trade stories about how they got messed over and about how insane it is to be married. It was billed at the time as a "musical novelty." But what was novel about the system-wide maltreatment of women, forcing them into the "Ozzie and Harriet" mode of living?

At the woman haters club meeting, you hear comments like, "they need quiet, not a riot." They meet for the 7th time to convince member of the club that romance is a crime. Check it out:

> Speak up like a hero
> Your speech not be rehearsed,
> It's Mr. Zero.
> "Alright I'll speak up first."

This may have been done for laughs, but men had no reason to hate women during that time or any other. The fact is, men of that era (and today) seem to hate the responsibilities that come with women. We want to be boys all of our lives, "kicking it" and having a good, or so it would seem, while she stays home with those bad ass kids that we helped to make, and that is why the battle of the sexes lingers on to this day.

Larry comes in and says, "Fellas I have to quit the club I joined last week," and explains that the reason he has to quit is that he fell in love. The response, led by Moe, is overwhelming:

> "What are you thinking of?
> If you violate the rules of the club
> you'll be just as good as dead.
> If you do, you'll b e carried out with a lump on your head.

Laughs? Of course. But sometimes that which is "said in jest is meant in earnest." Violence against a man because he falls for a woman? No more farfetched than the black fraternities who brand themselves, label themselves as "dogs" and abuse women, even though they have wives at home (the wives passively allow such behavior in far too many cases).

Larry is convinced by the words and the threat, and says he'll cut off the relationship, and to show that he's serious, he'll put up his bankroll and sign an agreement for life. The response?

> Now that you've signed
> Please bear in mind
> No women around of any kind.

In one particularly racist scene, a black porter asks Larry, "Is that all?" referring to Larrys' luggage. Larry replies, "that's all that I want with you." Then he tips him. At the same time, Moe and Curly are looking for Larry and ask the porter if they've seen a curly haired fella. "Sure did, she's hot stuff," says the black man. Say what?!

In my view, this was the worst "Three Stooges" short of all time. They tried a music and combined poetry, and it fell flat. When you add these two mistakes to the subject matter – hating on women – then it becomes clear that the Stooges improved as they found themselves – their comic niche, so to speak – and began to do movies that were less political and more physically abusive and slapstick-oriented.

You have to remember something about television that was true in 1934 just as it is true today in 2016. Somebody had to write that poem and then somebody read it and a committee of people approved it. Then somebody put it in television dialogue format, ran it past the "Three Stooges" and got them to memorize the script. This was a group effort, and it is doubtful if a single woman was involved in the production. And here we are some 83 years later still able to watch it during re-runs on various television stations. Sexism, like racism, won't end until the white man admits that not only does it exist, but that it is perpetual and will continue.

Now that we understand how deeply misogyny runs, we can gain a better understanding of why misandry exists and how it manifests itself in the form of what could be called "socioeconomic payback."

On-Going Misandry Gets "Flipped"

Sexism, as one writer might put it, is nothing short of "fragmentation of the human whole" (no pun intended). But there is another term that is rarely used, but is more prominent than one might believe. The term is "misandry," and it basically means "the hatred of men." Some background is in order before moving on and showing the link between the hatred of women and how women continue to get "laid and paid."

According to one source,

Misandry, a word which appeared in the nineteenth century, is parallel in form to 'misogyny'. The form "misandrist" was first used in *The Spectator* magazine in April 1871. It appeared in *Merriam-Webster's Collegiate Dictionary* (11th ed.) in 1952. Translation of the French "Misandrie" to the German "Männerhaß" (Hatred of Men) is recorded in 1803. *Misandry* is formed from the Greek *misos* (μῖσος, "hatred") and *anēr, andros* (ἀνήρ, gen. ἀνδρός; "man") (Wikipedia, 2016).

These white people knew that such hatred could exist, despite the stranglehold that men thought they had on women's minds, beliefs, values, pocketbooks and goals. And that's pretty much the way it is today: men thinking that they have all this control when, in reality, *they don't control anything more than what women dupe them into believing and thinking they control.*

The misandry has been disguised, camouflaged with sex and other forms of social control. Women pretend to submit, feign being "talked out of their panties" and fake orgasms. They have been doing this for centuries. And in return to this feeling of "machismo" that the white man (and others) feel he's "earned," they are given increasing amounts of leverage and leeway, access to bank accounts and token access to power. The white woman has learned her lessons well: "The hand that rocks the cradle rules the throne."

Farrell (1993) has written a book that gives scholarly verification to a fact that most men in the streets have long known: that being the fact that men are "disposable." He cites as evidence of this the fact that men are in the most dangerous occupations, of which he claims the military is one. He claims that life expectancy is lower in men and suicides are higher. These points are relevant in only one way: as a point for discussion. Other than this, this white man sounds more like an apologist for men than anything else. The reasons for short life spans is the preoccupation with trying to justify and live up to the bullshit that men have created about themselves – things that they knew weren't true from the get-go.

More on this later.

Misandry is very real. I, for one, tend to believe that the claims that man-hating is a myth is in itself, bullshit. Women DO hate men and they have every reason to do so. You can hate someone and still be passionate about them; in fact, hate involves passion as does love. The opposite of love is not hate – it's "ambivalence." If you can say you don't care one way or the other about a person, that is the opposite of loving them. If you say you "hate" someone, you are nevertheless passionately connected. That's why so many people end up killing people they love as well as hate. Don't believe it? Watch an episode of "Snapped" and you'll see what I'm talking about.

How are you not going to "hate" someone who sends your daughters and sons off to war and claiming it's being done to protect YOU? He didn't ask you shit! He just started some shit and then sent the woman's kids off to fight for him. These old white men who talk all that shit and start wars can't fight! So they send kids off to do it. You don't think women see this shit?

You don't think women know that they get paid less for doing the same job a man gets paid? You don't think that these women use their spare time to study what is going on around them? You don't think women are smart enough to PRETEND to be "the weaker sex" while all the time puss whipping the hell out of men to get whatever they want or need? If you know this, then you have the basis for passion and that makes it hate. Because there is no way that an oppressed person can be "ambivalent" about the person who is oppressing him/her!

So misandry has to be the basis; this doesn't mean it has to be expressed behaviorally or verbally. In fact, these white feminists and their dyke counterparts are playing right into the white man's hands when they use the word "hate." As a black nationalist I have never written or said that I 'hated' the white man. I deplore his ways and I despise his traditions and history. But spending time hating him is like an obsessed bitch who claims that it's over but continues to stalk the guy that she claims to hate. It's like the punk ass guy who claims that he "quit" that woman but nevertheless talks about her every chance he gets, hoping to convince other guys not to go after her. All that "hate" does is waste energy, time that can be spend planning the next setback of the person you are ambivalent about but still as yet someone who you know is harming your people.

Women get laid and paid because they know that these are the male's two weakest areas: his wallet and his dick. They know that if they can control these two areas, they can gain a stranglehold. The fact of the matter is that if they can effectively control one of the two, they can automatically gain access to the second one, no matter which one is first or second. They have it like that and the male weaknesses are just that universal and easy to gain access to.

In the introduction to *The Great Comic Book Heroes*, though only h80 pages long, Jules Feiffer makes some great points about the super heroes of the 1930 and 1940s comic books. One point in particular is relevant to the issue of how men are viewed. In this case, Feiffer makes the comment that this is Superman's joke on the rest of us. Clark is Superman's vision of what other men are really like. We are scared, incompetent, and powerless, particularly around women (Feiffer, 1965). And this is exactly how women see us as well.

Super man could have assumed any identity: a construction worker, a pro athlete or even a radio announcer. He chose being a reporter so that he could keep up with what was going on, but to also fly under the radar. In Clark Kent, he wanted to be, as the promotion for the television version told us, "a mild-mannered reporter for the Daily Planet." Why "mild-mannered"? Because Superman saw earth men as pussies, that's why. And just as he saw us is how women see men for the most part: as violence-prone pussies who are desperate for pussy and will do whatever it takes to get it.

Misandry is payback for centuries of the stronger sex being projected as being "the weaker sex." Even William Shakespeare, in several of his plays, makes the point that men ain't worth a shit and that women have to "settle" just to be able to marry one. You don't have to hate men to see them for what they are. But women are trying to eke out an existence in a sexist society and on some level they are going to have to "deal with" the male of the species. So they pretend like they respect and love us, admire us and then dupe us into believing that they've bought into this misogynistic system called a "democracy."

But misandry is at the root and we deserve to have it inflicted upon us. But as I say in the case of racists, stop pretending you care about black people. Call a press conference, tell the world, "we hate niggers" and be done with it. In the case of the misogynist, the point is somewhat different: they need pussy in order to survive (although even now they are working on test tube alternatives to the vagina) and as a result, they pretend like they respect women by putting more on television, more on the movies, showing them kicking male ass, allowing them into the military to right wars that men started and so on. Far too many of them are duped into believing that such actions are signs of progress when *nothing* could be further from the truth.

The Pussy Principle: Concepts and Characteristics

The pussy principle is very simple and has been in effect for centuries, across international boundaries, cultural boundaries and of course, enacted to perfection here in the United States.

Pussy and the craving of it is a part of the male onset for the overwhelming majority of his life. Even after being rendered impotent by disease, natural causes or some kind of accident, men still spend huge amounts of money for "female company." After all, as the women say, "If you can't use the hips, use the lips." And so it has come to pass: the "pussy principle" is not only alive and well, but it is thriving in present day America.

What I am about to share is how the premise of the "mistress" enables a number of women, married or single, to get laid and paid.

Let me provide some examples.

It All Begins With "Nigga-Shit"

Because what I am about to write impacts all men and their being manipulated by women, don't get the term "nigga-shit" confused. I am mainly speaking about the bruthas and how easy it is to control their lives, the futures and their wallets through the skillful manipulation of pussy. Before addressing athletes and entertainers specifically, let me provide a case study and some definitions of the "nigga-shit" that creates division among black men who, like dogs, will fight over a woman in a "territorial" kind of way.

Take the case of professional basketball player Matt Barnes. An October 7, 2015 article from the Hollywoodlife.com website pretty much provides information that exhibits the kind of "nigga-shit" that I alleged. Under the heading, "Matt Barnes Attacks Former Teammate Derek Fisher For Dating Wife Gloria," the insights – and my analyses – follow:

> How awkward! New York Knicks coach Derek Fisher is involved in a romantic relationship with the WIFE of former L.A. Lakers teammate Matt Barnes. When Matt found out about it, all hell broke loose and he attacked his former pal! (Shilliday, 2015).

Once these bitches get ahold of one wealthy celebrity or athlete, it's difficult to "dumb down" when the next guy has to be selected. By that time they have a certain lifestyle that they want to maintain, which is why Derek Fisher was the logical "next man up" for the beautiful Gloria Govan. This then, is the beginning of what we call "nigga shit."

The story unfolds:

> This will make for an interesting twist on *Baksetball Wives LA* next season*!* One of the stars, **Gloria Govan**, 45, is now dating **Derek Fisher**, 41. Which would be great, except for the fact that Derek once played alongside Gloria's estranged husband **Matt Barnes**, 35, when the two were teammates on Los Angeles Lakers. Matt went berzerk over the news and totally attacked his friend! (Shilliday, 2015).

"Estranged" husband means that you're still married. But these bitches don't care and the media doesn't tell the whole story. Can there be any doubt that Barnes was getting' some pussy on the side? And of course Gloria found out. Women know how to serve revenge: "Let's see now, who can I fuck with that will drive Matt out of his fuckin' mind? I know – a former teammate!" So Derek got his ass kicked for messing with this woman when he (Derek) had his pick of any woman he wanted.

Check out what happened:

> When Matt learned that D-Fish was at Gloria's Los Angeles house
> on Oct. 3, he drove 95 miles from Santa Barbara, California to
> "beat the sh*t" out of him" according to *Page Six*. Their source
> says Derek and Gloria have been dating for "a few months," after
> Fisher filed to divorce his wife of 10 years, Candace, last spring.
> Even though Matt and Gloria are separated and there were rumors
> **that he dated Rihanna**, 27, it doesn't sound like Matt is allowing
> his estranged wife to do the same and date other people. (Shilliday,
> 2015).

First of all, I doubt if it as "Gloria's house." She was still married to Barnes so it was THEIR house. Secondly, if Derek and Gloria were "dating for a few months," then it is clear that he fucked her. Third, since Matt filed for divorce, then he didn't have shit to say other than the fact that if it wasn't her house, she shouldn't be entertaining company. Matt and Gloria had been married for ten years and he was a pro basketball player, so you KNOW he got pussy on the side. And while he was out of town, on the road, you also KNOW that she was fuckin' behind his back.

But she felt comfortable enough to have a party and invite Derek over. The only problem was that when women "get laid and paid," they have to be discreet because there are a lot of men out there who just can't get that pussy out of their minds. Barnes was one of them. Observe:

> The source confirmed the relationship between Derek and Gloria
> while explaining that "Derek was in Gloria's backyard with about
> 10 people having a bonfire on Saturday." Apparently Matt took
> this as the ultimate betrayal, causing him to drive down to LA from
> his Memphis Grizzlies training camp to confront his former
> teammate. "He went crazy. He got in his car and went to the house
> and went after Derek," their source said about Matt. Another
> insider claims "Someone told Matt that Derek was at the house and
> he drove down there — he went over to confront Derek."
> (Shilliday, 2015).

Ironically, Derek Fisher sat in as a co-host on the May3, 2017 edition of "Inside the NBA" and the topic was never raised. So he got his ass kicked a few years back and now it's business as usual. Take note that the Los Angeles Clippers, who had brought Matt Barnes on board for the end of the season and playoffs after losing Blake Griffin to injury, would not be an issue because the Clippers had just been eliminated from the playoffs by the Utah Jazz. So as soon as that's done, here comes "D-Fish" for the first time. Was he dodging the issue? Were the other hosts trying to avoid Barnes coming to the studio or being interviewed and saying something about incident?

What was Barnes going to "confront" Derek about anyway? Was it his house? Check out what Shilliday (2015) wrote:

> A source close to Fisher confirmed the fight to *Page Six* but said, "Matt came after Derek but he only had a few scratches…Derek's not going to press charges, he's going to let it go." Derek left Gloria's house before police arrived. The Knicks tweeted on Oct. 6 that that Derek was "not at practice due to personal reasons — expected back tomorrow." He was in LA visiting his kids but it is possible that he paid Gloria another visit!

Fisher was scared shitless. Barnes is a thug known for mixing it up on the basketball courts, so you know what he would have done to Fisher. But Gloria is the one who gets the money and the sex from two men who are in shape and obviously infatuated with her; and believe me, she is FINE! But that's what makes these women able to "get laid and paid." That is what makes them marriage material. They set it up so they can get the big house, the children who go to the best schools, a car and bank account of their own (and his as well) and that's the reality of the "American Dream."

But remember: the bruthas who get duped are very childlike and their needs are few. They can't stay out of the arms of other women on the side and they can be "tamed" with a little head and some booty. Meanwhile, the seducing, reducing, inducing strategies and tactics continue on. But in reality, it boils down to being what is known on as the streets by the elders as "nigga shit."

Pro Athletes and "Mistresses"

Getting laid and paid is evident when it comes to the institution of marriage and these so-called "housewives" who control the family budget, but it's all over the place. Let's take a look at the article about and comments of this porn star named Lisa Ann, who was the focus of an article in the *Sporting News* in March of 2016. The headline was, "Porn Star Lisa Ann Warns 25 Percent of NBA Players Have Faced Blackmail." According to the article,

> NBA Pro athletes engaged in affairs with porn stars and strippers should watch their step, warns adult film star and director Lisa Ann. She estimates 25 percent of NBA players have faced blackmail at some point in their careers. Writing for Complex, the basketball aficionado warned that rich NBA stars, particularly married players, have become targets for hustlers looking to steal their money, wallets, jewels, even their Playstations. If they're not

stealing, they're trying to hustle players into paying their rent or
buying them fancy cars (McCarthy, 2016).

But let's place the blame where it belongs: cockhounding-ass black men who see a white bitch in the stands and lose their minds. White society knows what these Kardashian-oriented women are about, and so do the teammates of the men who spend that money. But who really cares? Do these men give a shit about having "wives" at home or children who may be affected? Of course not. And this is one more piece of evidence that backs up my later claim and contention that men are viewed as children by women: immature "boys" who chase pussy and need a "mommy-type" to take care of them.

The previous quote by Lisa Ann posits that, "rich NBA stars, particularly married players, have become targets for hustlers looking to steal their money, wallets, jewels, even their Playstations." Play stations? Grown ass men? Jewelry? Are these men or bitches? So all that material acquisition slowly directs these males toward what they REALLY are and what they really crave: pussy – preferably white pussy. The article adds that, "If they're not stealing, they're trying to hustle players into paying their rent or buying them fancy cars." I ask, how is this any different than what the housewife is doing? Blackmail won't work if the man knows what's going on in terms of his relationship at home. "Tell her – she already knows," should be the response. But these cowardly effeminate assholes are AFRAID of the women they married. And so they pay the blackmail to keep the ho quiet.

And what a "get laid and paid" scam it is. According to Lisa Ann,

> I've heard girls say they make sure he is married or in a
> relationship before going back to his hotel with him. Once there
> they wait for their moment alone with his wallet and take photos of
> all of his credit cards and his ID. The final part of the plan is
> blackmail. You would be shocked how many NBA players have
> had been blackmailed in an effort to keep their privacy. My guess
> is a minimum of 25 percent of NBA players have dealt with
> blackmail at some point in their career. I've heard girls brag about
> long-term hustles where they have a player paying their rent and
> expenses just to keep them quiet and out of their family
> life.(McCarthy, 2016).

Snitch-ass Kobe Bryant got busted by his woman after he "raped" a white bitch while he was undergoing therapy in Colorado. I mean he bent the bitch over a chair and everything. So she blackmailed his ass. He came clean at a press conference, but that wasn't good enough. He added that, "I should have just paid her off the way Shaq does with his women." Now Shaq was married at the time, and his wife has since divorced him. Did Kobe's comments have anything to do with it? Who knows. But I know this: Shaq had kids and those kids watched Kobe's press conference. So Kobe is a snitch and a bitch. And his fine-ass Latina wife threatened him and he had to go out and buy her a million dollar ring and hasn't "gotten out of line" since. She definitely got "laid and paid."

Getting laid and getting paid. And for what? Pussy? I understand that men have their needs, but the problem with far too many of us (black men) is that we let our needs dominate and direct our thought processes. White men probably do that as well, but I don't give a shit what happens to them. I am talking about the few brothers who get the chance to make big money and who should be donating that money to community-based organizations (not the church) to defend and develop the black communities that spawned most of them. Instead, they know that these women want their money because even the ugly muthafuckas like Dennis Rodman can get approached by these women.

But it's not just the cockhounds from the NBA who get "punked" right out there in the open for all to see (clad in underwear, standing and listening to a little white man tell them what to do, having child-like temper tantrums when the referee makes a call they don't like, etc.), it's also the men from the National Football League and pro baseball as well. But beyond sports, politicians buy into it as well. I will address women getting "laid and paid" by the politicians and how it has functioned using a few case studies.

Politicians and "Mistresses"

America is a conglomeration of its own contradictions, preaching morals on the one hand and fucking around like there's no tomorrow on the other hand. An article titled, "Twenty Presidents Who Were Rumored to Have Mistresses," by Caitlin Bussman, which appeared on a website called "rantpolitical," provides a basis from which we can clearly establish why America is on the moral decline.

In this section I show that it is not pussy that brought down these men or impugned their reputations; it is the desire to get pussy, to seek it out, to control it that is the problem. See, the thing is, you can never control pussy unless you control the woman who is carrying it. And despite the games and claims to the contrary, no man can EVER control a woman, and this is especially true once kids come into the picture.

Let me provide some examples, borrowed from an incorrectly headlined article titled, "Twenty Presidents Who Were Rumored to Have Mistresses," and analyze, in retrospect, the role that sex plays even when the guys are borderline impotent, ultra-busy or borderline gay. Even when men have unlimited power, the pussy principle kicks in and is always at work. It's about conquest and power, and in some cases, getting a nut. At any rate, this mentality and tendency lends itself to "how women get laid and paid."

George Washington and Venus

Who is the hell is "Venus," you may ask. According to Bussman (2014),

> George was rumored to have an affair with a slave named Venus, resulting in the birth of a son named Wes Ford. Descendants to this day deny it ever happened, and refused any kind of DNA research. (Bussman, 2014).

I don't know what black woman in her right mind would name a lovely black girl after a white mythical character. But there she was: enslaved and vulnerable and the white boy who is still considered, "the father of our country" was taking advantage of some under aged pussy. Do you know any white folks named Washington? There are, of course, probably tens of thousands but what is noteworthy here is that there are probably millions of black people with that last name. And in fact, when you hear that surname, you assume that the person was black.

The grade schools, middle schools and high schools offer history and civics classes boasting about their bullshit presidents. They lie and revise history to make them look like they were great men. But when you enslave another human being and then take pussy that shows your true character. The only response the white historians can offer are denials, revisionist lies, and shame.

Abraham Lincoln and Joshua Speed

The man who black people love so much and who is still attributed with "ending slavery" (a damn lie – he ended it in areas where he had no jurisdiction), was married and was probably a fag. According to Bussman (2014), "Yes, you're reading that right. The two lived together for four years, and were rumored to have shared the same bed. A second 'affair' was said to happen with his bodyguard David Derickson."

Now, in today's racist white popular culture, they have the gall to offer us movies like "Abraham Lincoln: Vampire Slayer." What? There is no such thing as a vampire, you stupid muthafuckas. But guess what? How about a movie called "Abraham Lincoln: Fudge Packer"? Or "Abraham Lincoln: The Rump Roaster Who Would Be President"? Again, I don't put anything past a race of people whose men walked around in powdered wigs and called themselves "judges." They were waging war and killing unarmed people by day and taking it up the ass and sucking dick by night. Now – put THAT in the history books!

John F. Kennedy and Mimi Alford

Whether you take pussy or buy pussy, you're lacking in game and character in my book. And when you're president of the United States and you're doing it, risking it all (can you say Bill Clinton?), there is something wrong with you. Check out the following:

> No president liked to wander more than JFK, which will become evident in this list. The biggest cheater to ever reside in the oval office, has a never-ending list of women who claimed to have had an affair with him. And unfortunately for Jack, several of them have been confirmed. One of his first conquests was White House intern Mimi Alford -- who was 19 at the time. The two had an 18-month relationship, until he became tired of her. (Bussman, 2014).

Why aren't there any theories about Kennedy's assassination being the result of a plot designed by Jackie and one of his bitches? Wouldn't it seem logical? She had to know what he was into because the women he was messing with were highly visible and fine.

Like Clinton, he decided to fuck a White House intern. But we can't put it all on him. Women know what they're doing and they know that men, regardless of their power and titles, are as weak-minded as hell. She probably hiked her skirt up, bent over so he could see her panties and he got a boner. He snatched into one of those back rooms and prematurely ejaculated all over her and then gave her the day off. She was only nineteen years old and that's how white men – and a growing number of black men – seem to like their women: young, dumb and ready to be filled with cum.

This was no "fling." I consider a year and a half to be a long time, especially when Kennedy was married and surrounded by body guards (who had to know about it) and Bussman claims "until he got hired of her." No way. That bitch got PAID. If he hadn't paid her it would have been all over the newspapers. He knew that. So he probably gave her a giant wad of cash and threatened her. And, like most white women who get laid and paid, she kept her fuckin' mouth shut.

John F. Kennedy and Marilyn Monroe

Now this was some class pussy right here. The only problem was she was fuckin' almost everybody! This bitch was giving up more pussy than the local pet store! According to Bussman,

> Well, let's knock this one out of the way, shall we? The two had a romantic rendezvous at Bing Crosby's house in Palm Springs shortly after meeting. It's reported that Monroe got in touch with the President's wife, Jackie, and told her about the affair. Jackie was well aware of John's wandering eye, and responded by telling her to move in and marry him, and then she would have all the problems! (Bussman, 2014).

I don't know how valid this statement by Bussman is because I believe that Jackie was a dyke all along and just used men like JFK and Onassis as a "front;" JFK wasn't fucking her and Onassis was too old to fuck. So Jackie, who couldn't divorce JFK because of the scandal that would be involved, probably just bumped pussies with some women behind closed doors. I really don't give a shit but I'm only citing this excerpt and others to prove one thing: bitches know how to get "laid and paid," and Jacqueline Kennedy-Onassis was no exception.

John F. Kenned and Judith Campbell Exner

Revisionist history keeps this pussy hound from being exposed for what he really was. Black people kissed his ass and many older blacks have pictures and paintings of John, his brother Robert, and Martin Luther King standing shoulder to shoulder. And rightfully so: all three fucked around on a regular basis, including the fact that Robert also fucked Marilyn Monroe ("sloppy seconds" behind his brother), and King was fucking white women galore behind Coretta's back.
But in the case of JFK and this woman Exner,

> Introduced by Frank Sinatra, the two began their affair in 1960 in Vegas. In interviews since the affair, Exner described him as being "so reckless" and even admitted to aborting his child, although those allegations have never been proven. (Bussman, 2014).

I believe Exner. I believe that JFK didn't use condoms and didn't give a shit if she was using birth control. When he wanted pussy he wanted it with the quickness and that is what she meant by his being "reckless." What did he care? If push came to shove, he could have that bitch capped. He was fucking her at the same time that the Rat Pack was hanging out, which means that Peter Lawford, Sinatra, Sammy Davis, Joey Bishop and the rest of the "hangers on" knew about it as well. JFK wanted to be a part of the group but couldn't because he had big dreams; but his past is secure because the revisionist historians who dominate the American publishing estate make sure that the truth about these dog-ass white boys never gets out. He'd better be glad that there was no social media back then, or he'd be busted just like that bastard Donald Trump is even now being exposed in 2016.

John F. Kennedy and Ellen Rometsch

Check out the following JFK debacle:

> If you're going to cheat non-stop, why not make one a prostitute? Rometsch was from Germany and resembled Elizabeth Taylor on a bad day. She attended secret naked pool parties at the White House and would routinely visit for quickies. Apparently, brother Bobby threatened to have her deported but it's not stated whether or not that followed through. (Bussman, 2014).

Laid and paid. This guy had all the pussy he wanted, was married, and still had to find a bitch that he PAID money to. This is white boys for ya. Since those days the concept of paying for pussy has attempted to become normalized in popular culture, led by that worthless Charlie Sheen and his popular TV show, "Two and a Half Men." Not only did he buy pussy, but he used his money and his beach house as a recruitment tool for hos! Then he would brag about it and even his under-aged nephew knew about it.

As it relates to JFK, how can you have a "secret naked party" at the White House? How did this asshole find out? Where were the secret agents and government men? Where the fuck was Jackie? It was no secret except to the public. These white people show their true nature when they get some power and can afford some semblance of security.

Grover Cleveland and Maria Crofts Halpin

Another child born behind the back of a president's wife. How can this be? This guy was unique in that, according to one source, he was an American politician and lawyer who served as the **22nd and 24th** President of the United States.[1] He won the **popular vote** for three presidential elections – in **1884, 1888,** and **1892** – and was one of the three **Democrats** (with **Andrew Johnson** and **Woodrow Wilson**) to serve as president during the era of **Republican** political domination dating from 1861 to 1933. He was also the first and only President in American history to serve two non-consecutive terms in office.(Wikipedia, 2016).

But that means nothing: these white men with all that power continue to pay for pussy and take huge risks. Those bitches know everything because the white man, like his woman, is a gossip. Check out the case of Grover Cleveland:

> The 1884 presidential elections got ugly. Cleveland's opponent James Blane alleged Cleveland had fathered an illegitimate child with Halpin while practicing law in New York. In Blane's defense, Cleveland had been paying child support to Halpin. In Cleveland's defense, Halpin admitted she was a whore who slept with the whole law office and had no clue who the father was. Cleveland paid because he was the only bachelor there, and just assumed... (Bussman, 2014).

Another president with a "whore." He later got cancer and had it operated on aboard a yacht while on vacation. These white boys not only got "laid and paid," but they got away with it on both counts.

Bill Clinton and Monika Lewinsky

I believe Clinton "paid" as well as got laid. According to recent accounts by his wife's opponent Donald Trump, he was fined $850,000. But we'll get to that later.

The fact is, Clinton seduced that young girl because he was president of the United States, a man who knew full well that this girl was the same age as his own young daughter, Chelsea. One source gives us the embarrassingly unbrotherly facts of the case:

> In 1995, Lewinsky, a graduate of Lewis & Clark College, was hired to work as an intern at the White House during Clinton's first term, and was later an employee of the White House Office of Legislative Affairs. While Lewinsky worked at the White House, Clinton began a personal relationship with her, the details of which she later confided to her friend and Defense Department co-worker Linda Tripp, who secretly recorded their telephone conversations.(Wikipedia, 2016).

Linda Tripp wasn't always overweight and ugly. But obviously her lackluster love life made her depressed and she turned into a hefty bag. So she was jealous when this young girl divulged that she had just sucked Clinton's dick, not just once, but several times. And Tripp couldn't keep her mouth shut and probably wanted some of the limelight. So here's what took place:

> When Tripp discovered in January 1998 that Lewinsky had sworn an affidavit in the Paula Jones case denying a relationship with

> Clinton, she delivered the tapes to Kenneth Starr, the Independent
> Counsel who was investigating Clinton on other matters, including
> the Whitewater scandal, the White House FBI files controversy,
> and the White House travel office controversy. During the grand
> jury testimony Clinton's responses were carefully worded, and he
> argued, "It depends on what the meaning of the word 'is' is,"[6] with
> regard to the truthfulness of his statement that "there is not a sexual
> relationship .(Wikipedia, 2016).

Clinton was already in trouble with Paula Jones – who also ended up getting paid. She is the one who got the $850,000. And here is now, in 2016, still trying to do harm to Clinton by appearing at Donald Trump's campaign debates with some other bitches that Clinton allegedly "sexually assaulted." Laid and paid, plain and simple.

Clinton looked like a complete ass in front of millions of people, lying his ass off. Then he had to recant his statement and admit that he lied to the country and to his wife. And don't think Hillary wasn't pissed. I don't think she's said a word to that muthafucka since 2001. Now she's running for President and is using him in her campaign, and will probably use him in her cabinet if elected. But her attention is on Chelsea, their daughter and her grand kids.

Bill Clinton was 49 years old at the time and Monica was 22, and a White House intern. He fucked her life up, although she tried to do some writing and did go away and get a degree. And what about Billy boy?

> President Clinton was held in civil contempt of court by Judge
> Susan Webber Wright for giving misleading testimony in the
> Paula Jones case regarding Lewinsky and was also fined $90,000
> by Wright. His license to practice law was suspended in Arkansas
> for five years and later by the United States Supreme Court
> .(Wikipedia, 2016).

So getting some head behind your wife's back cost him his law license and a bunch of money. I hope that this shows that it doesn't matter if you're the President of a pauper, if you want to get laid in America you are going to pay one way or the other.

James Buchanan and William Rufus King (probably)

I don't know what Bussman wrote "probably" because if it didn't happen, then he had no business printing it. I date a lot of pretty women and when nosey assholes see us out, the know my reputation and assume that I 'probably' fucked them. See what I mean? At anyrate, here is how this particular situation evolved, although it sounds like a homosexual tryst:

> After Buchanan's wife, Anne Coleman, died; he and future VP William Rufus King became very... close.King and Buchanan attended social functions and lived together, referred to themselves as a "communion", and Andrew Jackson called them "Miss Nancy and Aunt Fancy." After King died of TB, Buchanan became President and once wrote in his journal: "I have gone a wooing to several gentlemen, but have not succeeded with a one of them." (Bussman, 2014).

So Buchanan was gay, which means he was gay when he was married. And this is one more example of these powerful white men living double lives while their wives know what's going on but they enjoy the comforts and the status so they keep their mouths shut. Why? Because they may not be getting laid, but they are sure enough getting paid!

Buchanan was the 15th president of the United States and always favored the South in his decisions. He is quoted as having once said that, "slavery is of little practical importance." His woman knew this just like these other white women knew that their husbands were racist. But they kept their mouths shut and nodded their heads in approval. And why? Because they got "laid and paid"!

Warren G. Harding and Nan Britton

This president was known for his cockhounding and apparently didn't give a shit about who knew. The rumors were that he was of "mixed race," but whether he was or not, he was caught in a scandal that almost rivaled Bill Clinton's many years later. Check it out:

> Throwing it back to 20's for this cheating commander-in-chief who strayed more than once. His first conquest was Nan Britton. Britton claims that right before Harding took the presidency, he fathered her illegitimate child. She made the announcement of her daughter and the cheating scandal well after his presidency ended in 1928. She described him as a womanizer and swore til the day she died in 1991 that her child was Harding's. (Bussman, 2014).

Sound familiar? And you don't think this woman got paid? These women aren't giving away booty for free because these old white man can't be that great in bed. They were getting wined and dined and given money to pay this bill or that bill because this was back in the days when prostitutes were more frugal and practical than those "buy me a diamond necklace" type bitches that you see today.

Warren G. Harding and Carrie Fulton Phillips

> The most well-known of Harding's affairs. The two were together for a long period of time when Harding was just a senator. The affair between the two ended around the time he became president when she tried to blackmail him. Not only did she try to blackmail him, she was successful. (Bussman, 2014)

Again, key points that you are not going to find in any history book in the American school system. Why? Because their goal is to make their presidents appear to be as moral and ethical as possible. That is where the myth that "George Washington never told a lie" and "Abraham Lincoln chopped down a cherry tree" came from.

Dwight D. Eisenhower and Kay Summersby

> Kay Summersby was Eisenhower's chauffeur and secretary during World War II. Eisenhower was not President at the time, and the two went their separate ways when he returned to the United States. This affair was never confirmed, but the two spent more time together than anyone else and were rumored to be very close. (Bussman, 2014).

Of course they had an "affair," as it was called. These guys have all this power and oftentimes the only female in the office or in nearby proximity is their "secretary." She knows she's going to give up that booty and so does he – it's just a matter of time. Clinton had his interns, JFK had his intern and Grover Cleveland had his office worker and FDR had his secretary. And the list goes on. And the American people, even when they find out, they don't really care as they showed when they found out that Donald Trump openly admitted grabbing women by their pussies. What kind of country elects these kinds of men? I think it is pretty clear, and that is why women continue to get "laid and paid."

Thomas Jefferson and Sally Hemings

> One of the biggest affairs in Presidential history was between TJ and his slave Sally Hemings. It's been suggested that the couple had six children together, four of which survived and went on to be free. This could be the most scandalous of all on the list, seeing as

race relations then are definitely not what they are today. (Bussman, 2014).

To begin with, race relations today are really no different if you look at what is said behind closed doors when an interracial couple is spotted. And second of all, why would this matter? The fact is this is a man who felt black people were inferior, and was on record claiming that the enslaved male was "less amorous" toward his female than the white male. Well this is a lie, but if it were true, maybe it was because the black male had white men like Jefferson whipping his ass every day and when he (the enslaved) got back to the shack, some peckerwood was straddling the black woman!

Franklin D. Roosevelt and Lucy Mercer

> The affair between FDR and his secretary Lucy was discovered first by none other than Eleanor Roosevelt herself. She wanted a divorce, but the President would have none of it, fearing that the scandal would become public and put his political career in jeopardy. (Bussman, 2014).

The word was that Eleanor was a lesbian. Who knows and who gives a shit? The main thing is that she stayed put as do most white women. They talk all that shit about sexism and gender bias, but they all seem to have a price. Hillary Clinton sure had one, and evidently she wasn't alone.

James Garfield and Lucia Calhoun

> James Garfield went the younger route when cheating with his mistress Lucia who was 18 at the time. She was a NY Times reporter whom the president had much admired. When wife Lucretia found out, he was given the ultimatum of wife or mistress, to which he played smartly and picked his wife. (Bussman, 2014).

No, he "pretended" to pick his wife. That young white girl was having an affair with the President of the United States and she wasn't going to give it up. He was getting head from a young woman who was someone he could talk to, and he wasn't going to give that up so he could go home to Lucretia. He lied and said he'd give it up and then he had his aides and others falsify some "fake business trips" or other junkets that they claimed were related to the job, trips that he would take the young woman on. That's how it's done, folks.

John Tyler and the Majority of His Slaves

> John Tyler holds the record for having fathered the most children of any president. In his two marriages Tyler fathered 15 legitimate

children. What remains murky is the persistent rumor that he'd fathered children with many of his slaves. Oral history among slaves confirms this -- however it's nearly impossible to prove by DNA, since all the children were reportedly sold off. (Bussman, 2014).

The question is why this information is not discussed in the American history and political science courses around the nation. Why don't white kids learn about all this "illegitimacy" among the "founding fathers" and other famous white men? What is there to hide? I think we know the answer. Black women who were held in bondage had no choice and surely did not get paid. The white man's history is the one that legitimately made rape legal. This is a point that should be studied in the law and civics classes of America. After all, isn't the oath in court "to tell the truth, the whole truth and nothing but the truth"?

George H.W. Bush and Jennifer Fitzgerald

> Big daddy Bush's affair was never confirmed, but this rumored couple met within the White House walls. Jennifer was the White House deputy chief of protocol and the affair was reportedly discovered by an aide to Bill Clinton. How convenient?

Like father, like son. The White House, as we can see in this analysis, has always been a hotbed of lewd and lascivious behavior. And yet it remains hidden behind those closed doors and those falsely named "hallowed" halls.

Lyndon B. Johnson and Alice Glass

> No stranger to cheating, Lyndon Johnson did this routinely. One of his most infamous scandals was with Alice Glass, whom wife Lady Bird has admitted to attacking. Nothing like a cat fight in the White House!

Another Texas loser gets into the white house (like Big Daddy Bush) and decides to sow his oats while his wife is right in the next wing. And these are the people who help perpetuate stereotypes about black people being sexually out of control, the myth of the black rapist and the myth of the loose black female. Meanwhile, these white men are in the White House and having sex with women who are getting laid and paid.

John F. Kennedy and Angie Dickinson

Dickinson was a slut that probably laid down with Sinatra and other members of the Rat Pack, of which JFK was an unofficial member. She played the role of a slut in the movies and on television and even in the TV flick "Police Woman," she was a loose cannon. Of course, JFK had also had affairs with Marilyn Monroe, Mimi Alford and Jill Cowen (both of them secretaries in the White House) and a stripper named Blaze Starr.

Mayor Marion Barry

While he was not directly a trick, he acted like one on enough occasions where, once he got hooked on crack, it appeared that Mayor Barry simply threw caution to the wind. According to Crilly (2014),

> He had had suffered a string of health problems in recent years,
> including diabetes, prostate cancer and a kidney transplant …
> Aside from his very public downfall - captured on video in a hotel
> room smoking a crack pipe in an FBI sting - he was always known
> as gregarious and charismatic, earning the title of Washington's
> "Mayor for life". (Crilly, 2014).

Bad health. A lot of crack heads experience that, and with Barry's track record, it could have been much worse. But as is far too typical of black people, we give assholes like this the benefit of the doubt no matter what they do. The same thing we did for Jesse Jackson and others of his misguided ilk. Crilly offers up the following assessment:

> Mr Barry managed to earn the title of the most notorious drug
> abuser in North American politics, long before Rob Ford was
> forced to take a leave of absence from his job as mayor of Toronto
> to deal with his drink and drug problems this year. Yet at one time,
> Mr Barry was a rising star of the Democratic Party, seen as one of
> America's most promising black politicians. He served three terms
> as mayor from 1979 before his personal life overtook his political
> career. (Crilly, 2014).

I don't know about that. Rob Ford smoked crack, talked shit on live TV, and admitted that he "copped" from drug dealers who were in the nearby vicinity. At least Marion Barry tried to keep his shenanigans under cover. But then again, this is a white reporter so what can you expect: when the issue is a negative they are more than willing to give black people "numero uno" status.

Marion had power and when you find a man with power you find someone who is more than willing to spend money on women. Many keep it under wraps but as in the case of Barry, who was like some kind of "godfather," he did his dirt and continued to do it, term after term.

Then came the point where "pussy politics" began to dominate and direct his life:

> In 1990 he met an ex-girlfriend, Rasheeda Moore, at a Washington hotel. Unknown to him, the room was rigged with hidden cameras. The 83-minute video captured him fondling Miss Moore and asking about the possibility of sex before taking two long drags on a crack pipe. At that point, FBI agents and police officers burst into the room. The court - sitting at the time of a crack epidemic and amid rising racial tensions - also heard allegations that the pair had used cocaine as many as 100 times. (Crilly, 2014).

The bitch set him up. She got paid after being laid many years earlier. Just the fact that he was able to fondle her shows that she knew what time it was. And if I remember correctly, she took a hit off the crack pipe as well. The only difference was that he was the political figure and was the one the authorities wanted to get tabs on. And that taped was aired on every major television station in the nation. And the bitch probably got paid after Barry got arrested. .

Continuing:

> Mr. Barry's lawyers accused law enforcement agents of entrapping the mayor and eventually the jury found him guilty of only one lesser charge of cocaine possession. He was sentenced to six months in prison. He later reflected on his troubled third term. In his autobiography, he described the build-up to another drug-fueled encounter at a party: "It was a mix of power, attraction, alcohol, sex and drugs". (Crilly, 2014).

He calls it "a mix of power, attraction, alcohol, sex and drugs." And reader, let me tell you: all five of these areas have something to do with the female persuasion. Men don't use drugs unless there is sex on their minds; men with power don't sit around drinking unless there is a woman somewhere in the vicinity. And in many cases these men are married, so that's one woman who's getting "laid and paid" from the get-go. But for some reason she's just not enough. And so it goes

Corey Booker, Newark Mayor and Senate Candidate

This guy, as of 2017, is being bandied about as a candidate for president in 2020. Really?

Booker was one of the speakers at the 2016 Democratic Convention in July and talked a whole lot of shit about how great America was and why the masses should throw their votes behind Hillary Clinton for president. But what it shows is that most people have short memories and as a result, Booker – like a number of black politicos in city after city – can do dirt and still get away with it. Look at the silly shit this black man, who was at the time running for a senate seat in New Jersey (which he won), got himself into:

> Could you call it a scandal? It's not exactly clear *who* is outraged. But Lynsie Lee, a Portland, Ore., stripper who once exchanged private Twitter messages with Senate candidate Cory Booker of New Jersey, is enjoying the attention while it lasts. The story is basically this: On Wednesday a BuzzFeed reporter -- perhaps with sexually challenged New York politico Anthony Weiner on the brain -- posted a story about Lee exchanging private messages with Booker, the bachelor mayor of Newark, N.J. (Pearce, 2013).

As I stated earlier, he won the Senate seat and he continues to be an articulate spokesman for the Democratic party. But I hope you can see why the white man has documentation that the white woman is the black man's "kryptonite." We just can't seem to keep away from those bitches, in person or on line. Why would this black man whose future is bright (in their system, of course) risk it all to engage in a Twitter exchange with a bitch who strips (and probably sells pussy) for a living?

The fact is you can be politically astute and say all the right words at press conferences, staff meetings and during talk shows and still be a complete and total clueless asshole in real life. Want proof?

> The private exchange with Booker, tweeted by Lee, was in February, after the mayor had done some characteristically goofy Twitter bantering with his followers. Booker tweeted to his followers that he wanted to be president of New Jersey's Star Trek club. Lee, who works at a vegan strip club in Portland, publicly tweeted at the ambitious mayor, "if you're ever POTUS I call dibs on First Lady." (Pearce, 2013).

And they wonder how these women end up getting laid and paid. They set these guys up, put on a short skirt and go after them. The guys will pay one way or the other, and it will more likely than not be a long-term "contract" whether the guy knows it or not. Elsewhere in this book, I include an article about the percentage of NBA players who are being blackmailed.

Corey Booker, like Jesse Jackson Jr., Marion Barry and so many other black men who think they are "politicos," can't seem to stop taking steps that will lead to their own undermining and eventual self destruction. And speaking of these types of bruthas, let's take a look at a man who claimed to be a "reverend" (just like Jesse Jackson) and ended up with his nuts in a vise.
\

Rev. Benjamin Chavis, NAACP

Speaking of getting "laid and paid," Rev. Ben Chavis, a long-time activist whose column I used to run weekly when I was editor of The Milwaukee Courier, got away from addressing issues of "environmental (toxic) racism" and ended up being selected to lead the NAACP.

In July of 1994, the following was reported:

> ATLANTA -- NAACP Executive Director Benjamin F. Chavis Jr. denied yesterday that he sexually harassed a former employee and said he agreed to pay the woman up to $332,400, without telling his board of directors, to "protect the NAACP." (Fletcher, 1994).

How can he protect the NAACP when he is the leader of it? By keeping his indiscretion away from his board of directors he was already violating policy – it's called "malfeasance." And whose money was he using to pay off this woman? More likely than not it was money that he earned as the director of the agency. So he was wrong on yet another count – unapproved expenditures of company funds. Let us continue with his "story":

> In his first public response to Mary E. Stansel's allegations in a lawsuit that she was discriminated against, sexually harassed and fired unjustly, Dr. Chavis told a news conference: "I made an administrative decision to protect the NAACP from exposure to false and slanderous allegations. I believe it would have been irresponsible of me . . . to have allowed this matter to linger."

No, what was "irresponsible" was for him to be screwing around with this woman in the first place. These women know what they're doing when they're secretaries to so-called "religious men." Ministers, preachers and the like are the biggest cockhounds there are. That skirt got hiked up a little higher and the compliments starting coming, responded to with a chickenshit smile. Then came the lunches and the late "snacks" in the office. And then he fucked her.

Just like Jesse Jackson, former HUD director Henry Cisneros (who would later be pardoned by President Clinton) and so many others before him, Chavis took the bait. And then when the tables got turned and the woman wanted to get paid, he tried to play the role of the victim.

Now pay close attention to the similar reactions by the wives of these cockhounds. They stand there while the man gives his side of the story, the same way that Vernon Jordan's wife did when she had to stand by his hospital bed after he got shot in the ass by a white man while he (Jordan) was on his way to some white woman's house "for lunch." Remember that? Now, check out the Rev. Ben Chavis situation:

> At times holding hands with his wife, Martha Rivera Chavis, who is pregnant with twins, the 46-year-old NAACP leader said that Ms. Stansel's allegations are "completely false and have no merit. . . . I do not minimize the harm of sexual harassment, when it happens." Ms. Stansel, a former legislative aide to Democratic Sen. Howell Heflin of Alabama, worked briefly as an interim employee at the NAACP in early 1993 but was dismissed. She had been a volunteer in the campaign to make Dr. Chavis the civil rights group's executive director.

Pregnant with twins and now holding hands with a man who was getting his dick sucked by a subordinate. She volunteered to help someone she believed in and it got turned into her getting on her knees – just like Bill Clinton did to Monica Lewinsky and Henry Cisneros did with his (paid) mistress. Women get laid and paid and they know how weak men are; it seems to be that the more power these men think they have, the more arrogant they become and the more likely they are to believe that they are above the law. Chavis, like Jesse Jackson, started out being a champion of the people and ended up being nothing more than a cowering cockhound.

And just as these women get laid and paid, the people who have to do the paying stand by and support the criminal perpetrator. The board of the NAACP did just what the wives of these scoundrels tend to do. Check it out:

> The 64-member NAACP board was not told of the deal that Dr. Chavis made with Ms. Stansel in November 1993. The out-of-court settlement committed the NAACP to pay her up to $332,400 unless Dr. Chavis helped find her a Washington-area job paying $80,000 a year.

The NAACP should have been disbanded a long time ago. Ever since Thurgood Marshall stopped winning cases, the organization has been under the control of their corporate and Jewish dominated board of directors and have taken control of local chapters by demanding that these local chapters "get permission" in order to pursue certain issues and cases. That slows up and convolutes the entire "civil rights" process – and the N AACP knows this. And meanwhile what is the Board doing: covering the ass of people like Chavis, as in the following example:

> Board Chairman William F. Gibson yesterday defended Dr.
> Chavis, saying that he had "complete, full executive authority" to
> make the deal with Ms. Stansel without consulting the board. Dr.
> Gibson said he knew in late 1993 of Ms. Stansel's threat to sue.
> "The board had not in the past dealt with such types of complaints
> and, in this case, there was no reason to deviate from standard
> operating procedures," he said, flanked by a handful of board
> members, including vice chairman Ben Andrews Jr.

And this is why the NAACP is now moribund – that is, at the point of death. The cycle of Neanderthal activity continues because these negroes are beholden to the white man who is their chief funding source. Their board of directors is chock full of powerful white people and most of them are Jews. But what can you expect when DuBois and others "allowed" these white folks to be a part of the start of the organization? What can you expect when you have a group that talks about advancing "colored" people? And in all those years they have not bothered to alter the name a single time. And therefore it should be expected that behavior like that of Chavis would continue to be covered up.

And when you know your actions, no matter how perfidious, are going to be protected by the President of the Board of Directors, what do you do? Check it out:

> Dr. Chavis refused to discuss in detail why he settled with Ms.
> Stansel. He also did not talk about the nature of his relationship
> with her; the news conference was limited to procedural questions
> surrounding the breach-of-contract suit.

Several of the "negro" board members called for Chavis to resign and others wanted to stall time to investigate, but it was clear Chavis would get away for the most part. The point to be made at this juncture is that the woman got both laid and paid, Chavis' wife went for the okey-doke (as did Vernon Jordan's wife, Bill Clinton's wife, Donald Trump's wife and so on) and this is how the cycle is perpetuated.

Henry Cisneros, Dept of Housing and Urban Development

An article titled, "Cisneros Pleads Guilty to Lying to FBI Agents" offers up evidence of at least another woman "getting laid and paid" by some high ranking politico. Using government money to pay for pussy? Come on. But it's not just the black bruthas doing it; Cisneros proved that Latinos make some of the same mistakes that negro leadership makes.

Check it out:

> Former housing secretary Henry G. Cisneros pleaded guilty
> yesterday to a single misdemeanor charge of lying to the FBI about
> money he paid to a former mistress, ending a wide-ranging
> independent counsel investigation that lasted more than four years
> and cost more than $9 million. (Miller, 1999).

So he lied and lied, just like Marion Barry was doing until they found him out on tape. Cisneros was accused of lying about the amount of money he had provided to former mistress Linda Jones, a political fund-raiser with whom he had an affair beginning in 1987. But in the case of Cisneros, all those lies were costing more money with the courts. And he still got off relatively easy. While Clinton was getting his dick sucked by an under-aged intern, Henry was battling in the courts to keep from getting butt fucked in a prison:

> Cisneros, 52, is the first Cabinet member of the Clinton
> administration to plead guilty in a case brought by an independent
> counsel, though the consequences of the plea proved relatively
> mild: Cisneros agreed to a $10,000 fine and a $25 court
> assessment, but he will serve no time either in prison or on
> probation and he will be free to seek elected office. (Miller, 1999).

He could still seek elected office if he chose to, and only had to pay a small fine. Not only that but,

> As part of the plea agreement, Cisneros was required to admit that
> he had knowingly given false information to FBI investigators. He
> told U.S. District Judge Stanley Sporkin that he regretted his "lack
> of candor" and added, "It is my hope that other people who aspire
> to and follow in public service will also perhaps learn . . . that truth
> and candor are important in the process of selecting people for
> governmental positions." (Miller, 1999)

So Cisneros was able to bullshit his way out of paying for buying pussy. And this woman got laid and paid. Miller writes that as part of his guilty plea, Cisneros, "admitted telling an FBI agent that he had paid Jones roughly $2,500 a month after their relationship ended, when in fact the payments were considerably higher. All told, prosecutors said that Cisneros provided Jones with more than $250,000 from 1990 until 1994." (Miller, 1999). What? Even after things were cut off she STILL got paid? That's bullshit. Why was he paying to keep her quiet and not get any pussy? Trying to adopt the role of the "white knight" check out Cisneros' reasoning:

> When the judge asked why he had lied, Cisneros answered, "For one thing, I wasn't sure about the numbers personally. I had never calculated them up. But beyond that, I was trying to protect [Jones], who didn't want the information out, and my own wife, who didn't know precisely what the number was. And in the final analysis I've attributed it to the pressure and confused sort of fog of the moment where I gave an incorrect number." (Miller, 1999).

But the fact is, Clinton was the standard bearer and a lot of the people in his administration got busted for criminal activity. For instance, Miller (1999) documents that, "Cisneros is one of several Clinton Cabinet officials to be targeted by independent counsel investigations. Former agriculture secretary Mike Espy was acquitted of corruption charges after a trial last year, and investigations of Interior Secretary Bruce Babbitt and Labor Secretary Alexis M. Herman are still ongoing." (Miller, 1999). It should be noted that Herman, who was accused to accepting kickbacks, was cleared of the charges.

Women getting laid and paid. It's as American as apple pie

Eliot Spitzer

This guy had credentials, juice and a good life. He had a law degree from Harvard and another degree from Princeton. He was a prosecutor in the Manhattan District Attorney general's office and had a job as a private attorney with several New York law firms. HE then served as Attorney General for New York from 1999 to 2006. As if that wasn't enough, this power-hungry sonofabitch ran for and then was elected governor of New York where he served for just over a year until the roof caved in: Eliot Spitzer definitely got laid and paid. But he paid a high price for it. As it was reported in March of 2008,

> On March 10, 2008, *The New York Times* reported that Spitzer had previously patronized a high-priced prostitution service called Emperors Club VIP[92] and met for two hours with a $1,000-an-hour call girl. This information originally came to the attention of authorities from a federal wiretap … Spitzer had at least seven or eight liaisons with women from the agency over six months, and paid more than $15,000 … (Hakim & Rashbaum, 2008).

You should have seen the picture in the New York Times: poor Mrs. Spitzer standing next to her man and then in another picture, holding his hand while they scurried away from the podium following his resignation announcement. All that money and power, and this peckerwood couldn't keep his dick in his pants. Just like so many of the others: they start thinking they're above the law, but there's a factor that most of the media seem to consistently overlook.

What about these women? They know who they're screwing and they lay out a plan. With them there is a "plan A" and a "plan B." Plan "A" is to screw this guy and get money for it. They know who he is and after the act is done, they want to make sure that its on-going and that he pays well. If he seems to be the "one night stand" type, then they can rig it so that they get him on film or in some way convince him that he is going to keep paying or they will jeopardize his career. This is one of the ways that these women "get laid and paid."

What was with this guy: no pussy is worth a thousand dollars an hour unless you're getting an hours worth! These guys are prematurely ejaculating and then lying there waiting to get some head. They might load up on Viagra, Cialis or Levitra and keep a long-time boner, that that's still an issue of give and take! These women have convinced these men that having sex is a one-way street and that they (the men) are one-way beneficiaries of some kind of "gift." They (the women) are getting dicked as well! What's up with that?

Continuing:

> According to published reports, investigators believe Spitzer paid up to $80,000 for prostitutes over a period of several years while he was Attorney General, and later as Governor … Spitzer first drew the attention of federal investigators when his bank reported suspicious money transfers under the anti-money laundering provisions of the Bank Secrecy Act and the Patriot Act … The resulting investigation, triggered by the belief that Spitzer may have been hiding bribe proceeds, led to the discovery of the prostitution ring … (Hakim & Rashbaum, 2008).

He was manipulating bank accounts, deceiving his wife, lying to his family and buying pussy even while he was working in the attorney general's office. How sick can you get? This means that he had sex on his mind around the clock, and his bank account proved that to be the case. What was his wife doing all this time? Was he even sleeping with her. She was no beauty but still they had three daughters and had been married for 26 years (1987-2013) before divorcing. How can you have three little girls at home sitting on your lap, a wife slaving away in the kitchen and taking care of your over-sized home and still have the gall to be staring down on the head of a prostitute while she sucks your dick?: This, in my book, describes a man with absolutely no conscience and waaaaaayyyyy too much time on his hands!

But he threw all caution to the wind, betraying the constituents of the largest state in the union. And it eventually came to a resounding conclusion:

> In the wake of the revelations, Spitzer announced on March 12, 2008, that he would resign his post as governor at noon on March 17, 2008, amid threats of his impeachment by state lawmakers … "I cannot allow for my private failings to disrupt the people's work," Spitzer said at a news conference in New York City. "Over the course of my public life, I have insisted – I believe correctly – that people take responsibility for their conduct. I can and will ask no less of myself. For this reason, I am resigning from the office of governor" … (Hakim & Rashbaum, 2008).

And that's how it ended. And now people have forgotten because such scandals are common place. Donald Trump may be a lousy human being, but he is not the first nor will he be the last. And that is the point I want to make. There is an old saying that, "all men and most rivers are crooked because they choose the path of least resistance." My version of that quote is that, "all rivers and most men walk around wet because they get all kinds of pussy and forget to wash their ass afterwards." I didn't say it made sense.

Anthony Weiner

Three years after the Eliot Spitzer incident and even more bizarre resignation took place in New York, this one involving a man who couldn't stop showing his dick to under aged girls on the internet. His name, quite appropriately, was "Anthony Weiner."

> American politician Anthony Weiner, former member of the United States House of Representatives from New York City, has been involved in two sexual scandals related to sexting, or sending explicit sexual material by cell phone. The first, sometimes dubbed **Weinergate**, led to his resignation as a congressman in 2011. The second, during his attempt to return to politics as candidate for mayor of New York City, involved three women Weiner admitted having sexted after further explicit pictures were published in July 2013. (Wikipedia, 2016).

There had to have been money involved on some level. Why not mention it? This guy is showing his dick to under-aged girls and anyone who wanted to see it and you mean to tell me that these women didn't see that money could be made? It was so bad that he had to resign, so why did he do that? What prompted him to step down? What was the threat? His reputation had already been besmirched. Was there some extortion or bribery involved? You mean to tell me that of the three women involved, none of them practiced the art of "getting laid and paid" and went after this well-heeled politician?

Continuing:

> The first scandal began when Democratic U.S. Congressman Weiner used the social media website Twitter to send a link to a sexually suggestive picture of himself to a 21-year-old woman from Seattle, Washington. After several days of denying media reports that he had posted the image, he admitted to having sent a link to the photo, and also other sexually explicit photos and messages to women both before and during his marriage. (Wikipedia, 2016).

Have you seen Weiner's wife? This woman is beautiful and dark-skinned. She is powerful, a close friend and confidante of Hillary Clinton. He had it made. But this perverted bastard decides to flash himself on social media. Where is the money? It has to be somewhere because he did it without even going after any booty – or so he claimed:

> He denied ever having met, or having had a physical relationship with any of the women. On June 16, 2011, Weiner announced his intention to resign from Congress with his official resignation occurring on June 23, 2011. (Wikipedia, 2016).

So he was a straight-up pervert. His wife Huma Mahmood Abedin of six years (2010-2016) was busily working in politics just as he was. But he was so sick and disrespectful of this woman of color that he just threw caution to the wind. When they got married Bill Clinton officiated the wedding ceremony which, to me, was the kiss of death right there. Weiner and this beauty – who is a Muslim by faith – had a son, Jordan Zain Weiner. But you are what you associate with; by being close to Bill Clinton some of the perversion was bound to rub off on Weiner. But Clinton finally got caught and ended up paying off some of his former mistresses; Weiner was a different story:

> A second scandal began on July 23, 2013, after Weiner returned to politics in April 2013 by entering the New York City mayoral election, when more pictures and sexting by Weiner were released by the website *The Dirty*. They were allegedly sent under the alias 'Carlos Danger' to a 22-year-old woman with whom Weiner had contact in late 2012, and as late as April 2013, more than a year after Weiner had left Congress. (Wikipedia, 2016).

The alias of "Carlos Danger"? What kind of "contact" did he have? There had to be a money exchange somewhere because he had plenty of it and any woman that would "meet with" a pervert like this has to have a financial plan of some kind. But what he did was not forgiven: "Weiner admitted sexting at least three women during this period, and although called on by the *New York Times* editorial board, among others, to leave the mayoral race, he remained in the race until the end, when he took fifth place in the Democratic primary, with 4.9% of the vote" (Wikipedia, 2016).

The previous sampling is random enough to make it clear that when it comes to politics, it is the male who is the "mitch" and the women who are totally in control. Again, "you cannot have political freedom without an economic base." The female of the species, led by the vulturism of the white female, has access to BOTH.

Forbes' wealthiest women in the world 2016

How could I write a book about women getting "laid and paid" without sharing with you what I view as the key underlying dynamic of both? Men's lust is exploited and pimped by women and the values of the society. Even the Bible is filled with lies and bullshit that place women in a subservient position. What they have been able to do is take their vaginas and place a market value on them; at first it was through marriage and the provision of a house, land and other assets, which of course they had to pay for by bearing children. But if those children were girls, they were able to train them about boys and men and how easy it is to manipulate both.

Wealth is defined as, "abundance of valuable material possessions or resources." Back in the day in Europe and Africa there were "arranged marriages," but the man had to have some kind of wealth: land, money or otherwise. Once married into that family, the woman had to "obey" and do her "womanly duties." This meant giving up a whole lot of booty whenever the man wanted it. If he prematurely ejaculated, so what? If she didn't get a nut, so what? James Browns' rather sexist 1966 song, "It's a Man's World" pretty much lays out the foundation for the global system of gender discrimination. Remember?

This is a man's world, this is a man's world
But it wouldn't be nothing, nothing without a woman or a girl
You see, man made the cars to take us over the road
Man made the train to carry the heavy load
Man made electric light to take us out of the dark
Man made the boat for the water, like Noah made the ark
This is a man's, man's, man's world
But it wouldn't be nothing, nothing without a woman or a girl

Man thinks about our little bitty baby girls and our baby boys
Man made them happy, 'cause man made them toys
And after man make everything, everything he can
You know that man makes money, to buy from other man
This is a man's world
But it wouldn't be nothing, nothing, not one little thing, without a woman or a girl
He's lost in the wilderness
He's lost in bitterness, he's lost lost

While admitting that this "man's world" would be nothing without a woman or a little girl, what the lyrics seem to overlook is that every man is born of a woman and raised by one. So it's actually a woman's world and it is my belief that they knew this all along. But without power what could they do? Men were physically stronger and if women stood up, they'd get their asses kicked or labeled as witches or burned at the stake.

Wealth then came through marriage and even then, the male-run courts made the decision regarding the division of property if the man died or there was a divorce. In fact, women couldn't even own land or property in some cultures. So they waited and over the centuries, increased their impact and influence on powerful men who, in turn, through a pussy whipped stupor, passed laws that began to ease the burden that had been placed on the female of the species.

Now with my rather bizarre interpretation of history out of the way (the truth can oftentimes be viewed as "bizarre"), let's fast forward to today's world and a March 7, 2016 article by Bartie Scott titled, "Forbes' Wealthiest Women in the World." I share this article and the list with you so that you can see that on some level, these rich women "got laid and paid" and came into their wealth. Now, remember the lyrics to James Brown's song. And even with women using "pussy power" to gain more and more control, it remains a "man's world" because he continues to control the wealth.

As importantly the male also controls the policies and the politics of wealth. That means he can lie, distort and control the contractual elements involved in business and the economy, This is what she exploits: the knowledge that she has to have her own money so that she can do things her way. Put another way, "you cannot have political freedom without an economic base" (Karenga, 1967). And in the case of almost every single one of these women, the big money came from some man, either directly or indirectly.

Let's take a look.

Liliane Bettencourt, whose wealth comes from L'Oreal. Her net worth is $36.1 billion, but get this: she maybe the richest person in the world but she's an "heiress." In other words, she got the company from somebody else. Research tells us that,

In 1909, Eugène Paul Louis Schueller, a young French chemist of German descent,[7] developed a hair dye formula called *Auréale*. Schueller formulated and manufactured his own products, which he then sold to Parisian hairdressers. On 31 July 1919, Schueller registered his company,[8] the Société Française de Teintures Inoffensives pour Cheveux (Safe Hair Dye Company of France). The guiding principles of the company, which eventually became L'Oréal, were research and innovation in the field of beauty. In 1920, the company employed three chemists. By 1950, the team was 100 strong; that number reached 1,000 by 1984 and is nearly 20,000 today.

So another woman gets "paid" because some male founded a company and she somehow stumbled into it. The specifics are not even important. This French company shows that the white man is paying for pussy just like his American counterpart. Now this rich woman has been paid. And what is their slogan? It's "Because I'm worth it." Name one woman who doesn't believe in this maxim.

Alice Walton is the second richest woman in the world, worth $32.3 billion and is the daughter of Sam Walton, the founder of those Wal-Mart stores.(Scott, 2016). So she is the product of a woman who got laid and now she has gotten paid.

Jacqueline Mars is worth $23.4 billion and is the daughter of the man who inherited the Mars candy empire along with some pet food companies. In other words, another "heiress." She has brothers who share in the inheritance, but remember this: all of them came from the woman who seduced and then married. According to Forbes magazine,

Jacqueline Mars (born October 10, 1939) is an American heiress, and investor. She is the daughter of Audrey Ruth (Meyer) and Forrest Mars, Sr., and granddaughter of Frank C. Mars, founders of the American candy company Mars, Incorporated. In 2014, *Forbes* described Mars as the 20th richest American. (Forbes, 2014).

Mars has evolved according to the research. According to Yahoo.com, "The Mars bars were sold as such in the US until 2002 when its name was changed to Snickers Almond Bar. It contained then, and still does, plain nougat, almonds, caramel and milk chocolate." Snickers remains a favorite for the most part, and Jacqueline and her brothers keep raking in the dough.

Maria Franca Fissolo of Italy is worth $22.1 billion. She's another candy heiress, this one with Nutella and related chocolates. An obvious case of "getting laid and paid." According to Scott (2016), "She is the widow of Michele Ferrero, who built Ferrero Group and died on Valentine's Day 2015. The private company is owned by Fissolo and her son Giovanni, the CEO; its products include the popular Nutella spread, Kinder chocolates and Tic-Tac mints." So she hooks up with some rich Italian, gives up the booty and has kids by h im, qualifying her to inherit all his shit. Now she's the owner (along with her son. See how it works?

Susanne Klatten is the daughter of a woman who got laid and paid, and is the owner of BMW after her mother died. Although Klatten is credited with steering German pharmaceutical and chemical company Altana AG toward $2 billion in annual sales, the fact has to remain that the "roots" of her wealth come from being the daughter of a woman who, again, "got laid and paid." Like Donald Trump, she was born with a silver spoon in her ass … oops! I mean MOUTH. You can afford to be an innovator when money is never an object.

Then there's **Laurene Powell Jobs**. Name sound familiar? It should. While she's an accomplished woman, she is also the widow of the late Steve Jobs, founder of Apple Computers, and it worth $16.7 billion. According to the research,

> Laurene Powell Jobs is an American businesswoman, executive and the founder of Emerson Collective, which advocates for policies concerning education and immigration reform, social justice and environmental conservation. She is also co-founder and president of the Board of College Track, which prepares disadvantaged high school students for college. Powell Jobs resides in Palo Alto, California, with her three children. She is the widow of Steve Jobs, co-founder and former chief executive officer of Apple Inc. She manages the Laurene Powell Jobs Trust.(Scott, 2016; Wikipedia, 2017).

See how it's done. She's blonde and cute and allows him to talk her out of her panties. He becomes a billionaire, dies at an early age (she had to have found uot he was ill), the necessary paperwork is in place and then, voila! The one who use do get laid has now been paid. She also owns a chunk of Disney.

Abigail Johnson is worth $13.1 billion and her wealth comes from "money management." Again, we find someone who got her start based on what she got from a man – her grandfather. As one source informs us,

> Abigail Pierrepont "Abby" Johnson (born December 19, 1961) is an American businesswoman. Since 2014, Johnson is President and Chief Executive Officer of US investment firm Fidelity Investments (FMR), and chairwoman of its international sister company Fidelity International (FIL). Fidelity was founded by her grandfather Edward C. Johnson II. Her father Edward C. "Ned" Johnson III remains Chairman Emeritus of FMR. As of March 2013, the Johnson family owned a 49% stake in the company. In

> November 2016, Johnson was named Chairman and will remain
> CEO and President giving her full control of Fidelity with 45,000
> employees worldwide … Johnson's wealth of approximately $14
> billion making her one of the world's wealthiest women. (Healy,
> 2014).

So her grandmother set everything up by screwing her grandfather, who handed the empire to his son. Then, he handed control over to Abigail. So again, a woman gets a hand me down from a man who impregnated that woman's mother and gave her a lifestyle of wealth. Getting laid and paid.

Charlene de Carvallio Heineken is worth $12.3 billion. I know you recognize the last name. That's right, she's from the Netherlands and she's another heiress. Her parents had money as well. Check it out:

> Charlene de Carvalho-Heineken (born 30 June 1954) is a Dutch-
> English businesswoman and the owner of a 25% controlling
> interest in the world's third-largest brewer, Heineken International.
> Charlene Heineken was born on 30 June 1954, the daughter of
> Freddy Heineken, the Dutch industrialist, and Lucille Cummins, an
> American from a Kentucky family of bourbon whiskey distillers.
> She was educated at Rijnlands Lyceum Wassenaar, followed by a
> law degree from the University of Leiden.

So her mother got laid, impregnated and paid and this makes Charlene another heiress. See what I mean? This gives an entire new meaning to those James Brown lyrics I shared, especially the part where he croons, "This is a man's world/But it would be nothing/without a woman or a little girl." He was right. The man continues to the species after impregnating one of these women who then gets all of his shit when he dies. So she can then go out and find another guy who is well off and the plutocracy (government by the wealthy) therefore perpetuates itself: getting laid and pad.

Christie Walton is the daughter-in law of Wal-Mart founder Sam Walton. Her net worth is "only" $5.2 billion after dividing her late husband's estate with their 29 year old son, Lukas.

What have we learned? That the female is getting rich based on her "connections" with various types of relationships with men. She uses whatever it takes to get ahead; and if that includes giving head, then so be it: gifts, gams and ideological game. Because she craves power and she understands the pussy-based weaknesses of the male, is there any wonder why she "needs to get in touch with her 'mitches'?

The Grown Man as Child

During the airing of what was originally a January 2, 1962 episode of the western, "Laramie," we find that even back then, during the days of the wild, wild west, the tendency was to treat men like children in order to be an "acceptable" woman.

In this episode, "After saving the life of an Arapaho girl in a fire and helping acquit her in a trial for killing a man, Slim (Sherman, played by John Smith) finds her his possession due to Arapaho law. When she won't leave him, he takes her in but soon finds he has feelings for her." At one point the beauty, whose name is Winona, draws Slim a warm bath without him having to tell her. They walk into his room and he asks her, if she learned this kind of treatment of a man back on the reservation. She tells him, "They taught us how to bathe small children. And what is a man but a small child grown up?"

And there you have it. At first it may seem like a contradiction: the big, bad macho man making sure that the female remains his social, cultural, political, educational and physical inferior. But there is one thing that he overlooked: she has always been his intellectual superior. And because of that, his machismo and political cravings are always manipulated by her and committed in her name. Keep in mind that, "the hand that rocks the cradle rules the throne."

This has always been the case. Don't be fooled into thinking that the rise of white bitches like Hillary Clinton, Elizabeth Warren, Nancy Pelosi is something new: white women have been in control of the men who appear to be in control. And they do it because behind closed doors, they treat him like a child. And he likes it and accepts it. And black people have mocked this pattern of behavior in the way the women treat the men and society has taken notice. Especially the advertising world.

Witness this spate of insurance commercials. What do you see? These mealy-mouthed effeminate "men" (husbands) kissing their wives asses and acting as if they don't know what to do. Companies like Metropolitan Life, Colonial Penn, Liberty Insurance, Mass Mutual, and many others have targeted black elderly married couples, scaring the shit out of them about dying and leaving behind huge funerals bills, and do it by showing the woman large and in charge while the man, admitting that "his health" might be a problem and may impede their qualifying for life insurance, stands back like some scatter-brained bitch while she makes the decision that yes, indeed, they may well need such insurance.

And it's not only the case with health and life insurance. Just look at the family on television: the man is the perennial fuckup, the excuse-maker and the clownish buffoon. On one such commercial, Liberty Mutual insurance commercial this white boy talks about he is leaving for work with his ten gallon jug of coffee and he's backing out of the driveway and then "accidentally bumped into his

wife's car while she was watching," and that "she forgave him later on --
eventually" and then goes about attacking the insurance company. Forgave him?
He didn't do it purposely so why should he have to apologize to that bitch? A true
pussy.

Oasisi Express Cash features this effeminate sounding black man who
promtes the product. Another one named "William M." comes on sounding even
more bitch-like than the narrator. Mark S. is another one, who calls Oasis Financial
"a blessing" is the third "coon" that comes on the air sounding like he was in need
of a panty shield. And the list goes on and on. And here is what you have to
remember: these "men" were selected over scores of others who auditioned to tell
these lies. They were chosen by a committee of white men who weighed their
attributes and how they would "come across." This effeminate shit you're *seeing is
all by design.*

Or how about the Buick commercial (aired during the summer of 2016)
where the young white couple is on vacation. Clad in bathing suits they sit in the
shade next to a pool. She asks him if he remembered to handle an issue with their
Buick, he assures her he did. Even as the words are uttered she then asks him if he
remembered to close the windows in the apartment. He claims he did as she
whispers, "You're the greatest." But out of her vision is this chickenshit look in his
face as he re-thinks his position on the windows. Cut to the apartment with pigeons
flying in and are all over the place.

Again, the woman is the responsible one (although she should have shut the
damn windows herself) and the man, who is probably paying for the vacation
where she is relaxing, is the asshole. She is large and in charge and of course,
getting g laid and paid.

In other commercials, the ones where the man is not totally left out while the
single mother who looks like a Victoria Secret model is shown having it all under
control, the man is a simpleton. Swiffer wet mops shows this giant of a man
mopping up behind his bad-ass half-white kid instead of putting his foot in that
kid's ass the first time he fucked up. Another time the little half-white daughter is
concerned about her daddy's heart so after talking with her white mommy, the
daddy, who is asleep on the couch, wakes up and finds Cheerios all over his
fuckin' chest. The little girl was told that Cheerios are good for your heart.

In addition, these effeminate rapper faggots are really a trip. They walk
around in skinny jeans acting like children. You've got the likes of Pharrell
Williams, Usher, Young Thug, 50 Cent, P-Diddy and so many others either
actually gay or what they might refer to as asexual, pansexual, and/or bisexual.
What does this have to do with being a "child"? It begins with denial of black
manhood. Once you do that, you can be used or manipulated into being anything,
including gay and a child. That's the connection. And it's being exploited by white

people because they have always had childish tendencies and orientations and it is reflected in the way they act, think and talk once they reach maturity.

RISE OF THE CHICKEN HEADS: EVEN UGLY WOMEN CAN GET "LAID AND PAID"

Under a separate heading I wrote this essay as, "The Rise of the Chicken heads: When Beauty IS a Beast!" At any rate, the point being made here can be found in an anonymous maxim: "Showing cleavage doesn't fix your face."

Ugly women are the new fine hos. Seriously. At least, that's the way it is in their minds and in this culture. Look at television and you can see it: white, black Asian, Latina – whatever. If you can walk in a pair of five inch heels and wear a skirt up to your panty line without actually exposing the panties (thanks to the thong, a thing will keep your panties from showing,), then you qualify.

Aiding these chicken heads in their quest for "pseudo-beauty" is the white man, who is the expert. After all, he's succeeded in making his pale, no breasted, flat-booty woman a standard of beauty for the world. And now the women of color all over this country are trying to look like her, but let me not get ahead of myself. First, we share what makes a woman ugly.

To begin with, it's her shallowness and attitude. And some of these fashions that I've alluded to aid and abet her in this "crime." She's flinging back her fake hair and has her hands on a waist held in place by a girdle and truly thinks that she's 'the bomb.' There are men who find this attractive. But he's encountering someone who has serious esteem issues and who is so obsessed with being accepted by her friends and being with the "in crowd," that she also mimics the attitude that will get her noticed as being "independent," "a down chick," "a strong woman" and so on. What it does is bring attention to what she really is: a modern day emotional troglodyte.

Now after the shallowness and attitude issues we come to the image issues which piles on additional dimensions of shallowness. How do I notice thee? Let me count the ways.

First, the extensions and the wigs. I venture to guess that more than 60% of black women in this country between the ages of 18 and 60 have some fake shit in their head. But the fact is, these women are putting it in the heads of their young daughters as well. Maybe they're too damn lazy to comb it, but the other day I saw a little girl about nine years old with extensions in her head – including blonde ones! What is this telling her about herself and culture? First it was the straightening comb, now it's this shit! (And black men: don't forget those "conks" that you used to put in your head so you could have textured hair like that cracker).

Anyway, these women are spending hundreds of dollars on this shit. Just so they can flip it back in anger or when they turn their heads – the way they've seen the white woman do for decades. And what's so cold about it is that they really seem to think the shit is theirs! And if you ask them (which I will do every time I get the chance) they'll say something flippant like, "yeah it's mine – I paid for it!" Self-image issues, pure and simple.

So it's not just the extensions and wigs, but many of them add color. I've seen more honey-blonde black women in the past five years than I saw during the previous 53 years of my life, combined. Even worse, the young generation has added new colors to their fake-ass repertoire: green, blue, blood red (and maroon), platinum and I've even seen purple. The older ones whose hair is graying refer to it as "silver" and then do whatever it is they do to make it appear as if they have more than they've got. I think they're called "hair pieces."

Now the eyes, which are supposed to be the "gateway to the soul." Based on the length of these eyelashes these women are wearing, I'd have to say that the gateway to the soul needs a pruning! Some of these eyelashes are a full half an inch long! Then they glue them to the ones they've got and they still look like shit. These women's eyelashes are so long that when you kiss them, you know when they open their eyes because the lashes brush your face!

The eyeliners and all that color, including glitter that they use – man, save that shit for the circus! This is the kind of makeup that used to be reserved for the bride of Frankenstein, Clayface and other feature creatures! They don't spare the nose: now it's vogue to have your nose pierced, sometimes on both sides, which prompts a thinking person to ask: what happens to the buggers and snot? And in Jewish culture it is a tradition to give the young girl a nose job when she reaches her teens, straightening it so that they can look for "Anglo" in appearance. Don't take my word for it: ask 'em!

Moving on, for a long time earrings have been modified in the name of being "hip." These women went from studs to earrings the size of bicycle rims. I mean, they are huge and some of them have the nerve to wear three and four earrings in one ear! When they do that you can hear the jingling and jangling halfway down the hallway!

And then, the breastseses. I am one of the men who can spot the "type" of breast no matter what you try to do to veil them. There are small breasts embellished with a padded bra – oftentimes complete with fake nipples. There are the sagging ones (I call them "droopers") that are pulled up and out with these new-fangled bras that have been developed. The breasts look alright with that bra on, but when they take it off, those things fall to their knees. There's the bra that helps them look larger, more full and can push those puppies right up under their chins, which is the way women seem to be wearing their blouses these days.

Without those bras, far too many women's breasts look like two side-by-side bowling balls held in a pair of fishnet stockings!

Speaking of blouses, there is an increasingly popular style that accommodates these "tittie-fakers." You've seen 'em: these newfangled blouses and shirts that are deep-V cut and allow propped up breasts to be exposed. They're not really "new," because trollops, saloon girls, street hos, women at dance clubs and other night crawler types wore them back in the day. But this "look-at-my-tits" style is even now being accepted in the workplace. And when they hit the club or some social event, you can almost see everything but the nipple.

The waist line can be equally well disguised. They've got these body suits that serve double duty: prop up the boobs and hold in the butt at the same time. They've got the girdles that hold in the gut and firm up the butt. They've got the ones that bring in your waistline only. There's so many looks to choose from, but let us not get it twisted: all this shit is about two types of deception: self-deception and social deception. The former is aimed at convincing yourself that you "still have it" and the second is aimed at convincing others – friends, relatives – that you don't have any psychological issues about "losing it" in the first place. In both cases, they are dead wrong.

Now before moving on, consider this: imagine getting up and having to put all this shit on, manage and arrange it and then live in pain all day along, thinking about avoiding certain things, the lies – both implicit and explicit – that you have to live each and every day. Now can you see why black women are always pissed off? They're not mad at you because you never asked them to do all this shit: they're mad at themselves and their mad at other women, white and black, for looking so "good" that they have to put on these fronts and facades in order to "fit in." Feel me?

So we've got the hair, the ears, the eyes, the nose, the breasts, waist, hips and ass. Let us move on and describe more evidence of the "image issues" that permeate far too many females in this society.

The feet. Most black women have big feet and they apparently don't like the fact. I think many have accepted it, because it's the only way to explain why they bring so much attention to those feet. They paint their toenails and then wear open toed shoes. Fine. But why do that when you're bringing attention to something that is bringing you pain, namely, those damn shoes!

These women are wearing five- and seven-inch heels, man! They're towering over everybody just so they can "look good" (or so they think). They are in pain because the human foot wasn't made to have all that weight (and some of these women are huge) on the falls of the foot. It's almost laughable how they maintain balance and some will even walk on gravel and uneven surfaces rather than taking their shoes off. Some even have the nerve to wear ankle bracelets, which bring even MORE attention to those feet.

The underalls which serve to also hold in the butt cheeks and give shape to sagging, unflattering asses, also serve to shape the legs in many cases.

There we have it: a female version of Frankenstein, Jr.! What could the psychological and emotional implications be for someone who is so manufactured, so fake, so committed to accepting the falsity of their looks? We know this much: it cannot, on any level, be positive. Psychologically, you are creating another person's because the person that you are, the way that you look, are realities that you simply cannot accept or deal with.

Emotionally, it's even deeper. You have to maintain this shit when you enter a relationship or go visit the family during the holidays. You have to keep this front up when you go out with the girls. You have to keep all this stuff up to snuff when you have an important engagement or go to work or to church. In other words, you have to be fake in order to be emotionally secure. But you cannot be emotionally secure unless you accept the fact that everything about you is fake.

The only people who see the "real you" (other than yourself) are your children, and they can't stand you with your "image issues" having self. Why? Because you chastise them and kick that ass for them being "bad" or out of control when it's YOU who's out of control. So much to the point that while they're getting ready for school, you're putting on all that fake shit I just described. When they're home doing their homework, you're stripping out of all that "goon gear" I just talked about. The quality time that you ought be spending with them is spent "relaxing," which is really nothing more than "decompressing" from the freak show that you have become.

Somebody with image issues needs you to affirm her womanhood. Well, they really don't "need" it, but they think they do. And when it comes to women, what they think is their world. That's why they when they enter a relationship they feel it's their goal to "fix," "repair, "mend" or otherwise "improve" the male. And why is that? Because they can't let you go on being your "natural" self while they go through the transformations that I've just described! They want control and the only way they can control you is to make you think you're just as f----ed up as they are!

No matter how much makeup or camera filters you shoot them through, a chickenhead is a chickenhead. Wanna name names? I'll offer a few so you won't think that what I've just provided is nothing more than a cacophony of emotive labeling. Here we go: Margaret Cho (comedienne), Sarah Jessica Parker ("Sex in the City"), Cheryl Underwood ("The Talk"), Jamie Lee Curtis, Lisa Rinna, Tori Spelling, Joan Rivers, Carla Hall ("The Chew"), Renee Zellweiger, Gwyneth

Paltrow, Kristen Stewart, Barbara Walters, Courtney Love, Hunter Tylo, Amy Schumer, Whoopi Goldberg and Sandra Bernhard.

Can I make it any plainer?

The Reality of Alimony: Ka-Ching!!!

As someone who has studied sociology at the doctoral level and written extensively on a number of sociological topics ranging from marriage and family, collective behavior and social stratification to culture, urban activity and deviance, I found the on-going defense of "alimony" an interesting one. So I looked into it and found that much of what is written does not really fit into its actual practice and application in the real world. Let me share with you some of my findings, observations and perspectives.

To begin with, what is "alimony." Involves a great deal of judicial and legal "discretion." I have found in my studies that when it comes to discretion in the hands of white people, it means carte blanche when it comes to fines, penalties and meting out punishment, especially when it comes to the application of the law and how to use it as a means of "control." Controlling women and entire families is another area where judicial discretion can be applied with extreme prejudice.

According to the on-line Free/Legal Dictionary, alimony is described thusly:

> The purpose of alimony is to avoid any unfair economic consequences of a Divorce, even after property is divided and Child Support, if any, is awarded. Courts set few specific guidelines to attaining this broad goal: instead of telling judges how and when to award alimony, most courts simply grant them broad discretion to decide what is fair in each case (Burton, 2007).

When the words "fair" and/or "unfair" are used by this American system, what it really means is what constitutes "fairness" in the minds of white people. And since discretion is a part of determining what is fair, that gives them free reign to be unfair to those groups they don't like. Women are one such group.

I am no feminist but I am a brilliant analyst. And there is something inherently unfair about a system that first of all lies about the "value" or "morality" of monogamous marriage. The ceremony is replete with lies about "'til death do us part" and loving someone "in sickness and in health" and other lies that humans usually fall short of. The fact that the divorce rate is near 60% proves my point.

But after that act of ersatz morality, and things don't work out, we can apply and accurately test the validity of the previous definition. To begin with, keeping in mind that this is a system run by men even though women are the numerical majority, read again this statement: "The purpose of alimony is to avoid any unfair economic consequences of a Divorce, even after property is divided and Child Support, if any, is awarded." This is a system that finds on-going disparate pay for women, a glass ceiling in the workplace and perpetual rapes and abuses a part of its culture. How can such a system therefore view women with anything even remotely approaching objectivity or "fairness"? This is a system that didn't even "allow" women the right to vote until 1920!

So "fairness" is defined by the people who make the rules. When property is divided, what is it based on? To many people, a fifty-fifty split of property is fair. But is it? To get half of what the family assets amount to is not fair to men who may have paid in much more during the marriage. But it is not fair to women either: they have to keep the children in many cases and that means that they have to deal with school, child support and child-related expenses. But even in that, women still manage to get "laid and paid" on an optimum level and I'm going to show you how. The late actor John Barrymore once quipped, "You never realize how short a month is until you pay alimony."

The divorce is final and alimony is doled out, usually to the woman (but not all the time). But this book is about women getting paid and that is my focus at this point. Women use that alimony to care for the child and in most cases, they also have to maintain the house, which they are usually rewarded. Now keep in mind that no matter how well off a woman may appear to be, she is still living in a society that is controlled by male rules. She knows that. So what is the male's main weakness? Pussy. So although it may appear as if the man is now free to cock hound now that he's divorced, the woman actually has the advantage even if she does have the children.

You see, she is getting a monthly payment and doesn't have to leave the house to get it. If she works, that's just icing on the cake. Children or no children, she's got a guaranteed income and even while paying for child care and related children's expenses, she's not going broke. The court will make sure that the former husband pays his alimony and if he doesn't, then he'll go to jail. So the man loses on that count as well.

Now the previous definition adds that in the case of alimony decisions, "instead of telling judges how and when to award alimony, most courts simply grant them broad discretion to decide what is fair in each case." Again, we find that word "fair" and what did we learn about its application when gender issues are involved? We learned that the female will always receive short shrift, either immediately or down the road.

So the alimony has been awarded, and she is now free. The alimony is going to continue until she re-marries, and this is the key: she is not required to re-marry. So now she is free to collect alimony, recruit and get free dick, get the money that the "new" relationship (or relationships) can generate and basically live the life of

Riley. She gets to raise the kids which is not the "curse" that some people try to make it out to be, because once those kids grow up, they are going to kick in and take care of mommy dearest as well. And this gives her time to continue poisoning the minds of the kids against their father while making herself out to be some kind of saint, savior or self-sacrificing victim who "bore the brunt" of a bad marriage.

By the time she re-marries – if she decides to make that mistake again – she's not broke. Women outlive men on average anyway: alimony is a cash cow if the woman manages it correctly. Since she's out looking for a new dick she's going to dress better, look better and has learned from any mistakes she made during the previous marriage. And the new guy is none the wiser.

I've always said that where there is white discretion, there is racism and gender bias. This is perhaps most true in the case of the court system in general and the family courts, in particular. Burton (2007) writes that, "No mathematical guidelines exist to tell courts how to calculate alimony. In addition, each state legislature sets its own policy regarding whether and when alimony may be awarded.

And according to the US Legal. Com website, The Uniform Marriage and Divorce Act (UMDA) was an attempt by the National Conference of Commissioners on Uniform State Laws to make marriage and divorce laws more uniform. This is also known as the Model Marriage and Divorce Act. UMDA was extensively amended in 1973. UMDA is a 1970 model statute that defines marriage and divorce. The greatest significance of UMDA is that it introduced irreconcilable differences as the sole ground for divorce. UMDA has been partly enacted only in a handful of states. However, it has had an enormous impact on marriage and divorce laws in all states.

More specifically,

> The Uniform Marriage and Divorce Act (UMDA), which many states use as a model, recommends that courts consider the following factors: the financial condition of the person requesting alimony; the time the recipient would need for education or job training; the standard of living the couple had during the marriage; the length of the marriage; the age, physical condition, and emotional state of the person requesting alimony; and the ability of the other person to support the recipient and still support himself or herself (Burton, 2007).

Let's look at these factors that the courts are going to "consider" before deciding whether or not this woman is going to walk away with a shit load of cash and assets.

The financial condition of the person requesting the alimony. So if the man has a good job, he's gonna get taxed. If she has a job, that don't mean shit: she's still going to get a part of his shit as well. If there's a house, usually she gets it if there are children, even if its in his name. Some judges will have the assets liquidated and then the proceeds are divided between the two, with her getting the lion's share. This is but a small part of what I call "the reality of alimony." It's like what Peggy Joyce one said: "Alimony is a system by which, when two people make a mistake, one of them keeps paying for it."

Another variable considered by the courts is the time the recipient would need for job training or education. If she gets alimony, she can keep getting it until she gets a job or completes training for a job. In this day and age of scam training programs and proprietary (for profit) colleges, the recipient of alimony should be able to bullshit her way through a program by taking her time, changing her major course of study, or "getting pregnant." All of this shit works and as long as she's getting training, she keeps on getting alimony from you – which is automatically deducted from your paycheck.

The couple's standard of living during the marriage is another way to determine the amount of alimony doled out. So the better off you are, the more money she is going to get. This is true only because men fall for the okey-doke and hang on to that antiquated belief that, "no wife of mine is going to work." Well the fact is, when he goes out and makes that money and she's at home, she's going to get paid anyway! If she's married to him when the money was made then, by law, she is entitled to HALF. The only salvation is a prenuptial agreement and most of these women aren't going to sign one: they wouldn't be getting married if they couldn't get PAID! What do you think this is about: LOVE?

Then there is the length of the marriage, which is an extension of the previous situation. The standard of living usually increases the longer the couple is together. And if they both work, this is definitely the case. The length of time oftentimes makes men lose their mind and enter into "joint accounts" with their wives: what a mistake. He thinks he can keep an eye on what she's spending when, unbeknownst to him, she has her own personal account PLUS his shit! She's getting laid, having kids that make him even more dependent on the relationship, and she's also getting paid.

And check this one out: "the age, physical condition, and emotional state of the person requesting alimony." Most women are going to be in better condition than men as they age. Women see to that. Remember that saying, "The way to a man's heart is through his stomach"? Who do you think was cooking that fatback, those pork chops, those steaks and all that ham? She was. She knew what she was doing and we sat there rubbing our distended bellies telling her, "that was good, honey." Meanwhile, she's going on walks and jogging with her gal pals while he's at work, stressing out and making that high blood pressure go even higher. By the time he finds out he's fucked up, she's got the reins on the money, what the split will be, who gets what and has another dude waiting in the wings – with a better job!

And the final point for consideration is "the ability of the other person to support the recipient and still support himself or herself." See? Even when the divorce takes place she STILL gets paid. The studies show that she gets all the burden because she has to have the kids and he's free to start over. First of all, if he starts over with another woman right away he's out of his damn mind. Furthermore, she might have the kids, but that alimony enables her to pay a good child care provider and she has the house as well. In other words, even when she's not getting laid by him, she's getting laid by somebody; and he has to pay, so in a way he's getting FUCKED as well.

Burton (2007) concludes thusly:

> Courts have at times awarded alimony when an unmarried couple separates, if the relation-ship closely resembled marriage or in other circumstances, such as in keeping with the couple's intentions and verbal agreements. Awards of this type are informally called palimony. Private separation agreements negotiated between divorcing individuals also can contain alimony provisions. For these reasons, it is difficult to estimate accurately the size and frequency of awards through the most common method, U.S. census data.

Alimony makes sense if there are young children being left behind by one of the spouses. But these women are using it to make a living, not for the kids, but for themselves. Some of these women are getting thousands of dollars a month that goes beyond food and clothing and shelter. The rich ones are taking men to the bank, literally. And this is just one more way that despite all the rampant gender bias, the glass ceiling and the general abuse of women, they inevitably get the last laugh – through the courts.

Speaking of courts, let's look at some instances where "child support" also represents a revenue stream for the so-called "fairer sex."

Child Support Payments: Ka-Ching!!!

A woman meets a man she likes. She makes him beg and pay for pussy through dinner dates, movies, concerts, outright "help" with rent, phone bills or car payments, and then when she thinks the time is right and she believes him to be a "keeper," here comes the news: "we're pregnant!"

We? Bitch, I don 't remember asking or telling you to have a kid! But she's made the decision and now is when the real battle begins. Back in the day a reliable scam was if you got the pussy and then ditched her, she'd come back with an excuse that she was "with child" and ask you for the $400 that it cost for an abortion. The average nigga ain't thinking: he's going to do what it takes to get the bitch out of his face. You'd be surprised at how many bruthas fell for that bullshit.

But now we come to the bruthas who have to deal with child support, so-called "wealthy" and "celebrity" black men who ought to know better.

<u>Little Bow-Wow</u>

In the gradually declining black music culture, it has become popular to refer to black men as "dawgs"; even if you are talking about a friend, that person becomes "my dawg." Therefore it should be no surprise when a young rapper came to the fore by the name of, get this: "Little Bow-Wow."

He started off and went to the top and that included money. Where you find rich black men you find gold digging women. One article reminds us of his start:

> When <u>Bow Wow</u> (formerly Lil' Bow Wow) appeared on <u>"The Oprah Show"</u> in 2003, the then-16-year-old <u>rap star</u> was living the high life. He bought fancy cars, wore expensive jewelry and even revealed that he had a $6,000-per-month allowance. Fast-forward 10 years. Now age 26, <u>Bow Wow</u> has said goodbye to his once-flashy lifestyle and has also become a father. (Huffington Post, 2013).

As is typical of far too many young people, especially young black people, their white (Jewish) agents pacify them with money and stand back and watch them "invest" their money in trinkets and other trivia. Bow-Wow was no exception. He had a $6,000 allowance – the same single mother that allowed this kid to have that insulting nickname was the one who thought that six grand a month was a fair amount for a 16-year-old kid. His real name, Shad Gregory Moss, is really no better. Then some girl/woman "got pregnant" (set-up) and as this section of the book makes clear, that is the way that a lot of these women "get laid and paid."

Moving on:

> In this clip from "Oprah: Where Are They Now?", Bow Wow opens up about how dramatically his life has changed since his days of teenage stardom. For one, he says, he stopped focusing so much on material things. "We called it 'stunting,'" Bow Wow says of parading around his large purchases. "I don't even wear that

stuff no more. I'm so laid-back and just chill." (Huffington Post, 2013).

He claims he's matured. The question is, what took so long? After you spend all that money on gold chains, watches, cars and the like, after you've cruised through ghettos and low-income areas to flash it all in front of the poor, then it gets boring. He claims that he's "so laid-back and just chill," but he's still the same immature punk that he always was. And he's still getting gamed on via the paternity route:

> … Bow Wow's perspective on material things isn't all that's different about the entertainer. He became a father in 2011, when his former girlfriend, Joie Chavis, gave birth to a little girl, Shai Moss. Bow Wow says he is still adjusting to the idea of being a parent, especially given the fact that he and his daughter, now 2 years old, live on opposite ends of the country. "Shai lives in Los Angeles and I'm in New York full-time," Bow Wow says in the clip. "It's so hard. I Skype with her and I just wish that I could just reach in there and grab her little self. [But] I can't." (Huffington Post, 2013).

So he's an absentee father, what we call a "Disneyland daddy." He comes around with gifts to shower on his daughter and hopes to curry favor with her. But the mother has her all the time and if he does something she doesn't like, she will poison that little girl's mind against him – and she will see to it that those child support payments are jacked up. Ka-ching!
Continuing:

> Bow Wow's career as a rap artist, <u>TV host</u> and all-around entertainer also makes fatherhood more of a challenge, he says. "I missed [Shai's] first step because I was in Australia on tour," he says. "I missed her first word." (Huffington Post, 2013).

Life is about choices. He has agents who can book his gigs. He has no real talent, a point that can be imposed on most of those guys who call themselves "rappers." They are poets with "beats" that they usually steal from old school artists. Be that as it may, he's a biological father, but he's just going through the motions like most single parents. According to an article in the Huffington Post, "Bow-Wow says that since he can't be with his daughter all the time, he understands how precious it is when they *can* get together. "For the times that I'm with her... I always try my best to take full advantage of it," he says."
Meanwhile the baby's mother is basking in the lap of luxury, no doubt

I don't know what has taken place since that time, but my research uncovered that this happy father was paying $3,000 a month in child support for a while. And that was in 2013. Who knows how much it is now?

Jermaine DuPri

Another runt. These short black guys make money and they can't keep the women away. That's because the women want one thing from them: their money. This 5'4 brutha is listed in his credits as, "an American hip hop recording artist, record producer, songwriter and rapper." You can add one more title to that: sucka or, more clearly, "trick."

On May 10, 2011 the following was reported on a website under the title, "Jermaine Dupri Sued by Stripper for Child Support. Check this out:

> According to AccessAtlanta, troubled music producer Jermaine Dupri Mauldin has been sued by a woman for missed child support payments. Earlier this year, a judge ordered Dupri, 38, to pay former stripper Sarai Jones $2,500 per month in child support based on the results of a paternity test for Jones' 7-month-old daughter. Dupri was also ordered to pay Jones an additional $7,500. (Rose, 2011).

See? These women know what they're doing. This woman strips for a living meaning that she knows she has the kind of body that men are going to glare at. She also knows how to "shake her groove thing." Runts like Dupri come into a club and then approach the woman, thinking that their "rap" is enough to get them laid. They buy some expensive drinks and flash some jewelry and take the woman home. She sets them up knowing that she's not using birth control. And she gets him horny enough to lose his mind and abandon his condoms. Next thing you know: pregnancy and that means eighteen years of child support.

He fronts and talks a big game, but Jermaine has had some financial problems. Check out the following:

> But Dupri, whose money problems are well-documented, has yet to come up with the money, so Jones went back to court to force him to pay up. Dupri reportedly met Jones during one of his many side trips to Atlanta strip bar Magic City, where Jones worked as a stripper under the name "Obsession". (Rose, 2011).

Her working name was "Obsession" but her real name was Sirai Jones. She knew what she was doing and she knew his track record as a DJ and a cockhound. She also knew that this guy has no morals whatsoever. He dated Janet Jackson for seven years and was messing around all along. All that money Janet had couldn't get him to fly right.

Moving on:

> According to a source close to Dupri, the diminutive producer often hid Sarai (and her stripper friends) in the back room of his Atlanta recording studio while Janet visited with him in the main studio. Friends say that Janet knew Jermaine was spending her money on strippers (and she even participated in ménage à trois with them), but her attitude at the time was, *"whatever makes him happy."* (Rose, 2011).

So Janet was weak-minded and this guy was able to convince her to engage in a threesome. This is what happens when there is money to burn and guys like Dupri have less dough than the main female. But Jones had less than Dupri, so she decided she'd get hers the old fashioned way: she'd *earn* it.

So Jones set Dupri up and then all hell broke loose:

> Jermaine's world began to unravel quickly when Jackson learned of Sarai's pregnancy and ended her relationship with Dupri before moving back to California. Without Janet as collateral, Jermaine could no longer secure financial loans and creditors began pursuing him aggressively through the court system for their money. (Rose, 2011).

All flash with no cash. For instance in 2011 it was reported that,

> Last week, Dupri's $2 million Mount Paran Road mansion in Northwest Atlanta was saved from the auction block when Dupri came up with cash at the last minute. WSB-TV obtained documents showing that Dupri owes more than $493,000 in back taxes for 2007. Plus he owes more than $12,000 in property taxes on the Fayetteville home where his mother currently lives. (Rose, 2011).

But this woman Jones is going to get paid. She was getting laid and turned that into a pregnancy that links Dupri to that child for eighteen years. And then he's got all this other debt. He is going to have to let his work control him rather than the other way around. He is going to have to earn of else go to jail. And at 5'4", he'd better come up with that dough or he's going to end up being somebody's prison bitch.

He comes off as a bum. Check out the following:

> Dupri's longtime friend, local club owner Alex Gidewon, helped
> Dupri out by hiring him to deejay at the Gold Room and other
> clubs last year. According to sources, Durpri is paid up to $10,000
> for deejaying gigs around the country. (Rose, 2011).

He's going to wear himself out one way or the other. These bruthas are tying themselves to these women and in the case of DuPri, finding women who are weak minded enough to fall for the okey-doke. But as old playas know it wears you down after awhile. As the old sports maxim teaches, "There are old quarterbacks and there are bold quarterbacks. But there are no old, bold quarterbacks."

<u>Chief Keef</u>

Rappers talk a lot of street shit, sell woof tickets about how many women they have and how much "cheese they have stacked" (translation: money they've made) but when all is said and done, most of them are pussy-crazed suckas who pay for the premature ejaculation that they boast about in their videos. They talk about not giving a shit and about how many women they have sucking their dicks and then once outside of the studio, these 'tricks' end up getting "tricked." Such is the case of Chief Keef (whose real name is Keith Cozart).

In other words, this no-talking muthafucka is pronouncing his first name incorrectly – as so many members of their generation tend to do. They can write lyrics as long as the words are spelled all fucked up, but they can't even pronounce their own names. And this is somebody's father?

A November 29, 2013 article by Tayla Holman titled "Chief Keef Ordered to Pay Child Support for 10-month Old After DNA Test" proves my point:

> Chief Keef has been ordered to pay child support after a DNA test
> confirmed that he is the father of a 10-month-old baby. The
> Chicago rapper is currently in a drug rehab facility in California
> for the next three months to address his marijuana addiction. His
> attorney appeared before Bridgeview Judge Russell Hartigan to
> review the results of the DNA test, according to Cook County
> state's attorney spokeswoman Lisa Gordon. (Holman, 2013).

So he had doubts that he was the child's father. Why? Because more likely than not the woman was a slut. She was in a club with one of those pussy-hugging micro skirts on, ass sticking out, titties up under her neck, and he thought that she was "special." These women know what they're doing, and the men who design their clothes know too. All you have to do is design something for a young girl and these grown as women will go out and buy it as well. Why? Because young girls are their competition! These "tricks" like Bow-Wow and Chief Keef are the guys these older sistahs want because these guys don't know the game the way the old hands do. They fall for the okey-doke and get just enough fellatio to get them in the mood to forget to put on a condom. From there, whether it's his or not, he's going to get the blame. Chief Keef got caught.

And the marijuana didn't make it any better. He's just a thug who came out with some poetry that he set to music and made some money. He was lost, probably quasi-illiterate, and walking around trying to be a "gangsta." The story continues:

> "An order was entered finding him to be the father," Gordon said.As reported by the *Chicago Tribune*, Hartigan ordered Chief Keef, whose real name is Keith Cozart, to pay $2,500 a month beginning December 1 for the next 10 months, as well as a lump sum of $25,000 by December 31. He must also obtain medical and life insurance for the baby, Gordon said. Chief Keef is due in court on January 27. Apparently, Chief Keef never denied that the child was his. (Holman, 2013).

And now this "sucka" has a child that he is responsible for and that means that the woman who carried the child and then had it is also taken care of. This is just one more case of women getting "laid and paid." And this guy, Chief Keef, is just a baby himself. An irresponsible one, making you wonder just where in the hell HIS mama is at. Check this out:

> The 18-year-old has been served with two paternity cases in less than a year. In January, a middle school student who said Chief Keef impregnated her in 2011 sued him for child support, health insurance, and other medical expenses. The girl gave birth to a daughter, Kayden Kash (Kay Kay), that same year. Kayden turned two on November 28, but the mother's age is currently unknown. A judge ordered Chief Keef to pay $2,600 a month in child support, plus $500 for daycare expenses, payments he repeatedly failed to make. (Holman, 2013).

Poor kid, In 2013 he was eighteen years old meaning that now he's about 22 or 23. The mother's age is "unknown" because the media chose not to make it known. The courts know her age and I'm willing to bet that she's much older than Keef is. If he never denied that the kid was his, then what was the paternity test for? It's because he was going by what the woman said and his attorneys were going by what they found out about this woman's past. The courts don't like this shit and now we know that he's got TWO baby's mamas. And from the pictures I've seen, both of them are butt-ugly.

As for the on-going saga involving the first kid,

> A judge sentenced Chief Keef to jail in September for failing to
> show up for a child support hearing. On October 21, **Chief Keef**
> **was ordered to pay $11,000**, which he did last week, managing to
> avoid jail time. He is due back in court on December 10 to address
> his failure to show up for multiple court dates. (Holman, 2013).

And that's how it goes. Paternity suits. Shelling out money to women you can't stand. Little girls growing up having their mother's put your name in the streets and condemning all men – along with teaching their "ho tricks" to their daughters. And the cycle of getting "laid and paid" is therefore perpetuated.

Now comes the second child:

> Chief Keef is currently expecting a son, Mon'e, with another
> woman. According to his Instagram, the child is due in January.
> When the rapper finishes his stint in rehab, which he has to pay for
> himself, he will head back to Illinois to work at a horse therapy
> facility for disabled patients. (Holman, 2013).

A loser with a hit record. Just like Jermaine DuPri and the others – totally lacking in penis control.

Allen Iverson

At just over six feet tall, this NBA scoring phenom entertained fans and made opposing defenses look ridiculous. But like so many before him, he got married at an early age and then got into major trouble with the child support people. The gossip show "TMZ" reported the following at the end of August of 2013:

> **Allen Iverson**'s ex-wife is sick and tired of dragging him to court
> to squeeze out child support ... she's asking a judge to make him
> cough up the next 13 years worth RIGHT NOW -- a cool $1.2
> MILLION. TMZ broke the story ... after the couple's nasty divorce
> Iverson was ordered to pay $8000/month in child support for their
> 5 kids. Problem is, Tawanna has gone to court on numerous
> occasions because A.I. won't pay. (TMZ staff, 2013).

Five kids meaning that she knew his weaknesses. The kids were probably conceived during his off-time from the basketball season. She knew what she was doing and she knew what he liked. She wasn't using birth control and evidently neither was he. Five kids. And then he turns around with his multi-million dollar contract and refuses to pay? Continuing:

It came to a head in July when a judge **threatened Iverson with jail**, unless he forked over $40,000 in back support -- **which he did**. But Tawanna says she doesn't want to keep running into the same problem. (TMZ staff, 2013 – emphasis original).

Laid and paid. They call it "child support," but these women are the ones spending the money on the child! The check doesn't come directly to the child. It comes to HER, and she blows it on herself and the child – in that order. How do I know? Because most of these women are broke until they latch onto one of these professional athletes. Even before they get to the pros, these women know who's got the potential to get the big contract and who doesn't. Even ugly niggas like Dennis Rodman can get booty because they make the big bucks. The only thing about him is that he doesn't like black women. But it's all the same when the lights go out.

TMZ even added up the dollars that Iverson is going to owe. Check it out:

On August 1st she filed docs asking a judge to make A.I. cover ALL the support through October 2026 (when their youngest turns 18). After the math, it comes to $1,272,000 ... which Tawanna wants put in a trust for the children. A court has yet to rule. (TMZ staff, 2013)

It really doesn't matter how the court rules. Putting money in a "trust fund" for the kids doesn't mean anything when the woman is in control. She continually programs the kids with negative information about their father and about how she's "sacrificed" so much. This stuff begins to take hold after a while and even if the money is in a trust fund, she can borrow on it. That's what a lot of people don't seem to understand: these women get "the hookup" with some well-to-do trick and can borrow on that money in the name of the children. These women got laid and they will make sure that they get paid.

Terrell Owens

I saw this asshole on his television show, surrounded by two young black women who were his "advisors." The 2012 program was called, "The T.O. Show" and I watched him walk into a jewelry store and plop down $167,000 for a pair of diamond earrings. That's right – like the true fag that these niggas appear to aspire to be, "earrings."

An article titled, "Terrell Owens Makes Payments" on an ESPN website tells another story of a professional athlete turned "trick." Check it out:

ATLANTA -- Former NFL star **Terrell Owens** has made child support payments that he owed to the mother of his 7-year-old daughter, avoiding the threat of jail time. Owens appeared in Fulton County Superior Court in Atlanta on Thursday, after failing to appear for a court date in the case last week. His lawyer and a lawyer for Melanie Smith had come to an agreement before the hearing and signed it in front of the judge. Owens made the back payments he owed to Smith and agreed to pay her legal fees, according to court documents. (ESPN.go.com, 2012).

These coons have to be threatened with jail before they pay the child support that their own pussy-hunting trapped them in. These women know what they're doing, and the pain of childbearing is muted by the thoughts of a big money future. After going through all that, and then having their dreams threatened or dashed because some athlete refuses to pay? You think black women are going for that shit? No way.

Terrell Owens boasted and bragged all over the football field, almost demanded that he be admitted into the Hall of Fame (which he deserved) and ruined almost every locker room he ever entered. That was on the field. Off the field he was a pussy whipped piece of shit, a "trick" in the true sense of the world, and ended up at the mercy of attorneys and the courts:

"We're pleased. It's too bad it took this long," Smith's lawyer, Randy Kessler, said after the agreement was signed. "If he's not going to be there physically, he needs to be there financially." Owens left the court without speaking to reporters. A lawyer for Owens didn't immediately respond to an email seeking comment. (ESPN.go.com, 2012).

There is no doubt that the attorney was a white man. He says that if Owens is "not going to be there physically, he needs to be there financially." Doesn't this peckerwood realize that if he's "there financially," he IS there physically! That's his money, that's his check being cashed and that his young child who is benefitting from the resources being provided!

It gets worse: check this out:

A previous agreement requires Owens to pay Smith $5,000 a month. This was the third case Smith has brought against Owens for non-payment of child support, Kessler said. In previous instances, Owens has settled and paid up right before the cases were to go to court but then failed to make subsequent payments, Kessler said. (ESPN.go.com, 2012).

In other words, Owens went to Smith, flashed a couple of grand in her greedy ass mug, and shut her up. This woman is going to get $5,000 a month because she gapped her legs and set this professional athlete up. She had to know she wasn't marrying material; she had to know that like most athletes, he was a playa. But she wanted that money and she knew how to get it. So she got pregnant and now she's got an income without lifting a finger. This is another example of how women "get laid and paid."

Now comes the "mommy dearest" contradictions that most of these skanks offer once they get the money they seek:

> Smith, who lives in northwest Georgia, is glad to have the signed agreement, but would really like for Owens to be more involved in their daughter's life, Kessler said."What she really wants is for him to have a relationship with his child," Kessler said. Smith, who was also present in court Thursday, said her daughter has seen Owens about eight to 10 times. (ESPN.go.com, 2012).

Take note that Owens "having a relationship with his child" was not as important as Smith getting that money up front! If she had managed to trap Owens into seeing her regularly, she could have gotten paid. Or would she? She probably knew that Owens was a piece of shit and as a result, there were no guarantees. She may want Owens to see that child, but trust me: that's for babysitting purposes. If he comes and gets the child for the weekend or takes the child out, that's more time for her (Smith) to get dressed in those micro-skirts that Owens paid for and sashay out to the bar to look for a new sucker … oops! I mean suitor.

Pretending to be broke (remember that $162,000 diamond earring set this asshole paid for?), Owens then made a number of moves where he made a complete and utter ass out of himself. He's already made one: impregnating a woman that he had no intention of staying with. But wait: there's more!

> Owens has raised the possibility of lowering his monthly child support payments since he's no longer drawing an NFL salary, and Smith is willing to discuss that, Kessler said. (ESPN.go.com, 2012).

Cutting deals to whittle down his payments after making tens of millions of dollars and wasting millions on jewelry, cars and expensive furnishings for his mansion. Check out this man's Hall of Fame-like stats:

> The 38-year-old Owens played 15 years in the NFL, most recently for the Cincinnati Bengals during the 2010 season. Before his single season with the Bengals, Owens played one season with the Buffalo

Bills, three with the Dallas Cowboys, two with the Philadelphia Eagles and eight with the San Francisco 49ers. (ESPN.go.com, 2012).

So many men, many of them black men, fall for the okey-doke. They say that for the want of money is the root of all evil. I disagree. I say that it's the want of pussy that is the root of all evil. Not because the women are bad, but because men are so screwed up, so animalistic in their lust for something that often smells like sardines, that we lose our damn mind. And then, when they choose, here comes a cute little baby that you can't help but love, but you're responsible for that tiny creature for 18 years according to the law. More evidence of how women "get laid and paid."

Evander Holyfield

Poor Evander Holyfield – another "trick" masquerading as a world class athlete. When all is said and done, even the mightiest fall to the almighty seductions of those who are in good enough shape to be able to convincingly sport a lift-up bra or a skirt with no draws on under it.

A September 18, 2012 story on FoxSports.com titled, "Report: Holyfield Held in Contempt" provides one more example of a woman getting "laid and paid."

> The financial blows keep coming for boxing legend Evander Holyfield. Celebrity news website TMZ reported, citing court documents, that the former heavyweight champion has been held in contempt of court in Georgia for failing to pay $563,900.91 in back child support.(FoxSports, 2012).

More than half a million dollars owed in back child support. He competed in boxing from 1984 to 2011, and according to the Xfinity.com (2017) website, "Evander Holyfield earned several hundred million dollars during a career that spanned more than two decades."

As it was reported in 2012,

> The latest charge stems from an initial payment of more than $372,000 that Holyfield owed in support of his 18-year-old daughter, Emani. TMZ reported that, according to court documents, that amount increased to $563,900.91, and Holyfield was held in contempt and ordered by a judge to pay $2,950 per month to clear the debt. Holyfield made an initial $17,700 payment, TMZ reported, but the judge also ordered that a

percentage of Holyfield's income be earmarked to pay down the debt.(FoxSports, 2012).

Public humiliation after being in the ring with some of the baddest men on the planet. Brought down by pussy payments. What else can you say? And he's not just being sued in one state, either:

> According to a biography on Holyfield's website, the former boxing star made more than $230 million in the ring. But he's faced numerous financial difficulties since. The Atlanta Journal-Constitution reported that Holyfield recently foreclosed on his Fayette County mansion and has been sued for thousands of dollars in child-support cases in Georgia, Texas and California. Holyfield has fought these cases, the AJC reported, claiming that his income has fallen off since his career ended. (FoxSports, 2012).

Broke, busted with a kid who grew up to hate your guts because, thanks to her mother's on-going lectures, she has been led to believe that you hated her guts, didn't want her, and had to be forced by the courts, to do the right thing. If Holyfield hadn't been in such world-class shape for most of his life, I'm pretty sure that all this financial and personal pressure would and could have led directly to a heart attack or a stroke.

Bobby Brown

Whitney Houston was one of the most beautiful women in the world. When I saw that she was hung up on and eventually married Bobby Brown, two words came to my mind: dick whipped. That's the only way to explain why she would marry someone so unattractive with a track record so abysmal. This woman was supposed to be from a Christian background, but I guess that just goes to show what a little crack cocaine can do.

Long after Whitney died, Bobby was still in trouble with child support. An article by Paysha Stockton Rhone that appeared in People.com on February 27, 2007, titled, "Bobby Brown Arrested in Massachusetts, proves the point and offers background:

> Bobby Brown, who was arrested and jailed in Massachusetts on Sunday for failing to appear in court and pay child support fines, will remain behind bars until he pays $19,150, a judge ruled Monday. (Rhone, 2007).

I don't know what was on Whitney Houston's mind other than two things: (1) getting dicked and (2) hitting that crack pipe. How else to explain a woman with all the potential in the world hooking up with a piece of shit like Bobby Brown. His track record speaks for itself. Check it out:

> Brown, 40, owes support to his former girlfriend Kim Ward, who
> lives in Massachusetts and with whom he has two teenage
> children: LaPrincia and Bobby III. The singer's attorney, Phaedra
> Parks, said she didn't expect Brown to get the money until
> Tuesday, and said he's been struggling to make the payments he
> owes to Ward. (Rhone, 2007).

All these kids. Once again, someone "famous" lands these sluts and starts dating them. Don't ask me why. When you travel all over the world you can do what you please and you have enough money to afford birth control. But these young guys (as I supposed we all did during our youthful days) see a short skirt and immediately begin wondering what the panties look like and more importantly, what the pussy looks like. Eighteen minutes (max) of pleasure for 18 years of pain once the woman claims you're the father. In the black community it seems like making babies is some kind of badge of courage and serves as an indicator of how potent you are. What it shows, in the final analysis, is how big a sucka you are.

And an un-talented sucka at that. Check this out:

> "Although this agreement was put in place when he was Bobby
> Brown the star, this agreement is being enforced when he is not
> always able to find work," Parks told the Associated Press. "He
> hasn't made an album in quite some years." (Rhone, 2007)

So what? Where are his agents and managers? Where are the people who are supposed to be watching and holding this man's money while he skips around town spending money on pussy, ordering Cristal Champagne and speeding around town in high-end sports cars? By not having any money to pay his child support this shows that he is not a responsible parent, which is what the courts look at when he eventually gets hauled up in front of them.

Continuing:

> Brown was also ordered to return to court on Thursday – the day
> when his next $5,500 support payment is due. "Kim always finds
> these hearing to be extremely difficult," Ward's lawyer, Linda
> Medonis, said. "This is not the route she wants it to go, but when
> he doesn't pay for a few months it becomes a real hardship for
> her." (Rhone, 2007)

Such bullshit. Kim doesn't find going to court "extremely difficult." Nobody knows that bitch from Adam's house cat. She's basking in the fame she gets just like she did when she went around bragging to all of her friends that Bobby Brown was screwing her. That's how these women are – the pregnancy was set up from the get go. They knew how irresponsible that punk was. That is why women like this don't complain when they find out that he's out on the road partying with other women. Once they get the pregnancy they seek, they could care less. Kim is not stupid and hardly afraid to walk into a courtroom and point her finger at a $5,500 paycheck.

Brown is such a loser that being arrested is pretty much an acceptable form of behavior. As one account points out,

> Brown was arrested Sunday evening outside his daughter's cheerleading competition, Patrick McDermott, clerk of Norfolk Probate Court in Canton, Mass., told PEOPLE. "He went very cooperatively," he says. "According to the constable, no one was really around." (Rhone, 2007).

Of course he went cooperatively – he had no case. He was as guilty as sin and he knew it. According to Rhone (2007), "Jerry Loomis, one of the constables who arrested Brown, said he stopped the singer in the parking lot "because we didn't want to embarrass him or anyone else in there." Asked if Brown was able to see his daughter perform Loomis said, "No. He was begging us to go in there, but we felt for safety reasons we couldn't allow him. It wasn't even in the cards." So he missed his daughter's cheerleading competition – undoubtedly not the first time – and acted like it was no big deal. Kids don't forget this kind of thing, especially with the mother reminding that kid, no a daily basis, that "yo' daddy ain't shit."

As a result,

> In October, a judge ordered Brown to be arrested if he stepped foot in the state after the singer skipped a court hearing over $11,000 in delinquent child support payments to Ward. Later that month, McDermott said that Brown had paid what he owed to Ward; however, the arrest warrant has remained in place – probably in case Brown fell behind again, McDermott said. (Rhone, 2007).

Black men, black women and the rift between us is a direct response to trying to survive in a capitalist system – with no capital. Black men's desire for sex is well-noted because it is a societal norm for all males. Those who have resources can get the women to marry them, date them or they can just buy it outright. Those who lack resources have to use "gifts and ideological game" in order to get it. But even in that capitalism creeps into the relationship to define it. Women have to get paid in order for them to get laid, and men have to get laid in order for those payments to continue. This may sound trite and tragic – but it is also true.

Bobby Brown is proof and he continues to pay as he cavorts from female to female. He impregnates her, which is part of her game in order to get paid, and then he has to dole out more money for child support. And supporting her is part of the deal. She got "laid" and now she will get paid. Want proof? According to Rhone (2007),

> Brown, who split from Whitney Houston in September, has a history of missed child support payments, and was even jailed in March 2004 for one day after missing several payments, which he subsequently paid.

As the old man taught George Jackson who wrote the quote down in his great book, Soledad Brother, "Every sickness ain't death, every goodbye ain't gone, and every big man ain't strong." Women know this, have internalized it, and keep it in mind as they forge these "alienated arrangements" with black men and as such, continue to get "laid and paid.

Dennis Rodman

Even an unattractive individual can get laid, fall for the okey doke and end up paying child support in today's America. Dennis Rodman is a classic example of what I call a "troll turned trick."

A March 4, 2013 article by Nate Wooley titled "Dennis Rodman Too Broke to Pay Child Support" documents that Rodman owed more than $800,000 in child support. The article, which appeared on the website InvestorPlace, claimed:

> Former basketball star and headline grabber Dennis Rodman told a court that he can no longer afford his child support payments. The player — who made news last week with his visit to North Korea, where he made friends with dictator Kim Jong-un — owes more than $800,000 in back child support, (Wooley, 2013).

Rodman is one of those black people who is evidence that a black child raised around white people is going to grow up fucked up. He was this tall kid raised by white folks who saw his potential and he became a community college star. He went on to professional ranks but unfortunately continued to think he was white. He was so daffy that his teammates couldn't stand him but white people around him always made him the center of attention so they could get some laughs and hopefully get some insulting commentary from the black players around the National Basketball Association.

Just the fact that he could get pussy shows that women place getting "paid" above "getting laid." What woman would go to bed with a nigga whose acne bumps were as big as watermelons? White bitches, that's who. Three of his most visible girlfriends prove my point: (1) Madonna (1994), who has been fucked so many times I'm surprised she can even close her legs; (2) Vivica A. Fox (1997), a true beauty but if she was dating 50 Cent and then amidst an argument charged him with being gay, continues to be someone with issues from DUIs to dating young guys and being called a "cougar"; (3) Carmen Electric (1998), another beauty who has made millions of dollars posing for Playboy, as a professional dancer and in real life, a full-time whore.

All three women have something in common: they need the photo ops that parading around with Rodman, a member of the championship Chicago Bulls teams, could bring them and they could get all the dick they craved. Judging from his face, that's probably all he was good for.

At any rate, according to Wooley (2013),

> Rodman's ex-wife Michele filed for the back payments to collect the total of $860,376 in child and spousal support. Rodman's attorney told the court that he is unable to pay due to his lack of funds. The attorney also cited Rodman's alcoholism as a reason for his lack of income and assets. (Wooley, 2013).

A 6'8", ugly alcoholic with millions of dollars to spend. In the world of the women who are "laid and paid," he is the perfect thrall. And his life has spiraled out of control because of all of his bad choices, his love of white folks and his psychosis, which white people treat as if he's merely "playfully eccentric." Just follow the money:

> Rodman — a member of the Basketball Hall of Fame and winner of five NBA championships — made more than $27 million during his NBA career. It is also believed that he earned as much or more than his salary in endorsements. (Wooley, 2013).

And now it's all gone. In the meantime he's posed publicly in women's clothing including a wedding gown, and he's gone to North Korea and kicked it with Kim Jong-un.

<u>Flavor Flav and Child Support</u>

In the same psychological nut-sack as Rodman is Flavor Flav, that zany member of the otherwise incredible rap group, Public Enemy. Another unattractive black man who attracts money-grubbing women, mostly white, Flavor Flav is as eccentric as Rodman in the world of reality.

A June 19, 2012 article by Joseph Gibson titled, "Flavor Flav Pays More Than $100K In Child Support To Stay Out Of Prison", that appeared in a website called Celebritynetworth.com" provides us with a sampling of how this guy fell into the "laid and paid" scenario.

> Flavor Flav's career has taken many different turns over the last 25
> or so years. He first found fame as the comic relief/hype
> man/sidekick to Chuck D in the rap group Public Enemy, before
> beginning a slow slide into late night talk show punchline and
> reality TV star. Those ups and downs come with their own price –
> in Flav's case, more than $100,000 in child support payments
> which he had previously owed. (Bibson, 2012).

Some background is in order because this is really some weird shit, even BEFORE we get into the issue of child support and the like.

According to one source, "After falling out of the public eye for a number of years, he reappeared as the star of several VH1 reality series, including The Surreal Life, Strange Love, and Flavor of Love." I don't know what possessed the white man to give Flavor Flav (whose real name is William Jonathan Drayton, Jr.) and this blonde bombshell Brigette Nielsen a show where they were in a relationship, cuddled up, kissing and generally making asses out of themselves. Here's some more background:

> *Strange Love* is a reality series featuring Brigitte Nielsen and
> Flavor Flav that aired on VH1. Sparked by their on-screen
> romance in the third season of VH1's *The Surreal Life*, it is a spin-
> off that focused solely on Brigitte and Flav. The series premièred
> on January 9, 2005 and ended its run on April 24, 2005.
> (Wikipedia, 2017).

It may have been a short-lived "reality show," but the fact is that this black man got not one, but three reality shows – and got paid for it. This is straight up freak value by white people. Brigitte Nielsen has been appearing in some pretty mediocre movies herself, including one called "Mercenaries" (with Vivica A. Fox and Cynthia Rothrock) where she played a prison guard with the bad guys. And trust me: she looked like shit boiled over.

Nielsen obviously has some issues as well, as does model Beverly Johnson, the lovely black woman who, for some reason, was kicking it with Flav for years. He's also been married twice: one to a sister named Angie Parker and then to Karen Ross.

So what happened to the "Strange Love" show? According to Wikipedia,

Due to mutual jealousy, the couple was constantly fighting and yelling, and they went their separate ways in the end, with Nielsen choosing instead to live with her Italian boyfriend, Mattia Dessi. Flavor Flav would go on to have his own reality show, *Flavor of Love*, where he continued to search for love.

It should be stated here that Brigette Nielsen wasn't the sharpest knife in the drawer either. She seduced Sylvester Stallone and ended up with a major part in the "Rocky IV" movie, and they got married thereafter. It didn't last long and then the next thing you know, she's screwing Flavor Flav. But let us not get ahead of ourselves.

I am no big fan of Stallone. Two decades ago I wrote a 50 page essay titled, "Sylvester Stallone: Warrior or Wimp?" I wrote it after reading a book about his life and this guy was screwed up from the beginning. His mother, Toni, was a nut that was hooked on astrology and Sylvester had issues. He used to wear a Superman outfit under his school clothes and one day the principal found out. The principal called a school assembly and made Sly take off his clothes and reveal the outfit. He as a laughing stock.

So ashamed of him was Toni that she PAID a college in Switzerland to let him in. When he was three credits from graduating he dropped out to become an actor. My point here is that he is as screwed up and in search of "machismo" as Brigette was in search of, who knows that.

This explains her jealousy over sharing star billing with the diminutive Flav. But there is more about Nielsen and Sly which gives us an understanding of Flavor Flav as well. According to the *Huffington Post,*

> When Brigitte Nielsen was 22 years old, she married *Rocky* star Sylvester Stallone. At the time, Stallone was one of the biggest movie stars in Hollywood, so when he left his first wife for a woman 17 years his junior, the tabloids took them to task. Publications depicted Nielsen as a gold-digger, accused her of infidelity and asserted that she was simply using Stallone as a stepping stone for her career. But Nielsen tells "Oprah: Where Are They Now?" says that was far from the truth.(Huffington Post, 2014)

Like I said, Stallone had some issues himself. He buffed up because he was so short in stature, butchered the English language with what appears to be some kind of quasi-speech impediment, and he married a woman that stood over him. They didn't stay married long because in my view she also had issues. The used him for roles in "Rocky IV" and in "Cobra" and then, like that, they were divorced. In her words,

> "The biggest misconception while I was with Sylvester was the fact
> that everybody thought I married him because of money," she says.
> "They didn't understand that he begged me to marry. He begged me!"
> (Huffington Post, 2014).

If she didn't want to do it all the begging in the world would not have convinced her. What I figure is that she saw all the money he had so that was what convinced her – she knew she could get half his shit (getting' laid and paid) if things didn't work out. So what happened?

> When they wed in 1985, Nielsen and Stallone had only known each
> other a matter of months, which the Danish actress says gave her
> pause about becoming so serious so quickly. "I remember thinking,
> 'This is too early. This is not right,'" she recalls. "At the same time,
> everybody was going, 'Who wouldn't want to marry Rocky?'" After 19
> months as husband and wife, Nielsen and Stallone divorced. With the
> clarity of decades of distance since the split, she admits that their
> union was a mistake. "If I would go back in time, I shouldn't have
> married him (Huffington Post, 2014).

That lyin' bitch. She married him for the money and she knows it. She was tall and blonde and couldn't get a gig in Hollywood outside of the porn industry. She was too tall and intimidating. She was a freak. So she married someone and used his connections. As I say, she did "Rocky IV," and then "Red Sonja" also in 1985. The next year she made "Cobra" and then in 1987 she was in the Eddie Murphy movie, "Beverly Hills Cop."

I don't know what happened between Brigette and Stallone and personally, I don't give a shit. All I know is that I was channel surfing one day and I saw this little black muthafucka cuddled up with this giant white woman. "Strange Love"? You ain't NEVER lied!

But that shit didn't last and they went their separate ways. She's white so she'll be alright. But Flav – with that stature and that face? He gets a lot of pussy and he keeps getting women pregnant.

> But, that's been taken care of now. Today, Flavor Flav showed up
> at Albany County Family Court to settle his debt with Angie
> Parker. Flav has fathered three children with Parker, and was
> facing a 180-day prison sentence if he failed to pay the $111,186 in
> child support payments he owed to her. While it's not known
> exactly how much of the sum he payed (sic) today, he must have
> cleared things up to the satisfaction of all the parties involved
> because he's out walking the streets instead of in prison. (Gibson,
> 2012).

How does somebody lay up in a studio with some white woman cracking jokes and arguing, sucking on caviar and all that other food that lays around the set, get chauffeured around and live the life, and "forget" that he's got three children to take care of? How does he get behind a hundred and eleven thousand dollars in support for those kids? If you're going to play the field and travel around the world, at LEAST make sure the kids are being taken care of properly!

And it's not over, apparently. Back in 2012 where all this child support is being bandied about, check out the following:

> Of course, this is a matter of ongoing and continuous child support, so this payment, however much it was, doesn't absolve Flav of future responsibilities. In fact, he has another court date in September of this year to make sure he's kept up with his child support payments in the ensuing time. (Gibson, 2012).

So now he's got the court system all in his business. These men, all of the ones I've featured are black, just can't seem to get the point. They see some woman with huge breasts or a skirt up to the crack of her ass, and they fall for it. They apparently do not care who she is, where she's come from or where she's been. These women of the 21st century are running credit checks on men when they meet them; they are conducting background checks. They want security and safety but most importantly they want to make sure that he is the kind of guy who, if they set him up with a pregnancy, is going to be able to pay on a long-term basis. That's the politics of the game, baby: getting' "laid and paid."

> As for Flav, it isn't apparent that he has much of anything going on in the immediate future, career wise. His most recent widely seen gig was in a Super Bowl commercial for Pepsi along with fellow music industry stalwart Sir Elton John. He does, however, have a new restaurant in Las Vegas, Nevada which goes by the name of Flavor Flav's House of Flavor . It opened on his 53rd birthday: March 16, 2012. So hopefully, Flav will have the financial means to keep up with his child support responsibilities and won't be facing any more prison time any time soon. (Gibson, 2012).

The restaurant didn't last. Before that he had one in Detroit, but there's still a website. But after that he had another place called, get this: "Flavor Flav's Chicken & Ribs." He and his business partners were eventually evicted from the location in a Detroit suburb called Sterling Heights because they weren't paying the rent. A loser like this, a clown on stage and a bad choice-maker in his personal life, should never even think about having children. And the women who set him up need their asses kicked as well. There should be a limit to what a woman will do in order to get "laid and paid."

<u>Shawty Lo</u>

Shawty Lo is another one of those rapper guys who I wouldn't know from Adam's House cat. But then again I don't know Donald Trump either, but if I was writing a book about assholes I would do the necessary research under that topic. Again, another tale of pity serves as the basis for the irresponsibility that these self-proclaimed macho types exude when on stage and in the studio:

> **Shawty Lo's** life is clearly loaded with struggle, besides all the children and baby mamas. The Atlanta rapper was arrested on Friday, January 18, reportedly for failure to pay child support. (Blanco, 2013).

Pitiful. But wait: there's more:

> DJ Smallz posted a photo of Shawty Lo in cuffs while he was being arrested. It appears that the "Dey Know" rapper was detained after taping an episode of CNN's *Showbiz Tonight* to discuss his on again, off again *All My Babies' Mamas* reality show (he is wearing the same clothing on the program that he has on while being arrested). (Blanco, 2013).

These white people are continuing to make asses out of black people on every single level."Basketball Wives," "The Housewives of Atlanta," "Love and Hip Hop" and so on. Some coon pitches an idea to some white man who does the market research and creates the ads to start running to promote the show. Then they head over to the Jews at the bank to get the money to fund the project which has been "greenlighted." This shit is taped and mailed all over the world for people to see just how sick black people are. Black men acting like bitches, black women getting into "cat fights," young blacks spending money on jewelry and expensive liquors and young black women dressed like whores. And you wonder why we are so disrespected around the world?

Shawty Lo is just another casualty of the white man's casting couch, fast talk and ability to write what these young bruthas consider to be "fat checks." In turn, now they get money in their pocket and they start engaging in conspicuous consumption-type behaviors and hitting the clubs to "make it rain" (throwing up money into the air in a crowd of people). Those who see this stuff know that these men are idiots and don't really care about their money. As the age old saying teaches, "A fool and his money are soon parted."

To add insult to injury he was then fodder for the media to announce (and crack up at) his total irresponsibility:

> The G-Unit affiliated rapper has been in the press lately because of
> the controversial, to say the least, *All My Babies' Mamas*.
> Although initially scheduled to appear on Oxygen, the network
> backtracked after all the controversy surrounding its glorification
> of a poor lifestyle and stereotypical content that features the artist's
> *11 children and 10 baby mothers.*(Blanco, 2013, - emphasis
> added).

Again, here is whitey pointing his camera at people who are more than willing to get on television at the expense of the race. They will humiliate themselves to no end just to be able to tell their peers "I'ze was own TV, y'all." Even the title of the show, "All My Babies' Mamas" is not only an embarrassment, but just remember that it is going to be circulated all around the world and will be placed in the archives and used whenever the white man sees fit. Not only that, but all this embarrassing footage is admissible in a court of law.

Eleven children with ten different women. After the second woman found out that he had other women, or after female number five found out about those other kids, the only possible reason why they wouldn't keep their legs shut is because he was the kind of willing dupe that they knew would have to pay in order to keep getting laid. And pay he did.

As for those bullshit television show, check out the following:

> Nevertheless, Shawty Lo started a petition to bring back the show
> and recently told TMZ that he has suitors from other networks that
> will bring the program to a television near you. "There are offers
> on the table," he said, before adding, "I take pride in having been
> actively present in all my children's lives — and I understand my
> family doesn't represent the typical American family, but it's my
> family and it works for us." (Blanco, 2013).

How sick can one brutha be? Doesn't he know that the first thing he should do is have a plan that goes beyond how much money he is offered? The first question should be "what is the desired effect or impact of the show I am about to put on the air"? Or, "what are the desired outcomes as it relates to the young people who will inevitably be my primary audience?" The same lack of forethought that he exhibited when he impregnated all these women with all these dependent children is the same thoughtlessness that is clearly most evident in his "plan." And there is no bigger snitch than the Jewish-run TMZ which is always more than happy to circulate anti-black gossip any chance they get.

Shawty Lo's logic is convoluted at best:

> … However, Shawty previously asking, "Would you rather see 11
> children struggle with mothers on welfare?," in his aforementioned

petition probably doesn't sit right with tax payers. Also,
showcasing wads of cash, eating King Crab dinners and flossing a
Rolex watch on Instagram … is a bad look if it's true that's he
behind on child support payments. However, he does share a photo
of him playing Monopoly with his daughters and plenty of family
pics on the 'Gram, though.

White people don't need comedy clubs or any other form of humorous entertainment when they can see and read about people like Shawty Lo or any other black athlete or entertainer who continues to fall for the okey-doke. These women who are getting "laid and paid" know what they're doing and showboating one's financial status the way these black celebrities do merely makes the "targeting" of suckas that much easier.

Look at Shawty Lo: high siding (as we call it) on the internet, which reaches out to millions. Flashing a Rolex watch and he has ten kids whose child support he is behind on. Eating King Crab dinners while the mothers of his children are probably getting food stamps or feeding the kids peanut butter and jelly sandwiches. And then the ultimate insult: to call playing a game of Monopoly with his daughters and taking "plenty of family pics" a sign of positive and productive fatherhood.

DON'T HATE THE PLAYA OR THE GAME: HATE THE SYSTEM THAT PRODUCED AND ENDORSES BOTH!

So we know that the men are prospective tricks because of the American culture they were raised in. And we know that the women, even if not outright ho's, still have a philosophy that will get them "laid and paid" when all is said and done.

The Side Chick

An article titled, "3 Reasons Why Side Chicks are Settling for Second Place … And Lovin' It" offers up some of the reasoning and rationale for "being number two" in exchange for money and other favors. Following are the key points of that article with my analyses filtering in and out:

What is a "side chick"? In my own simple terms, I define a side
chick as a female who is involved in sexual relations with a male
who is in a committed relationship with another person. One may
ask why on earth an individual would voluntarily choose to play

this role in life. It sounds degrading, trifling, and just downright wrong. However, in a society where the idea of "every man for himself" becomes more widespread and the concept of a monogamous, traditional marriage becomes less and less popular with time, the side chick starts to prevail (Danielle, 2013).

"Starts" to prevail? These bitches been around for as long as marriage has. In fact, they've been around longer. The fact of the matter is that a lot of these "side chicks" are married themselves and are just "stepping out" on their husbands for various reasons. Some of them just need some extra money or want to have "more fun" because the "man" in their life is, for whatever reason, ignoring their social and financial needs. A great many of today's "wives" were able to latch onto their husbands because they started off as "side chicks" with the man they "took" or with some other guy.

This article is biased against the side chick as are large numbers of hypocritical moralizers. Check it out:

> She has reared her ugly little head in pop culture media numerous times over the past year, and unlike the old days where she was plagued with a scarlet letter and owned humility, she now is bold, fierce, and daring to be judged. (Danielle, 2013).

This white man controls these media images and remember the words of Mao: "He who controls images controls minds, and he who controls minds has little, if anything, to worry about from bodies." This side chick is a star in American culture, despite her dubious deeds. She is what the "good girl" wants to be; she is in many cases, the employee in the "world's oldest profession" – prostitution! She is an adventurer and she is the one who is a metaphor for America: a slut who feigns a belief in morality but who will do anything for a dollar.

Because of the on-going mis-perception of her, a number of distorted assumptions are derived. Following are three of them:

> Why are side chicks settling for second place and loving it? I found three reasons:
>
> **Convenience** – It takes time to develop and maintain a healthy relationship with a significant other. Trust is a very important part of relationships and is established over time. Side chicks have the pleasure of not having to be concerned with the emotional stress behind opening themselves up to trust. They know their role in a clearly defined, simple sexual relationship and not much is required of them. They get theirs and get out, avoiding any headaches. (Danielle, 2013).

What was just described is the American way! These college bitches – that's how they roll. They date, get screwed and take money and if the guy is an athlete, that's all the better. Maybe they can set him up with a pregnancy. But the point is that as soon as they are about to graduate, the guy gets dumped, she goes back home or to another city where she feigns borderline virginity, and then turns out another who she can dupe into marrying her. On campus she's the side chick, but she's a side chick on a mission.

Now, reason number two why side chicks love their roles:

> **Thrill --** Some find excitement in living a secret life. Obviously to be in an undercover relationship, there are always strategic steps made in finding out the best time to partake in sëxual relations with their taken partner. A lot of the hookups may take place late at night, on long lunch breaks, out of town, etc. To side chicks, the "creeping" never gets old. They live for thrill of not knowing where or when the next orgasm may occur. (Danielle, 2013).

The next "orgasm"? These bitches don't care about busting a nut: they want to get paid! They know men ain't shit and the way to entice them and keep them coming back it to convince them that the man they're with is "all that and a bag of chips." Even if he CAN'T screw (and most can't), she'll lie and say he can and that's all he needs to hear because he sho' ain't satisfying the woman at home. If he was, he wouldn't be banging THIS bitch – and paying her for the right to do so!

The previous statement by Danielle tries to make something scientific and strategic out of something that is surreptitious and sluttish. The woman is a ho. She wants a man but she doesn't want to be controlled, told what to do or hounded. Men represent baggage. She just wants to make some money and maybe go on some interesting dates to concerts, high-end restaurants and trips out of town. What is so complex about that?

Third point is one that needs analysis. It is where Danielle offers the following:

> **Short-term Cure** – In an odd and crazy way, side chicks feel needed. They believe their secret lovers are in relationships where they are unhappy, so she fills an important void. (Danielle, 2013).

So one lonely person finds lonely picking up somebody else's leftovers? What kind of bullshit is this? It doesn't represent short term care; it represents sick desperation! This slut is no "good Samaritan" out there looking to give up booty so that a man can feel "whole." She's out there trying to get laid and paid, looking for something to do because her girlfriends have men in their lives. It is not rocket science: it's the way things have been for centuries. This article by Danielle calls them 'side chicks' when, in reality, they are just straight up hos. And so are the men who finance their charade.

Danielle clearly doesn't know her ass from a hole in the ground, as shown in her next attempt at morality:

> In closing, I personally feel that to lower yourself to this level of "importance" is sad. Those being fulfilled in this role suffer from insecurity issues. Feeling needed, living the thrill, and calling the situation convenient is all a cover-up for what is really a void inside of one's soul. I'm a firm believer in the famous Bible verse "do unto others as you would have them do unto you." The most important part in all of this is respect, honesty, and integrity for another individual … (Danielle, 2013).

First of all, side chicks are now "lowering" themselves any more than a housewife, who is nothing more than a legal prostitute with benefits. These women get these guys to marry them and in many cases use the incomes to buttress their own accounts in the name of "taking care of the household." A prostitute is someone who sells her body for money; what do you think these "married women" do before they tie the knot? They go out on dates, suck dick, give up pussy and pussy whip the man into dropping to one knee and asking for their hand in marriage. This shit has been going on for centuries and no one says anything. In my book, that's "lowering yourself" in a more long-term basis and not only that, but then you get children involved in the whole shebang.

Secondly she says that side chicks suffer from insecurity issues. Women, in general are insecure. And so are the men who believe that somehow they are not "whole" unless they find some woman to latch on to and play "mama" for them. Lay out his clothes, tell him when to come home, cook his food, tell him what to do, control the money. That's a mother –figure, man! How much more insecure can you get than that. Women are under equal pressure and are judged by their own female pals: if one of them turns thirty and hasn't been married, they assume something's wrong with her or she's a dyke. America is filled with insecure people looking to latch on to someone else to "fulfill" their lives. What you end up with is two unfulfilled muthafuckas.

Danielle must have gotten a case of the Holy Ghost, writing that, "The most important part in all of this is respect, honesty and integrity for another individual." That is bullshit. The most important part is to have all those things first, and foremost, *for your self!* If you don't love yourself, how can you love anybody else? The greatest number is one and number one is supposed to be YOU!

Danielle (mercifully) concludes with the following:

There are several victims involved in these circumstances. The one
being cheated on is not alone in suffering from betrayal, it is just
that the two cheaters are forcing betrayal on themselves. One
should always rise above the temptations and hold integrity and
respect at a higher regard. (Danielle, 2013).

The concept of "cheating" has to be looked at. The term implies that
marriage is somehow "fair" and the perfect goal of the game. It is not. It is a scam
where you have to sign up with the state, pay for various tests and other fees and
then stand before a crowd of people who claim to be your friends and lie your ass
off. "Til death do you part" is an ideal, but in reality very few of the people
probably go that far. In fact, when it gets to "in sickness and in health," most
people are ready to cut bait.

The fact of the matter is, you already had sex and it was so good and you
feel so comfortable that you want to keep on getting it. But now you bring in extra
baggage that is going to impede on those sexcapades: electric and gas bills, car
payments, mortgage payments and/or rent, kids and their clothes and food, related
costs. By the time you get through working a job (which it is almost required that
you have) who have time for fuckin'?

The "side chick" is no victim: she's playing it safe. She gets primo dick and
his money *sans* the responsibility and the brats running all over the house fuckin'
shit up.

CONCLUSION

The age-old adage teaches that, "Girls inherit the guile and knowledge of
older women."

Chairman Mao once wrote that, "He who controls images controls minds,
and he who controls minds has little, if anything, to worry about from bodies." The
white man knows this and has traditionally used his version of reality via movies
and television, to control the minds of the masses. He has set standards and
initiated trends and fads, and has basically established the "American values" that
so many people emulate and learn from.

Women getting laid and paid is nothing less than knowing the white man's
system from top to bottom and expertly exploiting his values and priorities while
lying about what the white male REALLY is. Women get paid to lie to men about
male virility, stability and their status. In return, they get to control the purse
strings. The white man in 2016 is so obsessed with global domination, profit and
control that he's willing to do anything to show everyone that he's still the one on
top. He uses a number of arenas to do this and one of those avenues is the media.

REFERENCES

Aesop. *Fables,* retold by Joseph Jacobs. Vol. XVII, Part 1. The Harvard Classics. New York: P.F. Collier & Son, 1909–14; Bartleby.com, 2001.

Blanco, Alvin Aqua (2013, January 20). Shawty Lo Arrested For Failure To Pay Child Support? Retrieved from http://hiphopwired.com/2013/01/20/shawty-lo-arrested-for-failure-to-pay-child-support-photos/#sthash.pzl1N13T.dpufNEWS,

Burton, W.C. (2007). *Burton's Legal Thesaurus.* Retrieved from http://legal-dictionary.thefreedictionary.com/Alimony.

Bussman, C. (2014, November 12). Twenty Presidents Who Were Rumored to Have Mistresses. Retrieved from http://www.rantpolitical.com/2014/11/12/15-presidents-who-were-rumored-to-have-mistresses/

Carr, Coeli (2014, August 14). The male bad-in-bed list. Retrieved from http://www.msn.com/en-us/news/other/the-male-bad-in-bed-list/ss-AAd6Aj?srcref=rss&FORM=MH146Q&OCID=MH146Q#image=11

Chancellorfiles (2006). Penis size and racial groups. Retrieved from https://chancellorfiles.wordpress.com/2006/12/10/penis-size-and-racial-groups/

Crilly, R. (2014, November 23). Marion Barry, scandal-plagued ex-mayor of Washington, dies. *The London Telegraph.* Retrieved from http://www.telegraph.co.uk/news/worldnews/northamerica/usa/11248647/Marion-Barry-scandal-plagued-ex-mayor-Washington-dies.html

Danielle, Patrice (2016, April 9).Naturallymoi.com. 3 reasons why side chicks are settling for second place … And loving it. Retrieved from http://naturallymoi.com/2016/04/3-reasons-why-side-chicks-are-settling-for-second-place-and-lovin-it/

ESPN.go.com (2012, July 19). Terrell Owens makes payments. Retrieved from http://espn.go.com/nfl/story/_/id/8180722/terrell-owens-agrees-pay-child-support-promises-more

Farrell, W. (1993). *The myth of male power: Why men are the disposable sex.* New York, New York: Berkley Publishing.

Feiffer, J. (1965). *The Great Comic Book Heroes Paperback*. Seattle, Washington: Fantagraphic Books.

Fletcher, Connie. (1990). *What cops know: Today's police tell the inside story of their work on America's streets*. New York: Pocket Books

Fletcher, M.A. & Bock, J. (1994, August 1). NAACP leader denies sexual harassment allegations. *Baltimore Sun*. Retrieved from http://articles.baltimoresun.com/1994-08-01/news/1994213100_1_chavis-harassment-naacp-board

Forbes magazine (2014, September 23). Forbes 400 – Facts and figures on America's wealthiest.

FoxSports (2012, September 18). Report: Holyfield held in contempt. Retrieved from http://www.foxsports.com/boxing/story/evander-holyfield-judge-court-orders-back-pay-child-support-debt-091812.

Gibson, J. (2012, June 19). Flavor Flav Pays More than $100K in Child Support to Stay Out of Prison. CelebrityNetworth.com. Retrieved from http://www.celebritynetworth.com/articles/celebrity/flavor-flav-pays-100k-child-support-stay-prison/

Hakim, D. & Rashbaum, W.K. (2008, March 10). Spitzer is linked to prostitution ring. *New York Times*. Retrieved from http://www.nytimes.com/2008/03/10/nyregion/10cnd-spitzer.html

Healy, B. (2014, December 5). Abigail Johnson, after years of training, gets to put her stamp on Fidelity. *The Boston Globe*.

Holman, T. (2013, November 29). Chief Keef Ordered to Pay Child Support for 10-month Old After DNA Test. *Inquisitr*. Retrieved from http://www.inquisitr.com/1046968/chief-keef-child-support-10-month-old/

Huffington Post (2013, April 30). Bow Wow Isn't 'Lil' Anymore: Rapper Opens Up About His Baby And Being A Dad. Retrieved from http://www.huffingtonpost.com/2013/04/30/bow-wow-lil-rapper-baby-dad_n_3181067.html

Huffington Post. (June 27, 2014). Brigitte Nielsen: I Didn't Marry Sylvester Stallone For The Reason Everyone Thought. Retrieved from http://www.huffingtonpost.com/2014/06/27/brigitte-nielsen-sylvester-stallone-marriage_n_5536778.html

McCarthy, M. ()2016, March 16). *Sporting News*. Porn star Lisa Ann warns 25 percent of NBA players have faced blackmail. Retrieved from http://www.sportingnews.com/nba-news/4697284-porn-star-lisa-ann-warns-25-of-nba-players-are-blackmailed

Miller, B. (1999, September 8). Cisneros Pleads Guilty to Lying to FBI Agents. The Washington Post. Retrieved from http://www.washingtonpost.com/wp-srv/politics/special/cisneros/stories/cisneros090899.htm

Miller, M.E. (2016, March 15). A Miami woman killed a teen burglar as he fled her home, police say. Should she be charged? The Washington Post. Retrieved from http://www.msn.com/en-us/news/crime/a-miami-woman-killed-a-teen-burglar-as-he-fled-her-home-police-say-should-she-be-charged/ar-BBqtGa8?li=BBnb7Kz&ocid=iehp

MSN.com (2016, March 11). The top 20 traits women want in a man. Retrieved from http://www.msn.com/en-us/lifestyle/lifestylewomen/the-top-20-traits-women-want-in-a-man/ss-AAeHzO0?ocid=iehp

Naturallymoi.com (2012, November 4). Gabrielle Union on marriage: "I just like saying 'my boyfriend'. Retrieved from http://naturallymoi.com/2012/11/gabrielle-union-on-marriage-i-just-like-saying-my-boyfriend/

Naturallymoi.com (2016, April 9). Ladies: 5 things you must know about dating a black man. Retrieved from http://naturallymoi.com/2016/04/ladies-5-things-you-must-know-about-dating-a-black-man/

New York Daily News (2016, July 6). New Iron Man is black – And a woman. Retrieved from http://www.nydailynews.com/entertainment/new-iron-man-black-woman-article-1.2701328

Page, A. (2013, July 13). Baby Drama! Celebrities With Major Child Support Issues. Retrieved from http://madamenoire.com/287670/baby-drama-celebrities-with-major-child-support-issues/15/

Pearce, M. (2013, September 26). Cory Booker's Twitterstripper: 'It's not a sex scandal!" Los Angeles Times. Retrieved from http://articles.latimes.com/2013/sep/26/nation/la-na-nn-cory-booker-stripper-20130926

Rhone, Paysha Stockton (2007, February 27). Bobby Brown arrested in Massachusetts. People.com. Retrieved from http://www.people.com/people/article/0,,20013443,00.html

Rose, Sandra (2011, May 10). Jermaine Dupri Sued by Stripper for Child Support. Retrieved fromhttp://sandrarose.com/2011/05/jermaine-dupri-sued-by-stripper-for-child-support/

Scott, Bartie (2016, March 7). Forbes' wealthiest women in the world. Forbes magazine. Retrieved from http://www.msn.com/en-us/money/savingandinvesting/forbes-wealthiest-women-in-the-world-2016/ar-BBqc8dC?li=BBnb7Kz&ocid=iehp

Shilliday, Beth (2015, October 7). Matt Barnes Attacks Former Teammate Derek Fisher For Dating Wife Gloria Govan. Hollywoodlife.com. Retrieved from http://hollywoodlife.com/2015/10/07/matt-barnes-attacked-derek-fisher-dating-gloria-govan-ex-wife-teammates/

Simmel, G. (1990) The philosophy of money. London, England: Routledge Books.

Stitt, R. (2016, January 19). NY Jets' Antonio Cromartie's Child Support Bill is $336,000 For His 8 Children. Financial Juneteenth. Retrieved from http://financialjuneteenth.com/ny-jets-antonio-cromarties-child-support-bill-336000-8-children/

TMZ staff (2013, August 31). Allen Iverson's ex-wife: I want $1.2 million right now. Retrieved from Retrieved from http://www.tmz.com/2013/08/31/allen-iverson-tawanna-iverson-child-support-1-2-million/

Wikipedia (2016). Misandry. Retrieved from https://en.wikipedia.org/wiki/Misandry

Wikipedia (2016). Anthony Weiner sexting scandals. . Retrieved from https://en.wikipedia.org/wiki/Anthony_Weiner_sexting_scandals

Wikipedia (2016). Eliot Spitzer. Retrieved from
https://en.wikipedia.org/wiki/Eliot_Spitzer#Prostitution_scandal

Womanist Musings. (2016). When Black Women Sell Out: "It's Free Swipe Yo
EBT." Retrieved from
http://www.womanistmusings.com/when-black-women-sell-out-its-free/

Xfinity.com (2017). From rags to riches: How 10 jocks went broke. Retrieved from
http://my.xfinity.com/slideshow/sports-richestorags/5/

Wooley, Nate (2013, March 4). Dennis Rodman too broke to pay child support.
InvestorPlace.com. Retrieved from http://investorplace.com/2013/03/dennis-
rodman-too-broke-to-pay-child-support/#.VyUKHMtwXcs

Newsweek's "Secret Lives of Wives": An Africentric Viewpoint

The myth on the streets is that pretty girls lose out because they are so pretty that guys don't approach them because the assumption is that they are going to be vain or that they already have a man. This sounds logical but it's bullshit. This society is based on women and their overall physicality and as I point out later in this book on ugly women, any woman in America can get laid any time she wants to, no matter how she looks. But it is the image of "the pretty girl," popularized by television, film and magazines that has so many young females feeling depressed and fucked up.

<u>The Myth of the "Pretty Girl's Curse"</u>

One of the biggest musical hits of all time was Roy Orbison's, "Pretty Woman." This 1964 hit described a man who was longing for this bitch, from beginning of the song to the end. His whole worldview was about trying to get this good looking woman to give him a chance. Following are the lyrics:

Pretty woman walkin' down the street
Pretty woman, the kind I like to meet
Pretty woman, I don't believe you
You're not the truth

No one could look as good as you
Mercy
Pretty woman, won't you pardon me
Pretty woman, I couldn't help but see
Pretty woman, and you look lovely as can be
Are you lonely just like me
Pretty woman, stop a while
Pretty woman, talk a while
Pretty woman, give your smile to me
Pretty woman, yeah, yeah, yeah
Pretty woman, look my way
Pretty woman, say you'll stay with me
Cause I need you
I'll treat you right
Come with me baby
Be mine tonight
Pretty woman, don't walk on by
Pretty woman, don't make me cry
Pretty woman, don't walk away
OK
If that's the way it must be, OK
I guess I'll go on home, it's late
There'll be tomorrow night
But wait, what do I see?
Is she walking back to me?
Yeah, she's walking back to me
O-Oh
Pretty woman

Pretty girl's "curse"? This hunk of bullshit is defined as a good looking woman not being able to get a lot of suitors because she is so fine that most men will assume that she has someone already and will bypass her for a woman who looks closer to "ordinary" or "attainable."

This myth says more about the people doing the pursuing than it does about the actual woman. To begin with, women know if they're fine or not. In fact, even ugly bitches think that if they slather on enough makeup, put on some false eyelashes, perhaps some contact lenses that make their eyes green, a wig or extensions. Some underalls and a pantyliner, a pushup bra, a super short micro skirt, and some "fuck me" pumps, they can land a man. And because men are so fucked up, in most cases they can do just that. It has nothing to do with "pretty" or "beauty" because beauty is in the eye of the beholder.j

But remember: so is "booty."

And that is what men pay for: pussy, not looks. Sure, looks help and the call girls that cater to a wealthy clientele look good as far as their faces are concerned. But white men are closet homoerotic assholes and they want their women's features to be tiny: small nose, no lips, flat asses, small breasts and so on. In that way they can pretend that they're having sex with a young girl. So it's the sexual desires of the men that enables women to get "laid and paid," not much else. Perhaps blonde hair doesn't hurt, but there are so many bitches dying their hair today there is no doubt in my mind that Clairol, Vidal Sassoon, L'Oreal, and Revlon – to name but a few – are making a virtual killing.

Where did the concept of a "pretty girl's curse" originate, one wonders? Who knows. More likely than not some loser – or a group of them – were having a hard time getting some pussy. So they came up with an excuse akin to that of the fox and the grapes. Remember that Aesop's fable? In case you don't, let me briefly recap:

> ONE hot summer's day a Fox was strolling through an orchard till he came to a bunch of Grapes just ripening on a vine which had been trained over a lofty branch. "Just the things to quench my thirst," quoth he. Drawing back a few paces, he took a run and a jump, and just missed the bunch. Turning round again with a One, Two, Three, he jumped up, but with no greater success. Again and again he tried after the tempting morsel, but at last had to give it up, and walked away with his nose in the air, saying: "I am sure they are sour." (Aesop, 2001).

In other words, since he couldn't reach them he had to convince himself that something must have been wrong with the grapes – instead of something being wrong with his abilities to reach them. So I believe this kind of failure created the "pretty girl's curse." And I only mention this because in this book on women "getting laid and paid," one might be led to believe that only the fine ones are benefiting. Let me tell you something.

Over the millennia, pussy is the only thing that never loses value. Women learned that a long time ago, even before capitalism was created. They also knew that men weren't about shit and were only good for physical labor, getting them pregnant, and menial chores. In the meantime, they (women) sat at home on their pussies and prepared food, cleaned the house and thought about just how stupid men, who seemed happiest when engaged in wars, bar room fights and other macho struggles, really were. And they waited and planned and have been getting "laid and paid" even before recorded history.

And this is taking place whether the woman is "pretty" or not.

The Pussy Principle: Concepts and Characteristics

The pussy principle is very simple and has been in effect for centuries, across international boundaries, cultural boundaries and of course, enacted to perfection here in the United States.

Pussy and the craving of it is a part of the male onset for the overwhelming majority of his life. Even after being rendered impotent by disease, natural causes or some kind of accident, men still spend huge amounts of money for "female company." After all, as the women say, "If you can't use the hips, use the lips." And so it has come to pass: the "pussy principle" is not only alive and well, but it is thriving in present day America.

What I am about to share is how the premise of the "mistress" enables a number of women, married or single, to get laid and paid.

Let me provide some examples.

It All Begins With "Nigga-Shit"

Because what I am about to write impacts all men and their being manipulated by women, don't get the term "nigga-shit" confused. I am mainly speaking about the bruthas and how easy it is to control their lives, the futures and their wallets through the skillful manipulation of pussy. Before addressing athletes and entertainers specifically, let me provide a case study and some definitions of the "nigga-shit" that creates division among black men who, like dogs, will fight over a woman in a "territorial" kind of way.

Take the case of professional basketball player Matt Barnes. An October 7, 2015 article from the Hollywoodlife.com website pretty much provides information that exhibits the kind of "nigga-shit" that I alleged. Under the heading, "Matt Barnes Attacks Former Teammate Derek Fisher For Dating Wife Gloria," the insights – and my analyses – follow:

> How awkward! New York Knicks coach Derek Fisher is involved
> in a romantic relationship with the WIFE of former L.A. Lakers
> teammate Matt Barnes. When Matt found out about it, all hell
> broke loose and he attacked his former pal! (Shilliday, 2015).

Once these bitches get ahold of one wealthy celebrity or athlete, it's difficult to "dumb down" when the next guy has to be selected. By that time they have a certain lifestyle that they want to maintain, which is why Derek Fisher was the logical "next man up" for the beautiful Gloria Govan. This then, is the beginning of what we call "nigga shit."

The story unfolds:

> This will make for an interesting twist on *Baksetball Wives LA* next season! One of the stars, **Gloria Govan**, 45, is now dating **Derek Fisher**, 41. Which would be great, except for the fact that Derek once played alongside Gloria's estranged husband **Matt Barnes**, 35, when the two were teammates on Los Angeles Lakers. Matt went berzerk over the news and totally attacked his friend! (Shilliday, 2015).

"Estranged" husband means that you're still married. But these bitches don't care and the media doesn't tell the whole story. Can there be any doubt that Barnes was getting' some pussy on the side? And of course Gloria found out. Women know how to serve revenge: "Let's see now, who can I fuck with that will drive Matt out of his fuckin' mind? I know – a former teammate!" So Derek got his ass kicked for messing with this woman when he (Derek) had his pick of any woman he wanted.

Check out what happened:

> When Matt learned that D-Fish was at Gloria's Los Angeles house on Oct. 3, he drove 95 miles from Santa Barbara, California to "beat the sh*t" out of him" according to *Page Six*. Their source says Derek and Gloria have been dating for "a few months," after Fisher filed to divorce his wife of 10 years, Candace, last spring. Even though Matt and Gloria are separated and there were rumors that he dated **Rihanna**, 27, it doesn't sound like Matt is allowing his estranged wife to do the same and date other people. (Shilliday, 2015).

First of all, I doubt if it as "Gloria's house." She was still married to Barnes so it was THEIR house. Secondly, if Derek and Gloria were "dating for a few months," then it is clear that he fucked her. Third, since Matt filed for divorce, then he didn't have shit to say other than the fact that if it wasn't her house, she shouldn't be entertaining company. Matt and Gloria had been married for ten years and he was a pro basketball player, so you KNOW he got pussy on the side. And while he was out of town, on the road, you also KNOW that she was fuckin' behind his back.

But she felt comfortable enough to have a party and invite Derek over. The only problem was that when women "get laid and paid," they have to be discreet because there are a lot of men out there who just can't get that pussy out of their minds. Barnes was one of them. Observe:

> The source confirmed the relationship between Derek and Gloria while explaining that "Derek was in Gloria's backyard with about 10 people having a bonfire on Saturday." Apparently Matt took this as the ultimate betrayal, causing him to drive down to LA from his Memphis Grizzlies training camp to confront his former teammate. "He went crazy. He got in his car and went to the house and went after Derek," their source said about Matt. Another insider claims "Someone told Matt that Derek was at the house and he drove down there — he went over to confront Derek." (Shilliday, 2015).

Ironically, Derek Fisher sat in as a co-host on the May 3, 2017 edition of "Inside the NBA" and the topic was never raised. So he got his ass kicked a few years back and now it's business as usual. Take note that the Los Angeles Clippers, who had brought Matt Barnes on board for the end of the season and playoffs after losing Blake Griffin to injury, would not be an issue because the Clippers had just been eliminated from the playoffs by the Utah Jazz. So as soon as that's done, here comes "D-Fish" for the first time. Was he dodging the issue? Were the other hosts trying to avoid Barnes coming to the studio or being interviewed and saying something about incident?

What was Barnes going to "confront" Derek about anyway? Was it his house? Check out what Shilliday (2015) wrote:

> A source close to Fisher confirmed the fight to *Page Six* but said, "Matt came after Derek but he only had a few scratches…Derek's not going to press charges, he's going to let it go." Derek left Gloria's house before police arrived. The Knicks tweeted on Oct. 6 that that Derek was "not at practice due to personal reasons — expected back tomorrow." He was in LA visiting his kids but it is possible that he paid Gloria another visit!

Fisher was scared shitless. Barnes is a thug known for mixing it up on the basketball courts, so you know what he would have done to Fisher. But Gloria is the one who gets the money and the sex from two men who are in shape and obviously infatuated with her; and believe me, she is FINE! But that's what makes these women able to "get laid and paid." That is what makes them marriage material. They set it up so they can get the big house, the children who go to the best schools, a car and bank account of their own (and his as well) and that's the reality of the "American Dream."

But remember: the bruthas who get duped are very childlike and their needs are few. They can't stay out of the arms of other women on the side and they can be "tamed" with a little head and some booty. Meanwhile, the seducing, reducing, inducing strategies and tactics continue on. But in reality, it boils down to being what is known on as the streets by the elders as "nigga shit."

Pro Athletes and "Mistresses"

Getting laid and paid is evident when it comes to the institution of marriage and these so-called "housewives" who control the family budget, but it's all over the place. Let's take a look at the article about and comments of this porn star named Lisa Ann, who was the focus of an article in the Sporting News in March of 2016. The headline was, "Porn Star Lisa Ann Warns 25 Percent of NBA Players Have Faced Blackmail." According to the article,

> NBA Pro athletes engaged in affairs with porn stars and strippers should watch their step, warns adult film star and director Lisa Ann. She estimates 25 percent of NBA players have faced blackmail at some point in their careers. Writing for Complex, the basketball aficionado warned that rich NBA stars, particularly married players, **have become targets for hustlers** looking to steal their money, wallets, jewels, even their Playstations. If they're not stealing, they're trying to hustle players into paying their rent or buying them fancy cars (McCarthy, 2016).

But let's place the blame where it belongs: cockhounding-ass black men who see a white bitch in the stands and lose their minds. White society knows what these Kardashian-oriented women are about, and so do the teammates of the men who spend that money. But who really cares? Do these men give a shit about having "wives" at home or children who may be affected? Of course not. And this is one more piece of evidence that backs up my later claim and contention that men are viewed as children by women: immature "boys" who chase pussy and need a "mommy-type" to take care of them.

The previous quote by Lisa Ann posits that, "rich NBA stars, particularly married players, **have become targets for hustlers** looking to steal their money, wallets, jewels, even their Playstations." Play stations? Grown ass men? Jewelry? Are these men or bitches? So all that material acquisition slowly directs these males toward what they REALLY are and what they really crave: pussy —

preferably white pussy. The article adds that, "If they're not stealing, they're trying to hustle players into paying their rent or buying them fancy cars." I ask, how is this any different than what the housewife is doing? Blackmail won't work if the man knows what's going on in terms of his relationship at home. "Tell her – she already knows," should be the response. But these cowardly effeminate assholes are AFRAID of the women they married. And so they pay the blackmail to keep the ho quiet.

And what a "get laid and paid" scam it is. According to Lisa Ann,

> I've heard girls say they make sure he is married or in a relationship before going back to his hotel with him. Once there they wait for their moment alone with his wallet and take photos of all of his credit cards and his ID. The final part of the plan is blackmail. You would be shocked how many NBA players have had been blackmailed in an effort to keep their privacy. My guess is a minimum of 25 percent of NBA players have dealt with blackmail at some point in their career. I've heard girls brag about long-term hustles where they have a player paying their rent and expenses just to keep them quiet and out of their family life.(McCarthy, 2016).

Snitch-ass Kobe Bryant got busted by his woman after he "raped" a white bitch while he was undergoing therapy in Colorado. I mean he bent the bitch over a chair and everything. So she blackmailed his ass. He came clean at a press conference, but that wasn't good enough. He added that, "I should have just paid her off the way Shaq does with his women." Now Shaq was married at the time, and his wife has since divorced him. Did Kobe's comments have anything to do with it? Who knows. But I know this: Shaq had kids and those kids watched Kobe's press conference. So Kobe is a snitch and a bitch. And his fine-ass Latina wife threatened him and he had to go out and buy her a million dollar ring and hasn't "gotten out of line" since. She definitely got "laid and paid."

Getting laid and getting paid. And for what? Pussy? I understand that men have their needs, but the problem with far too many of us (black men) is that we let our needs dominate and direct our thought processes. White men probably do that as well, but I don't give a shit what happens to them. I am talking about the few brothers who get the chance to make big money and who should be donating that money to community-based organizations (not the church) to defend and develop the black communities that spawned most of them. Instead, they know that these women want their money because even the ugly muthafuckas like Dennis Rodman can get approached by these women.

But it's not just the cockhounds from the NBA who get "punked" right out there in the open for all to see (clad in underwear, standing and listening to a little white man tell them what to do, having child-like temper tantrums when the referee makes a call they don't like, etc.), it's also the men from the National Football League and pro baseball as well. But beyond sports, politicians buy into it as well. I will address women getting "laid and paid" by the politicians and how it has functioned using a few case studies.

Forbes' wealthiest women in the world 2016

How could I write a book about women getting "laid and paid" without sharing with you what I view as the key underlying dynamic of both? Men's lust is exploited and pimped by women and the values of the society. Even the Bible is filled with lies and bullshit that place women in a subservient position. What they have been able to do is take their vaginas and place a market value on them; at first it was through marriage and the provision of a house, land and other assets, which of course they had to pay for by bearing children. But if those children were girls, they were able to train them about boys and men and how easy it is to manipulate both.

Wealth is defined as, "abundance of valuable material possessions or resources." Back in the day in Europe and Africa there were "arranged marriages," but the man had to have some kind of wealth: land, money or otherwise. Once married into that family, the woman had to "obey" and do her "womanly duties." This meant giving up a whole lot of booty whenever the man wanted it. If he prematurely ejaculated, so what? If she didn't get a nut, so what? James Browns' rather sexist 1966 song, "It's a Man's World" pretty much lays out the foundation for the global system of gender discrimination. Remember?

This is a man's world, this is a man's world
But it wouldn't be nothing, nothing without a woman or a girl
You see, man made the cars to take us over the road
Man made the train to carry the heavy load
Man made electric light to take us out of the dark
Man made the boat for the water, like Noah made the ark
This is a man's, man's, man's world
But it wouldn't be nothing, nothing without a woman or a girl
Man thinks about our little bitty baby girls and our baby boys
Man made them happy, 'cause man made them toys

> And after man make everything, everything he can
> You know that man makes money, to buy from other man
> This is a man's world
> But it wouldn't be nothing, nothing, not one little thing, without a woman or a girl
> He's lost in the wilderness
> He's lost in bitterness, he's lost lost

While admitting that this "man's world" would be nothing without a woman or a little girl, what the lyrics seem to overlook is that every man is born of a woman and raised by one. So it's actually a woman's world and it is my belief that they knew this all along. But without power what could they do? Men were physically stronger and if women stood up, they'd get their asses kicked or labeled as witches or burned at the stake.

Wealth then came through marriage and even then, the male-run courts made the decision regarding the division of property if the man died or there was a divorce. In fact, women couldn't even own land or property in some cultures. So they waited and over the centuries, increased their impact and influence on powerful men who, in turn, through a pussy whipped stupor, passed laws that began to ease the burden that had been placed on the female of the species.

Now with my rather bizarre interpretation of history out of the way (the truth can oftentimes be viewed as "bizarre"), let's fast forward to today's world and a March 7, 2016 article by Bartie Scott titled, "Forbes' Wealthiest Women in the World." I share this article and the list with you so that you can see that on some level, these rich women "got laid and paid" and came into their wealth. Now, remember the lyrics to James Brown's song. And even with women using "pussy power" to gain more and more control, it remains a "man's world" because he continues to control the wealth.

As importantly the male also controls the policies and the politics of wealth. That means he can lie, distort and control the contractual elements involved in business and the economy, This is what she exploits: the knowledge that she has to have her own money so that she can do things her way. Put another way, "you cannot have political freedom without an economic base" (Karenga, 1967). And in the case of almost every single one of these women, the big money came from some man, either directly or indirectly.

Let's take a look.

Liliane Bettencourt, whose wealth comes from L'Oreal. Her net worth is $36.1 billion, but get this: she maybe the richest person in the world but she's an "heiress." In other words, she got the company from somebody else. Research tells us that,

In 1909, Eugène Paul Louis Schueller, a young French chemist of German descent,[7] developed a hair dye formula called *Auréale*. Schueller formulated and manufactured his own products, which he then sold to Parisian hairdressers. On 31 July 1919, Schueller registered his company,[8] the Société Française de Teintures Inoffensives pour Cheveux (Safe Hair Dye Company of France). The guiding principles of the company, which eventually became L'Oréal, were research and innovation in the field of beauty. In 1920, the company employed three chemists. By 1950, the team was 100 strong; that number reached 1,000 by 1984 and is nearly 20,000 today.

So another woman gets "paid" because some male founded a company and she somehow stumbled into it. The specifics are not even important. This French company shows that the white man is paying for pussy just like his American counterpart. Now this rich woman has been paid. And what is their slogan? It's "Because I'm worth it." Name one woman who doesn't believe in this maxim.

Alice Walton is the second richest woman in the world, worth $32.3 billion and is the daughter of Sam Walton, the founder of those Wal-Mart stores.(Scott, 2016). So she is the product of a woman who got laid and now she has gotten paid.

Jacqueline Mars is worth $23.4 billion and is the daughter of the man who inherited the Mars candy empire along with some pet food companies. In other words, another "heiress." She has brothers who share in the inheritance, but remember this: all of them came from the woman who seduced and then married. According to Forbes magazine,

Jacqueline Mars (born October 10, 1939) is an American heiress, and investor. She is the daughter of Audrey Ruth (Meyer) and Forrest Mars, Sr., and granddaughter of Frank C. Mars, founders of the American candy company Mars, Incorporated. In 2014, *Forbes* described Mars as the 20th richest American. (Forbes, 2014).

Mars has evolved according to the research. According to Yahoo.com, "The Mars bars were sold as such in the US until 2002 when its name was changed to Snickers Almond Bar. It contained then, and still does, plain nougat, almonds, caramel and milk chocolate." Snickers remains a favorite for the most part, and Jacqueline and her brothers keep raking in the dough.

Maria Franca Fissolo of Italy is worth $22.1 billion. She's another candy heiress, this one with Nutella and related chocolates. An obvious case of "getting laid and paid." According to Scott (2016), "She is the widow of Michele Ferrero, who built Ferrero Group and died on Valentine's Day 2015. The private company is owned by Fissolo and her son Giovanni, the CEO; its products include the popular Nutella spread, Kinder chocolates and Tic-Tac mints." So she hooks up with some rich Italian, gives up the booty and has kids by him, qualifying her to inherit all his shit. Now she's the owner (along with her son. See how it works?

Susanne Klatten is the daughter of a woman who got laid and paid, and is the owner of BMW after her mother died. Although Klatten is credited with steering German pharmaceutical and chemical company Altana AG toward $2 billion in annual sales, the fact has to remain that the "roots" of her wealth come from being the daughter of a woman who, again, "got laid and paid." Like Donald Trump, she was born with a silver spoon in her ass … oops! I mean MOUTH. You can afford to be an innovator when money is never an object.

Then there's **Laurene Powell Jobs.** Name sound familiar? It should. While she's an accomplished woman, she is also the widow of the late Steve Jobs, founder of Apple Computers, and it worth $16.7 billion. According to the research,

> Laurene Powell Jobs is an American businesswoman, executive and the founder of Emerson Collective, which advocates for policies concerning education and immigration reform, social justice and environmental conservation. She is also co-founder and president of the Board of College Track, which prepares disadvantaged high school students for college. Powell Jobs resides in Palo Alto, California, with her three children. She is the widow of Steve Jobs, co-founder and former chief executive officer of Apple Inc. She manages the Laurene Powell Jobs Trust.(Scott, 2016; Wikipedia, 2017).

See how it's done. She's blonde and cute and allows him to talk her out of her panties. He becomes a billionaire, dies at an early age (she had to have found out he was ill), the necessary paperwork is in place and then, voila! The one who used to get laid has now been paid. She also owns a chunk of Disney.

Abigail Johnson is worth $13.1 billion and her wealth comes from "money management." Again, we find someone who got her start based on what she got from a man – her grandfather. As one source informs us,

> Abigail Pierrepont "Abby" Johnson (born December 19, 1961) is an American businesswoman. Since 2014, Johnson is President and Chief Executive Officer of US investment firm Fidelity Investments (FMR), and chairwoman of its international sister company Fidelity International (FIL). Fidelity was founded by her grandfather Edward C. Johnson II. Her father Edward C. "Ned" Johnson III remains Chairman Emeritus of FMR. As of March 2013, the Johnson family owned a 49% stake in the company. In November 2016, Johnson was named Chairman and will remain

> CEO and President giving her full control of Fidelity with 45,000
> employees worldwide … Johnson's wealth of approximately $14
> billion making her one of the world's wealthiest women. (Healy,
> 2014).

So her grandmother set everything up by screwing her grandfather, who handed the empire to his son. Then, he handed control over to Abigail. So again, a woman gets a hand me down from a man who impregnated that woman's mother and gave her a lifestyle of wealth. Getting laid and paid.

Charlene de Carvallio Heineken is worth $12.3 billion. I know you recognize the last name. That's right, she's from the Netherlands and she's another heiress. Her parents had money as well. Check it out:

> Charlene de Carvalho-Heineken (born 30 June 1954) is a Dutch-
> English businesswoman and the owner of a 25% controlling
> interest in the world's third-largest brewer, Heineken International.
> Charlene Heineken was born on 30 June 1954, the daughter of
> Freddy Heineken, the Dutch industrialist, and Lucille Cummins, an
> American from a Kentucky family of bourbon whiskey distillers.
> She was educated at Rijnlands Lyceum Wassenaar, followed by a
> law degree from the University of Leiden.

So her mother got laid, impregnated and paid and this makes Charlene another heiress. See what I mean? This gives an entire new meaning to those James Brown lyrics I shared, especially the part where he croons, "This is a man's world/But it would be nothing/without a woman or a little girl." He was right. The man continues to the species after impregnating one of these women who then gets all of his shit when he dies. So she can then go out and find another guy who is well off and the plutocracy (government by the wealthy) therefore perpetuates itself: getting laid and pad.

Christie Walton is the daughter-in law of Wal-Mart founder Sam Walton. Her net worth is "only" $5.2 billion after dividing her late husband's estate with their 29 year old son, Lukas.

The Grown Man as Child

During the airing of what was originally a January 2, 1962 episode of the western, "Laramie," we find that even back then, during the days of the wild, wild west, the tendency was to treat men like children in order to be an "acceptable" woman.

In this episode, "After saving the life of an Arapaho girl in a fire and helping acquit her in a trial for killing a man, Slim (Sherman, played by John Smith) finds her his possession due to Arapaho law. When she won't leave him, he takes her in but soon finds he has feelings for her." At one point the beauty, whose name is Winona, draws Slim a warm bath without him having to tell her. They walk into his room and he asks her, if she learned this kind of treatment of a man back on the reservation. She tells him, "They taught us how to bathe small children. And what is a man but a small child grown up?"

And there you have it. At first it may seem like a contradiction: the big, bad macho man making sure that the female remains his social, cultural, political, educational and physical inferior. But there is one thing that he overlooked: she has always been his intellectual superior. And because of that, his machismo and political cravings are always manipulated by her and committed in her name. Keep in mind that, "the hand that rocks the cradle rules the throne."

This has always been the case. Don't be fooled into thinking that the rise of white bitches like Hillary Clinton, Elizabeth Warren, Nancy Pelosi is something new: white women have been in control of the men who appear to be in control. And they do it because behind closed doors, they treat him like a child. And he likes it and accepts it. And black people have mocked this pattern of behavior in the way the women treat the men and society has taken notice. Especially the advertising world.

Witness this spate of insurance commercials. What do you see? These mealy-mouthed effeminate "men" (husbands) kissing their wives asses and acting as if they don't know what to do. Companies like Metropolitan Life, Colonial Penn, Liberty Insurance, Mass Mutual, and many others have targeted black elderly married couples, scaring the shit out of them about dying and leaving behind huge funerals bills, and do it by showing the woman large and in charge while the man, admitting that "his health" might be a problem and may impede their qualifying for life insurance, stands back like some scatter-brained bitch while she makes the decision that yes, indeed, they may well need such insurance.

And it's not only the case with health and life insurance. Just look at the family on television: the man is the perennial fuckup, the excuse-maker and the clownish buffoon. On one such commercial, Liberty Mutual insurance commercial this white boy talks about he is leaving for work with his ten gallon jug of coffee and he's backing out of the driveway and then "accidentally bumped into his wife's car while she was watching," and that "she forgave him later on -- eventually" and then goes about attacking the insurance company. Forgave him? He didn't do it purposely so why should he have to apologize to that bitch? A true pussy.

Oasisi Express Cash features this effeminate sounding black man who promtes the product. Another one named "William M." comes on sounding even more bitch-like than the narrator. Mark S. is another one, who calls Oasis Financial "a blessing" is the third "coon" that comes on the air sounding like he was in need of a panty shield. And the list goes on and on. And here is what you have to remember: these "men" were selected over scores of others who auditioned to tell these lies. They were chosen by a committee of white men who weighed their attributes and how they would "come across." This effeminate shit you're *seeing is all by design.*

Or how about the Buick commercial (aired during the summer of 2016) where the young white couple is on vacation. Clad in bathing suits they sit in the shade next to a pool. She asks him if he remembered to handle an issue with their Buick, he assures her he did. Even as the words are uttered she then asks him if he remembered to close the windows in the apartment. He claims he did as she whispers, "You're the greatest." But out of her vision is this chickenshit look in his face as he re-thinks his position on the windows. Cut to the apartment with pigeons flying in and are all over the place.

Again, the woman is the responsible one (although she should have shut the damn windows herself) and the man, who is probably paying for the vacation where she is relaxing, is the asshole. She is large and in charge and of course, getting g laid and paid.

In other commercials, the ones where the man is not totally left out while the single mother who looks like a Victoria Secret model is shown having it all under control, the man is a simpleton. Swiffer wet mops shows this giant of a man mopping up behind his bad-ass half-white kid instead of putting his foot in that kid's ass the first time he fucked up. Another time the little half-white daughter is concerned about her daddy's heart so after talking with her white mommy, the daddy, who is asleep on the couch, wakes up and finds Cheerios all over his fuckin' chest. The little girl was told that Cheerios are good for your heart.

In addition, these effeminate rapper faggots are really a trip. They walk around in skinny jeans acting like children. You've got the likes of Pharrell Williams, Usher, Young Thug, 50 Cent, P-Diddy and so many others either actually gay or what they might refer to as asexual, pansexual, and/or bisexual. What does this have to do with being a "child"? It begins with denial of black manhood. Once you do that, you can be used or manipulated into being anything, including gay and a child. That's the connection. And it's being exploited by white people because they have always had childish tendencies and orientations and it is reflected in the way they act, think and talk once they reach maturity.

RISE OF THE CHICKEN HEADS: EVEN UGLY WOMEN CAN GET "LAID AND PAID"

Under a separate heading I wrote this essay as, "The Rise of the Chicken heads: When Beauty IS a Beast!" At any rate, the point being made here can be found in an anonymous maxim: "Showing cleavage doesn't fix your face."

Ugly women are the new fine hos. Seriously. At least, that's the way it is in their minds and in this culture. Look at television and you can see it: white, black Asian, Latina – whatever. If you can walk in a pair of five inch heels and wear a skirt up to your panty line without actually exposing the panties (thanks to the thong, a thing will keep your panties from showing,), then you qualify.

Aiding these chicken heads in their quest for "pseudo-beauty" is the white man, who is the expert. After all, he's succeeded in making his pale, no breasted, flat-booty woman a standard of beauty for the world. And now the women of color all over this country are trying to look like her, but let me not get ahead of myself. First, we share what makes a woman ugly.

To begin with, it's her shallowness and attitude. And some of these fashions that I've alluded to aid and abet her in this "crime." She's flinging back her fake hair and has her hands on a waist held in place by a girdle and truly thinks that she's 'the bomb.' There are men who find this attractive. But he's encountering someone who has serious esteem issues and who is so obsessed with being accepted by her friends and being with the "in crowd," that she also mimics the attitude that will get her noticed as being "independent," "a down chick," "a strong woman" and so on. What it does is bring attention to what she really is: a modern day emotional troglodyte.

Now after the shallowness and attitude issues we come to the image issues which piles on additional dimensions of shallowness. How do I notice thee? Let me count the ways.

First, the extensions and the wigs. I venture to guess that more than 60% of black women in this country between the ages of 18 and 60 have some fake shit in their head. But the fact is, these women are putting it in the heads of their young daughters as well. Maybe they're too damn lazy to comb it, but the other day I saw a little girl about nine years old with extensions in her head – including blonde ones! What is this telling her about herself and culture? First it was the straightening comb, now it's this shit! (And black men: don't forget those "conks" that you used to put in your head so you could have textured hair like that cracker).

Anyway, these women are spending hundreds of dollars on this shit. Just so they can flip it back in anger or when they turn their heads – the way they've seen the white woman do for decades. And what's so cold about it is that they really seem to think the shit is theirs! And if you ask them (which I will do every time I get the chance) they'll say something flippant like, "yeah it's mine – I paid for it!" Self-image issues, pure and simple.

So it's not just the extensions and wigs, but many of them add color. I've seen more honey-blonde black women in the past five years than I saw during the previous 53 years of my life, combined. Even worse, the young generation has added new colors to their fake-ass repertoire: green, blue, blood red (and maroon), platinum and I've even seen purple. The older ones whose hair is graying refer to it as "silver" and then do whatever it is they do to make it appear as if they have more than they've got. I think they're called "hair pieces."

Now the eyes, which are supposed to be the "gateway to the soul." Based on the length of these eyelashes these women are wearing, I'd have to say that the gateway to the soul needs a pruning! Some of these eyelashes are a full half an inch long! Then they glue them to the ones they've got and they still look like shit. These women's eyelashes are so long that when you kiss them, you know when they open their eyes because the lashes brush your face!

The eyeliners and all that color, including glitter that they use – man, save that shit for the circus! This is the kind of makeup that used to be reserved for the bride of Frankenstein, Clayface and other feature creatures! They don't spare the nose: now it's vogue to have your nose pierced, sometimes on both sides, which prompts a thinking person to ask: what happens to the buggers and snot?

For a long time earrings have been modified in the name of being "hip." These women went from studs to earrings the size of bicycle rims. I mean, they are huge and some of them have the nerve to wear three and four earrings in one ear! When they do that you can hear the jingling and jangling halfway down the hallway!

And then, the breastseses. I am one of the men who can spot the "type" of breast no matter what you try to do to veil them. There are small breasts embellished with a padded bra – oftentimes complete with fake nipples. There are the sagging ones (I call them "droopers") that are pulled up and out with these new-fangled bras that have been developed. The breasts look alright with that bra on, but when they take it off, those things fall to their knees. There's the bra that helps them look larger, more full and can push those puppies right up under their chins, which is the way women seem to be wearing their blouses these days.

Speaking of blouses, there is an increasingly popular style that accommodates these "tittie-fakers." You've seen 'em: these newfangled blouses and shirts that are deep-V cut and allow propped up breasts to be exposed. They're not really "new," because trollops, saloon girls, street hos, women at dance clubs and other night crawler types wore them back in the day. But this "look-at-my-tits" style is even now being accepted in the workplace. And when they hit the club or some social event, you can almost see everything but the nipple.

The waist line can be equally well disguised. They've got these body suits that serve double duty: prop up the boobs and hold in the butt at the same time.

They've got the girdles that hold in the gut and firm up the butt. They've got the ones that bring in your waistline only. There's so many looks to choose from, but let us not get it twisted: all this shit is about two types of deception: self-deception and social deception. The former is aimed at convincing yourself that you "still have it" and the second is aimed at convincing others – friends, relatives – that you don't have any psychological issues about "losing it" in the first place. In both cases, they are dead wrong.

Now before moving on, consider this: imagine getting up and having to put all this shit on, manage and arrange it and then live in pain all day along, thinking about avoiding certain things, the lies – both implicit and explicit – that you have to live each and every day. Now can you see why black women are always pissed off? They're not mad at you because you never asked them to do all this shit: they're mad at themselves and their mad at other women, white and black, for looking so "good" that they have to put on these fronts and facades in order to "fit in." Feel me?

So we've got the hair, the ears, the eyes, the nose, the breasts, waist, hips and ass. Let us move on and describe more evidence of the "image issues" that permeate far too many females in this society.

The feet. Most black women have big feet and they apparently don't like the fact. I think many have accepted it, because it's the only way to explain why they bring so much attention to those feet. They paint their toenails and then wear open toed shoes. Fine. But why do that when you're bringing attention to something that is bringing you pain, namely, those damn shoes!

These women are wearing five- and seven-inch heels, man! They're towering over everybody just so they can "look good" (or so they think). They are in pain because the human foot wasn't made to have all that weight (and some of these women are huge) on the falls of the foot. It's almost laughable how they maintain balance and some will even walk on gravel and uneven surfaces rather than taking their shoes off. Some even have the nerve to wear ankle bracelets, which bring even MORE attention to those feet.

The underalls which serve to also hold in the butt cheeks and give shape to sagging, unflattering asses, also serve to shape the legs in many cases.

There we have it: a female version of Frankenstein, Jr.! What could the psychological and emotional implications be for someone who is so manufactured, so fake, so committed to accepting the falsity of their looks? We know this much: it cannot, on any level, be positive. Psychologically, you are creating another person's because the person that you are, the way that you look, are realities that you simply cannot accept or deal with.

Emotionally, it's even deeper. You have to maintain this shit when you enter a relationship or go visit the family during the holidays. You have to keep this front up when you go out with the girls. You have to keep all this stuff up to snuff when you have an important engagement or go to work or to church. In other words, you have to be fake in order to be emotionally secure. But you cannot be emotionally secure unless you accept the fact that everything about you is fake.

The only people who see the "real you" (other than yourself) are your children, and they can't stand you with your "image issues" having self. Why? Because you chastise them and kick that ass for them being "bad" or out of control when it's YOU who's out of control. So much to the point that while they're getting ready for school, you're putting on all that fake shit I just described. When they're home doing their homework, you're stripping out of all that "goon gear" I just talked about. The quality time that you ought be spending with them is spent "relaxing," which is really nothing more than "decompressing" from the freak show that you have become.

Somebody with image issues needs you to affirm her womanhood. Well, they really don't "need" it, but they think they do. And when it comes to women, what they think is their world. That's why they when they enter a relationship they feel it's their goal to "fix," "repair, "mend" or otherwise "improve" the male. And why is that? Because they can't let you go on being your "natural" self while they go through the transformations that I've just described! They want control and the only way they can control you is to make you think you're just as f----ed up as they are!

No matter how much makeup or camera filters you shoot them through, a chickenhead is a chickenhead. Wanna name names? I'll offer a few so you won't think that what I've just provided is nothing more than a cacophony of emotive labeling. Here we go: Margaret Cho (comedienne), Sarah Jessica Parker ("Sex in the City"), Cheryl Underwood ("The Talk"), Jamie Lee Curtis, Tori Spelling, Joan Rivers, Carla Hall ("The Chew"), Renee Zellweiger, Kristen Stewart, Barbara Walters, Courtney Love, Hunter Tylo, Amy Schumer, Whoopi Goldberg and Sandra Bernhard.

Can I make it any plainer?

The Reality of Alimony: Ka-Ching!!!

As someone who has studied sociology at the doctoral level and written extensively on a number of sociological topics ranging from marriage and family, collective behavior and social stratification to culture, urban activity and deviance, I found the on-going defense of "alimony" an interesting one. So I looked into it and found that much of what is written does not really fit into its actual practice and application in the real world. Let me share with you some of my findings, observations and perspectives.

To begin with, what is "alimony." Involves a great deal of judicial and legal "discretion." I have found in my studies that when it comes to discretion in the hands of white people, it means carte blanche when it comes to fines, penalties and meting out punishment, especially when it comes to the application of the law and how to use it as a means of "control." Controlling women and entire families is another area where judicial discretion can be applied with extreme prejudice.

According to the on-line Free/Legal Dictionary, alimony is described thusly:

> The purpose of alimony is to avoid any unfair economic consequences of a Divorce, even after property is divided and Child Support, if any, is awarded. Courts set few specific guidelines to attaining this broad goal: instead of telling judges how and when to award alimony, most courts simply grant them broad discretion to decide what is fair in each case (Burton, 2007).

When the words "fair" and/or "unfair" are used by this American system, what it really means is what constitutes "fairness" in the minds of white people. And since discretion is a part of determining what is fair, that gives them free reign to be unfair to those groups they don't like. Women are one such group.

I am no feminist but I am a brilliant analyst. And there is something inherently unfair about a system that first of all lies about the "value" or "morality" of monogamous marriage. The ceremony is replete with lies about "'til death do us part" and loving someone "in sickness and in health" and other lies that humans usually fall short of. The fact that the divorce rate is near 60% proves my point.

But after that act of ersatz morality, and things don't work out, we can apply and accurately test the validity of the previous definition. To begin with, keeping in mind that this is a system run by men even though women are the numerical majority, read again this statement: "The purpose of alimony is to avoid any unfair economic consequences of a Divorce, even after property is divided and Child Support, if any, is awarded." This is a system that finds on-going disparate pay for women, a glass ceiling in the workplace and perpetual rapes and abuses a part of its culture. How can such a system therefore view women with anything even remotely approaching objectivity or "fairness"? This is a system that didn't even "allow" women the right to vote until 1920!

So "fairness" is defined by the people who make the rules. When property is divided, what is it based on? To many people, a fifty-fifty split of property is fair. But is it? To get half of what the family assets amount to is not fair to men who may have paid in much more during the marriage. But it is not fair to women either: they have to keep the children in many cases and that means that they have to deal with school, child support and child-related expenses. But even in that, women still manage to get "laid and paid" on an optimum level and I'm going to show you how. The late actor John Barrymore once quipped, "You never realize how short a month is until you pay alimony."

The divorce is final and alimony is doled out, usually to the woman (but not all the time). But this book is about women getting paid and that is my focus at this point. Women use that alimony to care for the child and in most cases, they also have to maintain the house, which they are usually rewarded. Now keep in mind that no matter how well off a woman may appear to be, she is still living in a society that is controlled by male rules. She knows that. So what is the male's main weakness? Pussy. So although it may appear as if the man is now free to cock hound now that he's divorced, the woman actually has the advantage even if she does have the children.

You see, she is getting a monthly payment and doesn't have to leave the house to get it. If she works, that's just icing on the cake. Children or no children, she's got a guaranteed income and even while paying for child care and related children's expenses, she's not going broke. The court will make sure that the former husband pays his alimony and if he doesn't, then he'll go to jail. So the man loses on that count as well.

Now the previous definition adds that in the case of alimony decisions, "instead of telling judges how and when to award alimony, most courts simply grant them broad discretion to decide what is fair in each case." Again, we find that word "fair" and what did we learn about its application when gender issues are involved? We learned that the female will always receive short shrift, either immediately or down the road.

So the alimony has been awarded, and she is now free. The alimony is going to continue until she re-marries, and this is the key: she is not required to re-marry. So now she is free to collect alimony, recruit and get free dick, get the money that the "new" relationship (or relationships) can generate and basically live the life of Riley. She gets to raise the kids which is not the "curse" that some people try to make it out to be, because once those kids grow up, they are going to kick in and take care of mommy dearest as well. And this gives her time to continue poisoning the minds of the kids against their father while making herself out to be some kind of saint, savior or self-sacrificing victim who "bore the brunt" of a bad marriage.

By the time she re-marries – if she decides to make that mistake again – she's not broke. Women outlive men on average anyway: alimony is a cash cow if the woman manages it correctly. Since she's out looking for a new dick she's going to dress better, look better and has learned from any mistakes she made during the previous marriage. And the new guy is none the wiser.

I've always said that where there is white discretion, there is racism and gender bias. This is perhaps most true in the case of the court system in general and the family courts, in particular. Burton (2007) writes that, "No mathematical guidelines exist to tell courts how to calculate alimony. In addition, each state legislature sets its own policy regarding whether and when alimony may be awarded.

And according to the US Legal. Com website, The Uniform Marriage and Divorce Act (UMDA) was an attempt by the National Conference of Commissioners on Uniform State Laws to make marriage and divorce laws more uniform. This is also known as the Model Marriage and Divorce Act. UMDA was extensively amended in 1973. UMDA is a 1970 model statute that defines marriage and divorce. The greatest significance of UMDA is that it introduced irreconcilable differences as the sole ground for divorce. UMDA has been partly enacted only in a handful of states. However, it has had an enormous impact on marriage and divorce laws in all states.

More specifically,

> The Uniform Marriage and Divorce Act (UMDA), which many states use as a model, recommends that courts consider the following factors: the financial condition of the person requesting alimony; the time the recipient would need for education or job training; the standard of living the couple had during the marriage; the length of the marriage; the age, physical condition, and emotional state of the person requesting alimony; and the ability of the other person to support the recipient and still support himself or herself (Burton, 2007).

Let's look at these factors that the courts are going to "consider" before deciding whether or not this woman is going to walk away with a shit load of cash and assets.

The financial condition of the person requesting the alimony. So if the man has a good job, he's gonna get taxed. If she has a job, that don't mean shit: she's still going to get a part of his shit as well. If there's a house, usually she gets it if there are children, even if its in his name. Some judges will have the assets liquidated and then the proceeds are divided between the two, with her getting the lion's share. This is but a small part of what I call "the reality of alimony." It's like what Peggy Joyce one said: "Alimony is a system by which, when two people make a mistake, one of them keeps paying for it."

Another variable considered by the courts is the time the recipient would need for job training or education. If she gets alimony, she can keep getting it until she gets a job or completes training for a job. In this day and age of scam training programs and proprietary (for profit) colleges, the recipient of alimony should be able to bullshit her way through a program by taking her time, changing her major course of study, or "getting pregnant." All of this shit works and as long as she's getting training, she keeps on getting alimony from you – which is automatically deducted from your paycheck.

The couple's standard of living during the marriage is another way to determine the amount of alimony doled out. So the better off you are, the more money she is going to get. This is true only because men fall for the okey-doke and hang on to that antiquated belief that, "no wife of mine is going to work." Well the fact is, when he goes out and makes that money and she's at home, she's going to get paid anyway! If she's married to him when the money was made then, by law, she is entitled to HALF. The only salvation is a prenuptial agreement and most of these women aren't going to sign one: they wouldn't be getting married if they couldn't get PAID! What do you think this is about: LOVE?

Then there is the length of the marriage, which is an extension of the previous situation. The standard of living usually increases the longer the couple is together. And if they both work, this is definitely the case. The length of time oftentimes makes men lose their mind and enter into "joint accounts" with their wives: what a mistake. He thinks he can keep an eye on what she's spending when, unbeknownst to him, she has her own personal account PLUS his shit! She's getting laid, having kids that make him even more dependent on the relationship, and she's also getting paid.

And check this one out: "the age, physical condition, and emotional state of the person requesting alimony." Most women are going to be in better condition than men as they age. Women see to that. Remember that saying, "The way to a man's heart is through his stomach"? Who do you think was cooking that fatback, those pork chops, those steaks and all that ham? She was. She knew what she was doing and we sat there rubbing our distended bellies telling her, "that was good, honey." Meanwhile, she's going on walks and jogging with her gal pals while he's at work, stressing out and making that high blood pressure go even higher. By the time he finds out he's fucked up, she's got the reins on the money, what the split will be, who gets what and has another dude waiting in the wings – with a better job!

And the final point for consideration is "the ability of the other person to support the recipient and still support himself or herself." See? Even when the divorce takes place she STILL gets paid. The studies show that she gets all the burden because she has to have the kids and he's free to start over. First of all, if he starts over with another woman right away he's out of his damn mind. Furthermore, she might have the kids, but that alimony enables her to pay a good child care provider and she has the house as well. In other words, even when she's not getting laid by him, she's getting laid by somebody; and he has to pay, so in a way he's getting FUCKED as well.

Burton (2007) concludes thusly:

Courts have at times awarded alimony when an unmarried couple separates, if the relation-ship closely resembled marriage or in other circumstances, such as in keeping with the couple's intentions and verbal agreements. Awards of this type are informally called palimony. Private separation agreements negotiated between divorcing individuals also can contain alimony provisions. For these reasons, it is difficult to estimate accurately the size and frequency of awards through the most common method, U.S. census data.

Alimony makes sense if there are young children being left behind by one of the spouses. But these women are using it to make a living, not for the kids, but for themselves. Some of these women are getting thousands of dollars a month that goes beyond food and clothing and shelter. The rich ones are taking men to the bank, literally. And this is just one more way that despite all the rampant gender bias, the glass ceiling and the general abuse of women, they inevitably get the last laugh – through the courts.

DON'T HATE THE PLAYA OR THE GAME: HATE THE SYSTEM THAT PRODUCED AND ENDORSES BOTH!

So we know that the men are prospective tricks because of the American culture they were raised in. And we know that the women, even if not outright ho's, still have a philosophy that will get them "laid and paid" when all is said and done.

The Side Chick

An article titled, "3 Reasons Why Side Chicks are Settling for Second Place … And Lovin' It" offers up some of the reasoning and rationale for "being number two" in exchange for money and other favors. Following are the key points of that article with my analyses filtering in and out:

What is a "side chick"? In my own simple terms, I define a side chick as a female who is involved in sëxual relations with a male who is in a committed relationship with another person. One may ask why on earth an individual would voluntarily choose to play this role in life. It sounds degrading, trifling, and just downright wrong. However, in a society where the idea of "every man for himself" becomes more widespread and the concept of a monogamous, traditional marriage becomes less and less popular with time, the side chick starts to prevail (Danielle, 2013).

"Starts" to prevail? These bitches been around for as long as marriage has. In fact, they've been around longer. The fact of the matter is that a lot of these "side chicks" are married themselves and are just "stepping out" on their husbands for various reasons. Some of them just need some extra money or want to have "more fun" because the "man" in their life is, for whatever reason, ignoring their social and financial needs. A great many of today's "wives" were able to latch onto their husbands because they started off as "side chicks" with the man they "took" or with some other guy.

This article is biased against the side chick as are large numbers of hypocritical moralizers. Check it out:

> She has reared her ugly little head in pop culture media numerous times over the past year, and unlike the old days where she was plagued with a scarlet letter and owned humility, she now is bold, fierce, and daring to be judged. (Danielle, 2013).

This white man controls these media images and remember the words of Mao: "He who controls images controls minds, and he who controls minds has little, if anything, to worry about from bodies." This side chick is a star in American culture, despite her dubious deeds. She is what the "good girl" wants to be; she is in many cases, the employee in the "world's oldest profession" – prostitution! She is an adventurer and she is the one who is a metaphor for America: a slut who feigns a belief in morality but who will do anything for a dollar.

Because of the on-going mis-perception of her, a number of distorted assumptions are derived. Following are three of them:

> Why are side chicks settling for second place and loving it? I found three reasons:
> **Convenience** – It takes time to develop and maintain a healthy relationship with a significant other. Trust is a very important part of relationships and is established over time. Side chicks have the pleasure of not having to be concerned with the emotional stress behind opening themselves up to trust. They know their role in a clearly defined, simple sëxual relationship and not much is required of them. They get theirs and get out, avoiding any headaches. (Danielle, 2013).

What was just described is the American way! These college bitches – that's how they roll. They date, get screwed and take money and if the guy is an athlete, that's all the better. Maybe they can set him up with a pregnancy. But the point is that as soon as they are about to graduate, the guy gets dumped, she goes back home or to another city where she feigns borderline virginity, and then turns out another who she can dupe into marrying her. On campus she's the side chick, but she's a side chick on a mission.

Now, reason number two why side chicks love their roles:

> **Thrill --** Some find excitement in living a secret life. Obviously to be in an undercover relationship, there are always strategic steps made in finding out the best time to partake in sëxual relations with their taken partner. A lot of the hookups may take place late at night, on long lunch breaks, out of town, etc. To side chicks, the "creeping" never gets old. They live for thrill of not knowing where or when the next orgasm may occur. (Danielle, 2013).

The next "orgasm"? These bitches don't care about busting a nut: they want to get paid! They know men ain't shit and the way to entice them and keep them coming back it to convince them that the man they're with is "all that and a bag of chips." Even if he CAN'T screw (and most can't), she'll lie and say he can and that's all he needs to hear because he sho' ain't satisfying the woman at home. If he was, he wouldn't be banging THIS bitch – and paying her for the right to do so!

The previous statement by Danielle tries to make something scientific and strategic out of something that is surreptitious and sluttish. The woman is a ho. She wants a man but she doesn't want to be controlled, told what to do or hounded. Men represent baggage. She just wants to make some money and maybe go on some interesting dates to concerts, high-end restaurants and trips out of town. What is so complex about that?

Third point is one that needs analysis. It is where Danielle offers the following:

> **Short-term Cure** – In an odd and crazy way, side chicks feel needed. They believe their secret lovers are in relationships where they are unhappy, so she fills an important void. (Danielle, 2013).

So one lonely person finds lonely picking up somebody else's leftovers? What kind of bullshit is this? It doesn't represent short term care; it represents sick desperation! This slut is no "good Samaritan" out there looking to give up booty so that a man can feel "whole." She's out there trying to get laid and paid, looking for something to do because her girlfriends have men in their lives. It is not rocket science: it's the way things have been for centuries. This article by Danielle calls them 'side chicks' when, in reality, they are just straight up hos. And so are the men who finance their charade.

Danielle clearly doesn't know her ass from a hole in the ground, as shown in her next attempt at morality:

> In closing, I personally feel that to lower yourself to this level of "importance" is sad. Those being fulfilled in this role suffer from insecurity issues. Feeling needed, living the thrill, and calling the situation convenient is all a cover-up for what is really a void inside of one's soul. I'm a firm believer in the famous Bible verse "do unto others as you would have them do unto you." The most important part in all of this is respect, honesty, and integrity for another individual … (Danielle, 2013).

First of all, side chicks are now "lowering" themselves any more than a housewife, who is nothing more than a legal prostitute with benefits. These women get these guys to marry them and in many cases use the incomes to buttress their own accounts in the name of "taking care of the household." A prostitute is someone who sells her body for money; what do you think these "married women" do before they tie the knot? They go out on dates, suck dick, give up pussy and pussy whip the man into dropping to one knee and asking for their hand in marriage. This shit has been going on for centuries and no one says anything. In my book, that's "lowering yourself" in a more long-term basis and not only that, but then you get children involved in the whole shebang.

Secondly she says that side chicks suffer from insecurity issues. Women, in general are insecure. And so are the men who believe that somehow they are not "whole" unless they find some woman to latch on to and play "mama" for them. Lay out his clothes, tell him when to come home, cook his food, tell him what to do, control the money. That's a mother –figure, man! How much more insecure can you get than that. Women are under equal pressure and are judged by their own female pals: if one of them turns thirty and hasn't been married, they assume something's wrong with her or she's a dyke. America is filled with insecure people looking to latch on to someone else to "fulfill" their lives. What you end up with is two unfulfilled muthafuckas.

Danielle must have gotten a case of the Holy Ghost, writing that, "The most important part in all of this is respect, honesty and integrity for another individual." That is bullshit. The most important part is to have all those things first, and foremost, *for your self!* If you don't love yourself, how can you love anybody else? The greatest number is one and number one is supposed to be YOU!

Danielle (mercifully) concludes with the following:

> There are several victims involved in these circumstances. The one being cheated on is not alone in suffering from betrayal, it is just that the two cheaters are forcing betrayal on themselves. One

should always rise above the temptations and hold integrity and respect at a higher regard. (Danielle, 2013).

The concept of "cheating" has to be looked at. The term implies that marriage is somehow "fair" and the perfect goal of the game. It is not. It is a scam where you have to sign up with the state, pay for various tests and other fees and then stand before a crowd of people who claim to be your friends and lie your ass off. "Til death do you part" is an ideal, but in reality very few of the people probably go that far. In fact, when it gets to "in sickness and in health," most people are ready to cut bait.

The fact of the matter is, you already had sex and it was so good and you feel so comfortable that you want to keep on getting it. But now you bring in extra baggage that is going to impede on those sexcapades: electric and gas bills, car payments, mortgage payments and/or rent, kids and their clothes and food, related costs. By the time you get through working a job (which it is almost required that you have) who have time for fuckin'?

The "side chick" is no victim: she's playing it safe. She gets primo dick and his money *sans* the responsibility and the brats running all over the house fuckin' shit up.

CONCLUSION

Girls inherit the guile and knowledge of older women" - Anonymous

Chairman Mao once wrote that, "He who controls images controls minds, and he who controls minds has little, if anything, to worry about from bodies." The white man knows this and has traditionally used his version of reality via movies and television, to control the minds of the masses. He has set standards and initiated trends and fads, and has basically established the "American values" that so many people emulate and learn from.

Women getting laid and paid is nothing less than knowing the white man's system from top to bottom and expertly exploiting his values and priorities while lying about what the white male REALLY is. Women get paid to lie to men about male virility, stability and their status. In return, they get to control the purse strings. The white man in 2016 is so obsessed with global domination, profit and control that he's willing to do anything to show everyone that he's still the one on top. He uses a number of arenas to do this and one of those avenues is the media.

REFERENCES

Æsop. *Fables,* retold by Joseph Jacobs. Vol. XVII, Part 1. The Harvard Classics. New York: P.F. Collier & Son, 1909–14; Bartleby.com, 2001.

Blanco, Alvin Aqua (2013, January 20). Shawty Lo Arrested For Failure To Pay Child Support? Retrieved from http://hiphopwired.com/2013/01/20/shawty-lo-arrested-for-failure-to-pay-child-support-photos/#sthash.pzl1N13T.dpufNEWS,

Burton, W.C. (2007). *Burton's Legal Thesaurus*. Retrieved from http://legal-dictionary.thefreedictionary.com/Alimony.

Bussman, C. (2014, November 12). Twenty Presidents Who Were Rumored to Have Mistresses. Retrieved from http://www.rantpolitical.com/2014/11/12/15-presidents-who-were-rumored-to-have-mistresses/

Carr, Coeli (2014, August 14). The male bad-in-bed list. Retrieved from http://www.msn.com/en-us/news/other/the-male-bad-in-bed-list/ss-AAd6Aj?srcref=rss&FORM=MH146Q&OCID=MH146Q#image=11

Chancellorfiles (2006). Penis size and racial groups. Retrieved from https://chancellorfiles.wordpress.com/2006/12/10/penis-size-and-racial-groups/

Crilly, R. (2014, November 23). Marion Barry, scandal-plagued ex-mayor of Washington, dies. *The London Telegraph*. Retrieved from http://www.telegraph.co.uk/news/worldnews/northamerica/usa/11248647/Marion-Barry-scandal-plagued-ex-mayor-Washington-dies.html

Danielle, Patrice (2016, April 9).Naturallymoi.com. 3 reasons why side chicks are settling for second place … And loving it. Retrieved from http://naturallymoi.com/2016/04/3-reasons-why-side-chicks-are-settling-for-second-place-and-lovin-it/

ESPN.go.com (2012, July 19). Terrell Owens makes payments. Retrieved from http://espn.go.com/nfl/story/_/id/8180722/terrell-owens-agrees-pay-child-support-promises-more

Farrell, W. (1993). *The myth of male power: Why men are the disposable sex.* New York, New York: Berkley Publishing.

Feiffer, J. (1965). *The Great Comic Book Heroes Paperback*. Seattle, Washington: Fantagraphic Books.

Fletcher, Connie. (1990). *What cops know: Today's police tell the inside story of their work on America's streets.* New York: Pocket Books

Fletcher, M.A. & Bock, J. (1994, August 1). NAACP leader denies sexual harassment allegations. *Baltimore Sun*. Retrieved from http://articles.baltimoresun.com/1994-08-01/news/1994213100_1_chavis-harassment-naacp-board

Forbes magazine (2014, September 23). Forbes 400 – Facts and figures on America's wealthiest.

FoxSports (2012, September 18). Report: Holyfield held in contempt. Retrieved from http://www.foxsports.com/boxing/story/evander-holyfield-judge-court-orders-back-pay-child-support-debt-091812.

Gibson, J. (2012, June 19). Flavor Flav Pays More than $100K in Child Support to Stay Out of Prison. CelebrityNetworth.com. Retrieved from http://www.celebritynetworth.com/articles/celebrity/flavor-flav-pays-100k-child-support-stay-prison/

Hakim, D. & Rashbaum, W.K. (2008, March 10). Spitzer is linked to prostitution ring. *New York Times*. Retrieved from http://www.nytimes.com/2008/03/10/nyregion/10cnd-spitzer.html

Healy, B. (2014, December 5). Abigail Johnson, after years of training, gets to put her stamp on Fidelity. *The Boston Globe*.

Holman, T. (2013, November 29). Chief Keef Ordered to Pay Child Support for 10-month Old After DNA Test. *Inquisitr*. Retrieved from http://www.inquisitr.com/1046968/chief-keef-child-support-10-month-old/

Huffington Post (2013, April 30). Bow Wow Isn't 'Lil' Anymore: Rapper Opens Up About His Baby And Being A Dad. Retrieved from http://www.huffingtonpost.com/2013/04/30/bow-wow-lil-rapper-baby-dad_n_3181067.html

Huffington Post. (June 27, 2014). Brigitte Nielsen: I Didn't Marry Sylvester Stallone For The Reason Everyone Thought. Retrieved from http://www.huffingtonpost.com/2014/06/27/brigitte-nielsen-sylvester-stallone-marriage_n_5536778.html

McCarthy, M. ()2016, March 16). *Sporting News*. Porn star Lisa Ann warns 25 percent of NBA players have faced blackmail. Retrieved from http://www.sportingnews.com/nba-news/4697284-porn-star-lisa-ann-warns-25-of-nba-players-are-blackmailed

Miller, B. (1999, September 8). Cisneros Pleads Guilty to Lying to FBI Agents. The Washington Post. Retrieved from http://www.washingtonpost.com/wp-srv/politics/special/cisneros/stories/cisneros090899.htm

Miller, M.E. (2016, March 15). A Miami woman killed a teen burglar as he fled her home, police say. Should she be charged? The Washington Post. Retrieved from http://www.msn.com/en-us/news/crime/a-miami-woman-killed-a-teen-burglar-as-he-fled-her-home-police-say-should-she-be-charged/ar-BBqtGa8?li=BBnb7Kz&ocid=iehp

MSN.com (2016, March 11). The top 20 traits women want in a man. Retrieved from http://www.msn.com/en-us/lifestyle/lifestylewomen/the-top-20-traits-women-want-in-a-man/ss-AAeHzO0?ocid=iehp

Naturallymoi.com (2012, November 4). Gabrielle Union on marriage: "I just like saying 'my boyfriend'. Retrieved from http://naturallymoi.com/2012/11/gabrielle-union-on-marriage-i-just-like-saying-my-boyfriend/

Naturallymoi.com (2016, April 9). Ladies: 5 things you must know about dating a black man. Retrieved from http://naturallymoi.com/2016/04/ladies-5-things-you-must-know-about-dating-a-black-man/

New York Daily News (2016, July 6). New Iron Man is black – And a woman. Retrieved from http://www.nydailynews.com/entertainment/new-iron-man-black-woman-article-1.2701328

Page, A. (2013, July 13). Baby Drama! Celebrities With Major Child Support Issues. Retrieved from http://madamenoire.com/287670/baby-drama-celebrities-with-major-child-support-issues/15/

Pearce, M. (2013, September 26). Cory Booker's Twitterstripper: 'It's not a sex scandal!" Los Angeles Times. Retrieved from http://articles.latimes.com/2013/sep/26/nation/la-na-nn-cory-booker-stripper-20130926

Rhone, Paysha Stockton (2007, February 27). Bobby Brown arrested in Massachusetts. People.com. Retrieved from http://www.people.com/people/article/0,,20013443,00.html

Rose, Sandra (2011, May 10). Jermaine Dupri Sued by Stripper for Child Support. Retrieved fromhttp://sandrarose.com/2011/05/jermaine-dupri-sued-by-stripper-for-child-support/

Scott, Bartie (2016, March 7). Forbes' wealthiest women in the world. Forbes magazine. Retrieved from http://www.msn.com/en-us/money/savingandinvesting/forbes-wealthiest-women-in-the-world-2016/ar-BBqc8dC?li=BBnb7Kz&ocid=iehp

Shilliday, Beth (2015, October 7). Matt Barnes Attacks Former Teammate Derek Fisher For Dating Wife Gloria Govan. Hollywoodlife.com. Retrieved from http://hollywoodlife.com/2015/10/07/matt-barnes-attacked-derek-fisher-dating-gloria-govan-ex-wife-teammates/

Simmel, G. (1990) The philosophy of money. London, England: Routledge Books.

Stitt, R. (2016, January 19). NY Jets' Antonio Cromartie's Child Support Bill is $336,000 For His 8 Children. Financial Juneteenth. Retrieved from http://financialjuneteenth.com/ny-jets-antonio-cromarties-child-support-bill-336000-8-children/

TMZ staff (2013, August 31). Allen Iverson's ex-wife: I want $1.2 million right now. Retrieved from Retrieved from http://www.tmz.com/2013/08/31/allen-iverson-tawanna-iverson-child-support-1-2-million/

Wikipedia (2016). Misandry. Retrieved from https://en.wikipedia.org/wiki/Misandry

Wikipedia (2016). Anthony Weiner sexting scandals. . Retrieved from https://en.wikipedia.org/wiki/Anthony_Weiner_sexting_scandals

Wikipedia (2016). Eliot Spitzer. Retrieved from
https://en.wikipedia.org/wiki/Eliot_Spitzer#Prostitution_scandal

Womanist Musings. (2016). When Black Women Sell Out: "It's Free Swipe Yo
EBT." Retrieved from
http://www.womanistmusings.com/when-black-women-sell-out-its-free/

Xfinity.com (2017). From rags to riches: How 10 jocks went broke. Retrieved from
http://my.xfinity.com/slideshow/sports-richestorags/5/

Wooley, Nate (2013, March 4). Dennis Rodman too broke to pay child support.
InvestorPlace.com. Retrieved from http://investorplace.com/2013/03/dennis-
rodman-too-broke-to-pay-child-support/#.VyUKHMtwXcs

Newsweek's, "The Secret Lives of Wives:"An Africentric Viewpoint, July, 2004, Completed: November, 2011

Executive Summary

> Does it make sense to be married to the
> same person for your ***entire*** life?
>
> *--Ashton Kutcher,*
> *"Just Married" (2003)*

That, my friends, is the $64,000 question.

The July 12, 2004 issue of Newsweek is one that has generated controversy because of the manner in which the authors dealt with their topic, "The Secret Lives of Wives." According to their bold faced thesis situated above the article after the preface, "Why They Stray," the statement posits that, *With the workplace and the Internet, overscheduled lives and inattentive husbands – it's no wonder more American women are looking for comfort in the arms of another man."* This "breakthrough" is nothing that men of color haven't known for some time about white women – who are, after all, the numerical majority in this country.

Before the Internet, before they even entered the workplace, white women were committing adultery. This is not to say that other women were not; it is to say that these women who wrote the article interviewed white girls and then generalized to make it appear that all women are equal in sluttishness. They are not. The white woman, whether poor or rich, single or married, is present in disproportionate numbers in black bars, lounges and taverns. Many, if not most, of them, are married. In other words it is, as it is in other areas where whites only want to see the best of themselves, we – as men of color – know the real deal. Just like women of color know the sicknesses and perversities of the married white man. If this "report" would have been genuinely committed to addressing issues, it would have addressed the fact that the white woman complies with vows that she knows full well do not make any sense.

I have done my own ethnographic studies. I have seen how these white girls act on university and college campuses all over this nation. I've seen them in action at the University of Iowa, the University of Wisconsin, the University of Nebraska, the University of Missouri-Kansas City, Emory University, Northeastern University, University of Pittsburgh, Cleveland State and so on.

In each of these cases, they are available to black men and anyone else. In particular, the black athletes know who to go to for easy sex. She carries this reputation globally as well. Then, once she graduates or prepares to settle down, she moves to another city where available men won't know of her sluttish history. She gets a job and uses her wiles to allow men to "rap" to her. Such a history and tradition defies the very essence of what the wedding vows require. It should therefore be no wonder that one out of two marriages fails, and why white women are now being exposed for adultery. But don't be fooled: they've been at it for centuries, and even before this country was invaded by their race, they were carrying on the same way in various European countries.

In order to grasp the depth of an article about the "secret lives" of these wives (read: married white women), ***I re-typed the entire Newsweek article,*** so that I could respond to every nuance, assumption, theory, and claim of fact. As I got deeper into the article, I saw the need to draw on information from my think tank, the Uhuru Sasa Research Institute, and to use that information to put into perspective some of the claims made in this Newsweek piece.

Several points must be understood: there has never been an entire race of women as promiscuous and lascivious as the American white woman. An argument can be made that other American women follow suit; that indeed, sluttishness and licentious behavior are an American phenomenon that dates back to the days of the founders, evolved during the days of the saloon girls on the east and west coasts and is so widely accepted now that there are legal brothels in

Nevada and women, nearly nude, cavorting around almost every television program and film that this society produces.

For instance, during the same month that the article on "secret lives" of wives appeared in Newsweek, rival magazine time used its July 26, 200 issue to indeed, deal with why Las Vegas is not only America's number one tourist town but it also "hotter than ever." On the cover? Two white women dancing barefoot and clad in mini-skirts, atop a table in some bar or club (apparently the Tabu Clubb in Vegas). Mid-driffs exposed, these two blondes are clearly loaded, as are all of the people observing them in the background. Almost every person has a libation in hand. The message? Las Vegas is hot and these white women are part of the reason why!

A second point is this: how could these lives be "secret"? During slavery, black people knew what white women were up to. They saw the trysts and in fact, black men were the targets for some of those white women who "wanted some." Because no black could ever or would ever "tell" on a white man or woman, what their race considered to be "secret" really meant "secret among white folks" since blacks were considered chattel property and, at best, only "three-fifths of human being." Fast forward to the present-day.

A third point lies in the concept of these women, supposedly being "unfaithful" or "adulterous," are somehow "wayward." As I explicate throughout this work, what is truly "wayward" is a system that would promote monogamous marriage when its hedonistic, individualistic and selfish value system is diametrically opposed to such a union being successful for the long term.

Even Super-Uncle Tom and sellout Armstrong Williams was concerned about the contents of the article, and wrote down his concerns in a July 15 edition of the Myrtle Beach Sun Times:

> What's striking about the article is not that the rate of cheating by women is approaching that of men but that our so-called hard-news outlets are depicting the trend with so little introspection. The Newsweek article, for example, provides almost on counterbalance regarding personal or moral responsibility. The article mostly just invites the reader to peek over the windowsill and enjoy the vicarious gratification of other people's sexual subterfuge (Williams, 2004).

For once, Williams and I agree on something; since when does a fluff piece by two women, writing about women, get elevated to the status of "news"? This was a report that was limited in scope, filled with anecdotal evidence, conjecture and opinion. As I will show, even some of the "wayward women" from the annals of history and literature did not truly fit the definition. But Newsweek owed it to readers to at least address the issues of class and race as it relates to infidelity.

Instead, what do we find? White (and perhaps a "colored" one) female "scholars" and "journalists" writing and publishing articles about the "secrets" of white woman when, in reality, the only person who is out of the loop is the white man! The white woman is having affairs with his best friends, guys across town, the pool boy, the mail man and the black man in the nearby ghetto. Her car is seen leaving the barrio, and she's even getting it with the help of some of her friends. The "secret" that they claim exists is one that is being held back from the white male and a few others. But thanks to hi-tech surveillance, high profile legal cases, opening up the history books and the manner in which she acts and is treated in Hollywood and other media forms (including porno mags), it is clear who the "loosest" woman among American women continues to be.

Another key and core point is this: the methodology behind the article. According to a statement made in the piece, NEWSWEEK talked at lengthy to more thank a dozen women who cheated, and none of them wanted her real name used. A dozen women? And from that small group they generalize as if white women have "secret lives" when most people know full well that this is the woman who men all over the world perceive as being the biggest whore on the planet? By not using their real names, we have no idea if these women even existed, but one thing is for sure: the behavior of white women in America is no "secret" and the numbers of them who are being "unfaithful" to their husbands is sky high. They are probably also the national leaders when it comes to cohabitating and marrying out of their race. They are not the "lonely victims" that much of the literature makes them out to be.

Another key point: their fundamental theses regarding sneak around tactics and the like are probably way off base. The "strategy and tactics" that the writers proceed to provide are nothing but smokescreens for the real issues; the constraints of monogamous marriage, the neglect of the wife by the husband for a variety of reasons, the fact that white women have been getting away with "forbidden trysts" for centuries, and the reality that the white man – the husband – is either doing the same thing or just doesn't give a shit.

Bell Hooks (1990) writes that, "It should be possible for scholars, especially those who are members of groups who dominate, exploit, and oppress others to explore the political implications of their work without fear or guilt" (p. 124).

So be it.

The white girl. As I state later in this book, *Newsweek* buys into a double-standard with the article and these so-called examples and, in doing so, misses an essential point: *you can't make a whore into a housewife, but not for the reasons that the rappers claim. You can't do it or need to do it because if she's successful at the formere, she will inevitably join the ranks of the latter. Think about it as you read on.*

Introduction

The saying teaches us, "the hand that rocks the cradle rules the world." And yet those of us committed to launching counter-propaganda and defensive efforts aimed at negating the mythology that has so many black people brainwashed, continue to treat this race war as if it is the white man alone and for some reason, his woman is an innocent standing on the sidelines. Indeed, if the white man has a stranglehold on the world, then doesn't that mean that in reality, SHE is the one controlling the world? She controls how many children, if any, he will have; she controls his thoughts before he closes his eyes at night and dictates the mood that he will be in the following day. And we all know of the horrific damage that the American "white is right" campaign has done to the collective black psyche, much of it courtesy of and thanks to the white female and her "blondes have more fun" mythology.

Some will argue that all of this brainwashing is engineered by the white man and that the white woman is but a willing thrall. I argue that in this day and age of "women's liberation" and when one looks at the myths that permeate white female thinking, from the trailer parks to Beverly Hills, it becomes clear that she controls the white man's thinking sexually and he, in turn, has taken her sexuality and turned it on other men as a means of control. In more recent times, she has seen the value of sexuality and has put it to work to gain an advantage for herself.

This book will prove that.

To begin with, the white woman's promiscuity is no secret. The fact is, much of what she has done has been hidden, obscured, or otherwise re-defined by her man. Much of what he did to her has been justified by religion, dogma and brute force. But what must be understood is this: she had choices. The claim is that she was under his thumb and his sexist domination forced her to do this and do that.

Because the continuation and perpetuation of the white race was so closely linked to the goal of world domination that they BOTH shared in, she assumed the role of Robin to his Batman, Jane to his Tarzan, Spock to his Captain Kirk, and Kato to his Green Hornet. But take note that in each of my examples, the sidekick actually holds the real power: Kato drove the Black Beauty and was really the Green Hornet's physical superior; Spock was both stronger and smarter than Captain Kirk; Robin, the son of trained gymnasts, was younger and faster than Batman (although the mythology and camera angles made it appear otherwise), and Jane was the one who made it possible for Tarzan to have a son. You see?

Secondary roles that actually possess primary power. At any point either of these sidekicks could have overpowered or dominated the "hero." The fact that they did not was a matter of personal choice, not coercion.

And it's the same thing with the white man's sidekick, the white female.

They sit back and write about their sexuality and the white man suppresses it. Mary Shelly wrote **Frankenstein** and had to go through hell to get it out. These women were being held back, but they were still viewed as human beings, for the most part. Not only that, we must not forget that when the white man was planning the oppression of other people, she was right there and never voiced any opposition. As they murdered off Indian children and women, the white woman's job was to have a meal ready when they got back home. And that's what she did. She aided and abetted him in his crimes against black people. And now we are supposed to believe that she is somehow a "victim" in a society where she is privileged and more free than anyone else? Bullshit!

In this essay, inspired by a piece of drivel that appeared in the July 12, 2004 of *Newsweek* magazine, exposes what white folks want to say is a "secret." In this case it's the affairs that white women are having behind their husbands' backs. But we, as black men know it's no secret – many of them were having their affairs with us!

But the concept of it being "a secret" is a statement about the segregated state of this society. Once you segregate someone, you can control them with greater ease. But there are also other advantages offered, and they will be explained as an "evolution" of how girls in general, and white girls in particular, are socialized to behave once they get beyond the "eye" of their parents.

Creation of a Slut:
Four Evolutionary Observations

Over time, young girls in America are slowly transformed into the kind of young women who want to get away from home. While this may be a reality in many parts of the world, what makes America unique is that these girls want to get away from home for sexual purposes. What is even more hidden from public consumption is the fact that large numbers of this group cannot wait to violate their parents' number one taboo: sex with a person of another race. This holds especially true in the case of the white female.

The following vignettes offer a kind of "behind-the-scenes" description of how white women operate in certain contexts, a kind of "evolution of promiscuity" that few people want to seriously acknowledge. The fact is, "Girls Gone Wild!" is closer to being the collegiate norm than the acts of a "vacation-bound" minority.

The first vignette ("Go Big Red(necks)) deals with how white girls are used on campus to seduce black athletes and what happens when that athlete happens to be good enough to turn professional. From there is a trilogy, ("The Sluttification of Teen-Aged Girls"), and any parent with a teenaged dirty will know what I am writing about. I interject the variable of race and show how both white and black girls get caught up in this routine of glorifying the "hootchie mama."

The third component of the trilogy serves as the historical prelude to the analysis of the article, "The Secret Lives of Wives" that appeared in Newsweek magazine.

Go Big Red(necks)!
Nov 27, 1998

The recent spate of ass-whippings that the University of Nebraska at Lincoln has received at the hands of their opponents is part of a curse that I put on former coach Tom Osborne after his racist reaction to a proposal I submitted. Let me explain to you what took place, the gist of the curse and why my "Go Big Red (Neck) concept is one that is long overdue.

Last year on my hit cable TV show, "North Omaha Focus," I read a proposal that I had sent to Dr. Tom Osborne, then the coach of the UNL Cornhuskers. In that proposal I made it clear that he and his coaches bring in young black kids because they know they can't compete with crackers at the skill positions.

They tried, They know it won't work. I then suggested that an "annex" be set up in Omaha, where black athletes could come and hang out with black men and women in a major city, and stop chasing white bitches all over Lincoln.

In that proposal, and at a conference later that year, I told him that I knew that the ""Husker Hostesses" were really nothing but prostitutes. If you take off the last six letters of their name, you have what they really are: Husker HO's!! Clad in mini skirts with asses bulging from working on the farm, I hypothesized that these black kids had never seen white girls with "back" before. .

When they get here, they are greeted by these sluts who latch onto them in the name of "showing them around." After they clean the sperm from their mouths, these white girls become their "girlfriends' and most of these brothers, being sick, ignorant and country, fall in love.

Remember Turner Gill. He married one from Grand Island. Mike Rozier got turned out so bad that when he went pro, he brought a white woman -- who was married -- a new Camaro. And even now, future football star Mike Rucker is on his SECOND one.

I explained all this to Ozzie and suggested that he loan Triple One $500,000 to give these black athletes some alternatives. I sent a copy to him and one to Byrne, the athletic director.

Byrne responded first. He said he received the proposal and doubted the legalities and that they couldn't make such donations without the approval of the legislature. He thanked me and that was it. He also stated in his letter how much the football program cared about "Minorities" and so on. Yeah, right.

Ozzie's response came much later. He wrote that he got the proposal and blah blah blah. Toward the end of his letter his racism and vindictiveness came out. He said something like, "I'm surprised that you would write me asking for a favor when I heard that you referred to me as a New York Pimp."

First of all, I would explain both on my show and in another letter to this dry-mouthed cracker, I never said he was a New York pimp. One of his flunkies who listens to my show probably called him and said I made the statement. What I said was that he was a PIMP, and that he pimped black athletes who are basically his HO's, because at least prostitutes get PAID.

Secondly, I told him that I would never call him a "New York pimp," because I knew that with his countrified ass, he wouldn't last five minutes on the streets of New York. And after I blasted his ass and the program, I then put a curse on this year's team. And you see what's happening.

Remember the last time they lost three games? It was in 1977, the same year that I arrived in Omaha. Coincidence? I don't think so. And guess what: they're going to lose some more because the curse don't end until February!

Go Big Red(neck) is an idea whose time has come. I sicken of seeing these sick young punks walking around Lincoln's black community like they're better than everybody else. If not that, then they're coming up in some club with some Barbie Doll on their arm. And the Husker's host families give them money and "loan" them cars. I know because I used to write term papers for some of those sorry ass Husker players. And they paid cash.

I don't want UNL to win anything until black people in Omaha get some justice. When the city begins fairly allocating the Community Development Block Grant monies in Omaha and Lincoln, and our people begin to get jobs. When they start treating Senator Ernie Chambers with the dignity he deserves, instead of trying to silence him, that's when I'll lift the curse. And when those racist schools, UNO, UNL and Kearny hire some black faculty WHO ARE RELEVANT TO BLACK PEOPLE, that is when my hex will be reversed.

Not one minute before that. As long as black kids get the short end of the stick and are outnumbered by students from Japan, as is the case at UNO, no mercy for the Big Red. The only reason I'm cutting UNO's football team some slack is that they've got a black quarterback -- that's right -- Ed Thompson is black. I don't know if he's trying to "pass" for white or what, but I notice nobody says anything about it. So they've won a conference title and I'll cut them some slack so that this "brother" can get a shot at the pros.

But not the Big Red Necks. No siree. And the only time you'll hear me yelling, "Go Big Red" is when the complete sentence reads as follows: "Go [Straight to Hell] Big Red (Necks)!

The "Sluttification" of Teen-aged Girls:" Documentation and Discussion (Part I)

Information provided in a recent study by the National Council on Crime and Delinquency clearly shows that America is, once again, turning on itself. Funkadelic said long ago that, "America eats its young," and in this instance, the group being devoured are black women. According to the study, Black girls between the ages of 12 and 18 are more likely than all other American youth to be the victims of violence. The study concludes that the younger the girls are, the more vulnerable they are. For instance, one graph shows that black girls ages 12-15 are more than 30 percent more likely to be victims of violence than girls 16-19. The study also claimed that one in six women in this country are raped or victims of attempted rape, and that the greatest percentage of these are committed before the girl is 18 years old.

Omaha's WOWT-Channel 6 did a report on the issue of "Dating Violence." Tracey Madden, the author of the story, was allowed 3 minutes during the "In-depth" segment (somewhat of an oxymoron isn't it – 3 minutes to go "in-depth"?) to address the issue. Although I am sure she did as good a job as she could, when I called her she admitted that she hadn't heard of this study nor had she consulted the internet. In depth, huh? Another reason why black folks need our own media.

At any rate the study didn't address the core causes of this, but raised questions that went unanswered. Therefore this brief essay will provide several reason why young black girls are being victimized more now than ever before. The main reason is what I call the "sluttification of American teen girls."

Young girls are under attack, but not just by each other or by some stalker or rejected boyfriend. The national media paints images that young girls are being bombarded with and that far too many of them accept. Following is a cursory – yet relevant – popular culture (television and movies, in this case) presentation of what I call "The sluttification" of the American teenager.

The first image pre-dates the present day images but is still as yet germane. This image is the one where white men, no matter how old, are usually paired up with some woman 20 or 30 years their junior. The white man's biggest heroes, from Cary Grant ("Charade," "An Affair to Remember"), John Wayne ("True Grit," "Rio Lobo,"), Anthony Hopkins ("Desperate Hours," "The Edge," to Andy Griffith ("Matlock"), Carroll O'Connor ("In the Heat of the Night") and Sean Connery ("Never Say Never Again," "First Knight," "Entrapment") the old white man gets the "girl" – literally.

In Omaha there is an event called "The Ak-Sar-Ben Ball." State Senator Ernie Chambers wrote and talked about how these old businessmen are matched up with this young girls and then they promenade about at an expensive black tie ball until a "king and a queen" are crowned. These white men, for the most part, are married. These young girls are young, many of them virgins. Doesn't this play into the myth of "white male irresistibility", which serves as the nexus of the "sluttification" of the American female?

But it is the old fuddy-duddy in Hollywood who is stripping young girls nearly nude and raping them with his camera. That is, AFTER his "fashion designer" counterpart convinces them to slip into "screw me" pumps, a micro-skirt, wonder bras and various forms of lingerie. This then, is the "neo-prostitution" that the media endorses and that the entertainment industry praises and perpetuates.

TELEVISION

There are a number of television shows that I believe works to perpetuate the sluttification of the young female, and they came in "waves."

The first "wave" set the stage for the fact that it was the teenaged daughter, not the mother, who was the real apple of "white daddy's eye," the "little princess" of the family. Two programs come to memory. The first is "Father Knows Best" where Elinor Donahue played teenager Betty Anderson to Robert Young's fatherly role. Young, an insurance salesman named Jim Anderson, always referred to her as "princess" and to his younger daughter, Kathy, as "Kitten." One daughter named after royalty, the other one after pussy. How interesting.

The second one was the "Donna Reed Show," where Carl Betz' daughter, "Mary" was energetic and yes, a virgin who only had eyes for daddy. That's on the TV show. Later, in films, Ms. Fabares would appear in three Elvis Presley movies and still holds the record for the white female lead who appeared in the most Elvis movies.

But all that "sweet young thang" stuff changed with the coming of the first wave.

Soon, the daughter became independent and, indeed, came and went as she pleased. We find programs like "Diff'rent Strokes" which was about two black kids adopted by a white man. Mr. Phillip Drummond. But as the show progressed, the daughter – Kimberly (played by Dana Plato) wore less and less clothing. The same thing happened on two other shows. First, "Growing Pains" where Jason Severs (Alan Thicke) had a daughter named Carol (Tracy Gold) who little by little was transformed into a slut. In the latter years, several shows revolved around her "dates."

Also on this list should go "Happy Days," where Erin Moran played Joanie Cunningham, known affectionately as "cupcake" by Arthur "The Fonz" Fonzerelli, a family friend. Joanie was a good student, great daughter and barely visible – until she started growing breasts. Then the camera man started zooming in, out came her tongue straight into the mouth of Chachi Arcola (Scott Baio), Fonzi's cousin. The roles of Joanie and Chachi – expanded to the point where they had their own short-lived spinoff, "Joannie Loves Chachi." However, Erin Moran's breasts apparently got TOO big and the relationship was no longer believable (that she would stick with a wimp like Baio). "Happy Days" was soon cancelled soon thereafter.

But a classic example of the sluttification of a young girl is what ABC did to Kellie Shanygne Williams who played Laura Winslow on the show, "Family Matters." While her father Carl (a policeman) provided laughs and hijinks, Laura changed from an innocent girl with a great smile so a makeup wearing slut who chased after men and made out anywhere in the house she wanted to. This was one of the longest running black TV shows in history, and over the 9 seasons you can see what happens to Laura as her dresses get shorter, her blouses get tighter and her morals become looser.

Then came the second wave, led by the Fox network's Married … With Children" and its UPN clone, "Happily Ever After." When scantily-clad blonde Kelly Bundy marched out to wolf whistles (her father, Al Bundy, allowed it) out came Nikki Cox with even bigger breasts and less clothing as the daughter (Tiffany) on the latter show.

The third wave comes in two forms and is perhaps the most current. One form is prime-time television and the second is the day-time drama, or "soap opera." Both of these target the young female and "sluttinize" her at every opportunity. Following is a sampling.

The Current Crop: Prime Time

A number of shows that "sluttify" young women. These shows begin with "8 Simple Rules for Dating My Teenage Daughter." The fact is the father, Paul Hennessy (notice the name also refers to a high priced cognac) who is played by John Ritter, doesn't have any rules and doesn't have a clue. The blonde daughter (sound familiar?) is named Bridget and does what she wants to do and basically dogs out her father in front of her boyfriends.

"My Wife and Kids" stars Damon Wayans as Michael Kyle. The daughter started off with beautiful dark skinned Jazz Raycole playing the part of "Claire." But that wasn't good enough – she wasn't sluttish enough. So in came Jennifer Nicole Freeman, who brought with her long curly hair, larger breasts and the ability to act both stupid and slutty.

George Lopez has his own show and is one of the first Latinos to have his own sitcom. But he is playing into the sluttification format as his daughter, Carmen (played by Masiela Lusha) is now growing up and, just last week, they had a show that discussed how the girl's breasts were growing! While the show was trying to make the point that she should remain a virgin as long as she can, there is no doubt that the writers – like those on the other shows – play on the sexuality of these young teenagers and the camera angles are provided by the directors.

This "sluttification" cannot lead to any conclusion but one: that young girls are easy and waiting for the guy who can lie to them the best. These shows demonstrate how the use of the word "love" can seduce almost any young girl and make her give up whatever she's got.

The coup de grace comes with the 'rap videos,' which feature black girls shaking their asses and other attributes. They have bought into the "gangster ho" syndrome perpetrated by male rappers. They watch television and they wear the clothes that they see other black girls wearing. The white girls simply watch and copy. In a short time you have hours of videos with young female trying to out-do one another in "I-can-be-a-bigger-ho-than-you" competition. And off camera, it's the same thing because in the final analysis, men are in charge on the set. The orders are clear: "Bitch, if you wonts ta be in mah nex' video, din I sugges' dat you git wit' de program."

The Current Crop: The Daytime Dramas

The day time soap operas have contributed to "sluttification" of women of all ages for decades. From Erica Cain of "All My Children" and Nikki Newman of "Young and the Restless" to Lucy Coe of "Port Charles," women who whore around in the name of "independence" have played key roles in these dramas and have been rewarded for those roles. However, in the past five years or so, the soaps have made a conscious effort to reach out to the "youth segment" and to begin featuring themes that involve teenagers. Mass sluttification is the result.

On "All My Children" evidence that "the fruit never falls far from the tree" is clear. Erica Kain, a long-time slut, has given birth to Bianca Montgomery (Nathalie Paulding) and has a sister, Silver Kane (Claire Beckman) who screwed Erica's husband!

"The Bold and the Beautiful" is a soap about the modeling industry and how "the beautiful people" live. The teen slut on this one is Amber Forrester (Susan Hanrovy) a teenager who was hooked on drugs and had a kid. Not to fear: her mother screwed the baby's father and also got pregnant by the same guy!

"General Hospital" was a number of young girls who whore around and wear next to nothing. Georgie Jones (Lindzie Letherman) is the daughter of Felicia Jones, who turned into a slut when the father of her children, Frisco Jones, abandoned her so that he could go off and engage in adventures with the top secret WSB (World Spy Bureau). Elizabeth Luebber (Rebecca Herbst) is an independent minor who is not married but is having plenty of sex. Gia Campbell (Marisa Ramirez) is a super fine young sister who is not really a slut, but she promotes an image of promiscuity because she's screwing a guy she's not married to and is always taking off on her own without thinking beforehand.

"One Life to Live" has a major youth presence, and the youngest is only about 8 years old. Her name is Starr Manning (Kristen Alderson), and she is a precocious, spoiled brat who talks back to her parents, catches taxicabs all by herself and does whatever she feels like. While not a slut, her maverick style of behavior is no model for young girls and she has future tramp written all over her. Natalie Buchanan (Melissa Archer) is a red-headed slut who screws whomever she wants and is now in love with Christian Vega, a Latino brother who had already screwed two other white girls -- Jessica Buchanan and Jen Rappaport (Jessica Morris). The former, a rich white kid that gave it up, got pregnant and lost the baby, and the later a true slut who also got pregnant by one guy and lied and said the baby belonged to Christian so that Christian would marry her.

The "Sluttification" of Teen-aged Girls:" Documentation and Discussion (Part II)

As promised, there is more to say about what I view as the "sluttification" of teen girls in America and, leading the way, is the entertainment industry and the lack of relevant role models that young girls have to emulate. In part 1 of this essay, I discussed, in some detail, the "waves" that came and ushered in new "types" of roles that teenagers were to imitate; from Kitten and Princess on "Father's Knows Best" to the current wave featuring Bridget "8 Simple Rules for Dating My Teenaged Daughter" and Claire of "My Wife and Kids," young girls are being given sluts as role models. The shorter the dress, the taller the pumps, the bigger the hair—the better. At one point in history, what I just outlined would be the description of a prostitute. Today it's the description of prime-time prima donas who are anything BUT pristine.

The last installment focused primarily on television, but movies and music have contributed to the aesthetic attacks on today's young girls. But again, I view the models that were provided as symbols of the times, and that these images, like the previous ones discussed, came in waves. These waves, however, are also linked to "age." In this section I again offer three waves: 1) Old Wave Ho's, 2) Mainstream Skanks and 3) New Wave Hootchies.

Old Wave Ho's

From as far back as the Mary Pickford, Faye Wray and May West, a number of images were offered for women. These three, in particular, broke that image. They were under the thumbs of men but were also audacious "tramps" who did their own thing. They paved the way for the mainstream skanks that I will discuss later, but even before we arrive at the skanks, a second "mini-wave" was ushered in by the women just mentioned. They were sexier, more flexible in terms of their roles, but also more than willing to be exploited. These include Elizabeth Taylor, Zsa Zsa Gabor, Jayne Mansfield and Marilyn Monroe. With Taylor it was the violet eyes, Gabor was the exotic, and Mansfield and Monroe were the breast women. All of them had multiple marriages in real life but more importantly, they paved the way for what could be called "the slut with class."

Somewhat younger but also a woman that fell into this category was Lucille Ball, a red-head who allowed herself to be exploited, but she wanted to control the image, and control it she did. With Desi Arnaz in her corner, she re-defined comedy and did it using beauty and the family . Lucy, unlike the others, was willing to be exploited, but she made sure that the exploitation went both ways.

During this time period there were some sisters who played the roles of skanks but were really just trying to get work in Hollywood. Most of the Old Wave Ho's that you find during this period are singers: Pearl Bailey, Lena Horne, and even Della Reese – yep, at one time Della Reese was fine. All three have something else in common: at one time or another, they were all married to white men. That says something in and of itself.

Mainstream Skanks

The mainstream skanks are still going strong today, and they provide negative role models for teen girls in a variety of ways: music, film and television. They come at the young girls mainly with the "attitude" and they talk about being independent of men while at the same time painting negative images of females by their actions both on-stage and off.

I'm writing about the likes of Whitney Houston, and Whoopi Goldberg, for starters. They seem totally different, do they not? But look at the images and tendencies as what they do relates to impressionable teenagers. In the case of Whitney, the lesson is clear: marry for sex and sex alone, get hooked on drugs, let a man beat you because, after all, you're carrying his child. Bobby Brown and Whitney Houston are a match made in hell, and appear to have nothing in common. But those of us from the 'hood know that Bobby probably "laid it on her" and she liked it, so she takes the abuse – which is so bad, that it spills over from their bedroom into the public.

And Whoopi is no better, her message is I'll do anything for a dollar and she also implies that there is no black man good enough for her. She changed her name so she could appeal to Jewish interests and she's married two Jews. The dread locks mean nothing cultural to her – it's a gimmick. A former welfare mother that was hooked on drugs, her standup comedy routine made fun of people in the same situation. As she crawled her way out of the ghetto into Hollywood, she now looks down on her former life and does nothing to help any of those people she left behind. She is not only a poor role model but as close to a traitor to the race as you'll find in modern society.

But there are "mainstream skanks" who are worthy of mention here. What about lyin' ass Starr Jones. Here is this woman, a former prosecuting attorney and a judge, a woman with a hit show, who wants US to believe that she wears shoes from Payless Shoes? Never in the annals of history has there been such a mis-match between a product and the pitchman! But what makes her negative is her bourgeois attitude and her, "that white boy sho' looks good" mentality that she conveys on the show, "The View." She's pushing the scales at almost 300 pounds, wears enough makeup to choke a muskrat, but evidently forgets that she's black.

What Starr Jones and Whoopi Goldberg convey to young girls in the way of forgetting about the race, you can add Jennifer Lopez to the list in regard to what she does to young Latinas. Those girls look up to Jennifer, and the best she can offer back is a wannabe mobster in Puff Daddy; then, she ditches him when he needs her the most and proceeds to marry/date three consecutive white boys. At a time when Latino power is at its height, this _**pendeja**_ offers young girls a clear message: once you make it, forget about your own people.

Jennifer also has a line of clothes which clearly spell out the word, "S-L-U-T." The pants are cut so low that a girl would have to get a bikini wax in order not to expose her pubes. In the back is a clear view of the ass crack. So now only is Jennifer sending out an image of "white is right," while claiming to be from "the hood," but were it not for black-originated hip hop, she would have never come up with the name "J-Lo" on her own! Add to this the clothing and, without a doubt, Jennifer Lopez is the most negative Latino image since the Frito Bandito.

Then there's the likes of Fran Dreschler and Jennifer Tilly. All body, no brains. While young people might not remember them, let me refresh your memories: Dreschler is from the "Nanny," where she intentionally flaunted her sexuality and systematically seduced, then married, her boss. Each week, miniskirt after miniskirt, midriff blouse after midriff blouse, she broke down the resistance of this rich white man, who was a television producer. This is the lesson that "The Nanny" portrayed: throw yourself at the man of your dreams and you can use sexuality to find someone to take care of you. After all, she lied on her resume to get the job, she had no marketable skills and her laugh actually made her quite obnoxious. But the lesson for little girls is that you can, indeed, make a silk purse out of a sow's ear – if the sow has perfect breasts, long legs and a skimpy outfit.

In like manner, Jennifer Tilly is the woman with the great body and the funny voice who appears in a lot of the sexy movies that hit the stage every now and then. She usually plays the dizzy mob girl ("The Getaway," "Bella Mafia," "Bound" "Liar, Liar"). Teen girls love that "bad girl" image because it falls in line with the "Gangster thug" image that their boyfriends convey.

Add the three tramps from "Friends" – Lisa Kudrow, Courtney Cox and Jennifer Aniston – to this growing list of "mainstream skanks" who wear and say whatever their please without considering the consequences and the fact that they are influencing tens of thousands of young women with their tramp-like behavior.

With Old Wave Ho's and Main-Stream Skanks out of the way, we can now turn to the current crop of trollops and the images that contribute to the rise in young female juvenile delinquency, teen pregnancy and sluttishness: a group that I like to refer to as, "New Wave Hootchies."

New Wave Hootchies

Today's crop of hootchies far outdo their predecessors in terms of on-stage and on-screen sluttish behavior. At the same time young people are more impressionable now than ever before: decreased attention being paid by parents, increased media technology (videos, more movie choices, cable, satellite) and an on-going advertising campaign telling them that it's no fun to be young.

Straight up ho's can be found throughout the music industry. The Jews that allow and promote these images are borderline pedophiles, but are also sexists who promote these images for others but never for their own people. New Wave Hootchies who immediately come to mind are Christina Aguilera, Britney Spears, Mya, Shakira and Li'l Kim – with Beyonce Knowles not far behind.

Christina is a Latina who obviously suffers from an identity crisis. Although blessed with a beautiful voice, she seems most comfortable with appearing on stage nearly nude. In fact, her newest album is called, "Stripped." She wears so much makeup that late night talk show host Conan O'Brien has made jokes about her "whore makeup" a regular part of this opening dialogue. Britney is another in a long string of no-talent white girls who get a break because they have blonde hair and blue eyes. Mya is a talented girl who got sucked into the "in-order-to-be-a-star-you-got-to show-your-ass syndrome, and now she's right up there with the sluttiest of them; Shakira is a Latina who, like the previous two, is being put on stage with skin tight pants and low cut blouses. Li'l Kim came to an award presentation several years back with one of her breasts exposed, and followed up on that with several other risqué "costumes" worn on stage. A popular poster among the hip hop crowd is one of her squatted, legs gapped, with skin tight hot pants. What you see is what you get.

Beyonce Knowles is a genuine beauty who is part of the group, "Destiny's Child." But once the white man saw her, it took no time for her father to allow her to be sold out and, at age 19, was seen on covers of magazines and in the movie "Gold Member" with hardly no clothes on, strutting her stuff. Another sister, Ashanti – an Alliyah clone – seems to think that her singing is not enough to get her over. Her videos are borderline pornographic and her on-stage presence is more thighs and breasts (what little she's got) than thoughts or brilliance. Too bad.

Others of this same type include: Eve, no-talent tennis player Anna Kournakova, TV "vampire slayer" Sarah Michelle Gellar, no talent songstress Pink ("Let's Get This Party Started"), Julia Stiles, who appears to be making quite a name for herself kissing and getting in bed with the young brothers, Kirsten Dunst, and how can we forget the likes of Jennifer "Alias" Gardner or "Titanic" concubine Claire Danes?

These are just some preliminary notes. In a few months I'll present "Sluttification III: The Search for More Condoms." I'm sure that by that time, this system will have found new youngsters to pimp, new old ho's to dredge up, and new ways to make the women of this society feel that if they can't fit into a size 6, they are worthless. Stay tuned.

In July of 1991, the same magazine that contained this most recent distorted article on infidelity carried an article titled, "Girls Who Go Too Far." According to the subtitle, "affection starved teenagers are giving new meaning to the term boy crazy" (Newsweek, 1991: 58).

What was the article about? Sure, young girls have always been crazy about boys, but for the most part there was some semblance of control, with social norms locking in and their mother's reminding them that there is a fine line between where boy crazy ends and where outright dick-hunting begins. As of the 1990s, it seemed that that line had blurred, if not outright disappeared.

The article begins by informing us that,

Like a lot of 15-year-old girls, Crystal Wilson was boy crazy. But to Crystal's mother, and to the boys who were the objects of her affection, the Kansas City teenager's behavior gave a whole new meaning to that term … Late at night, Crystal would start calling boys. Sometimes she would accuse them of things she knew they hadn't done just to have an excuse to talk to them. Rejection didn't stop her. "The more you get pushed away," she says, "the closer you want to be" (Newsweek, 1991: 58).

Teachers, school counselors and therapists who treat adolescents say they are seeking more and more girls like Crystal – desperate teenagers who will do just about anything to get a boy. Some, like Crystal, are daughters of divorce, eager for any kind of relationship with a male. Others are responding to peer pressure to be sexually active, and to the barrage of explicit images on television and in advertising. Girls will latch onto provocative entertainers like Madonna as role models, says Gail Elizabeth Wyatt, a professor of medical psychology at UCLA, and end up "playing a stereotypical role of a highly sexualized woman. And below that is a confused and lonely youngster seeking approval" (Newsweek, 1991: 58).

At the other extreme are young girls who attempt suicide or threaten boys who have spurned them. Neil Bernstein, a Washington, D.C., psychologist, says he had a patient who sent her ex-boyfriend a live snake. He has also seen girls who slashed the tires of ex-beaus' cars, or even spread rumors that their former boyfriends had AIDS. The inability to tolerate rejection is clear sign of emotional disturbance, Bernstein says. "Some girls just can't take no for an answer" (Newsweek, 1991: 58).

Sluttification III: The Search for More Condoms -- Wayward Wives

Several years have passed since I wrote the original essay on the "Sluttification of Teenaged Girls." Now is as good a time as any to write the third and final installment, which will deal with "sluttification" of women as they are now grown up, and how this society promotes this image and how, apparently, women have internalized it and used it for their own personal gratification. Elsewhere in this paper, I address some of the movies that promoted adulterous behavior and, in particular, female infidelity.

I'm a man, so when I say this, I speak from first-hand experience and as a scholar: generally speaking, men are fucked up. If a person is fucked up, then that which he produces will be fucked up. That is why even the so-called Holy Books that exist dog out women. "That's the way it will always be – until the lion learns how to write." Men are good are constructing systems and the systems are reflections of their biases, preferences and aversions. The concept of monogamous marriage is one of the stupidest ideas ever concocted. That is why it is failing: serial monogamy – one marriage after another – is nothing more than the white man's version of polygamy and polygyny, pure and simple. Reducing human beings to one of ANYTHING is always a risk.

Infidelity is only immoral and adultery illegal in a system that is rooted in the mythical belief of "one mate for all time." The woman gets caught holding the bag because she falls prey to these manipulated manifestations of reality. She buys into it. By the time she realizes how stupid it is, she's trapped in a marriage that she wants out of. But in most cases, her greed and materialistic leanings prevent her from liberating herself from the constrictions she's placed on herself. If not that, then it's "for the sake of the kids" – as if children would benefit if they knew their mother was suffering because of them. Yeah, right.

"The search for more condoms" is a metaphor for the search for the longer and more satisfying orgasm. Gone are the days when you could get a spontaneous nut; now, you've got to have a condom or you're risking a death sentence. Fortunately, for me, I grew up when there was booty aplenty and no viruses that would turn me into Mr. Potato Head if I got a nut without wearing a hat. Blunt, yet true.

101: A Partial History

As part of the "Secret Lives" article that appeared in Newsweek, the article included sidebars with history snippets titled "Wayward Wives 101." Following is what was included, with my analyses appearing after the presentations of the ladies who are used as examples of being "wayward."

As I hope to show, to label these women as "wayward" is to insinuate or assume that white culture is moral and straightforward. Here is a culture that has long been steeped in sodomy, same-sex relationships, incest and a host of perversions (many of which they put on film and then sell throughout the world), not to mention their crimes against humanity. To be "wayward" would imply that at one time, they were on the up-and-up. No. These women are not "wayward;" they are simply supporters and responders to a wayward culture, wayward in relation to the rest of humanity. To put it bluntly, Europe was the home-base and hotbed or sexual perversity. And at the center of it was Mr. Macho himself, the white male.

I mention this because he is the one who creates systems. He is the one who writes the rules that punish some, while awarding others. He is the one who marries and has sex with his own relatives and then when they come to the throne, he wonders why many of them went mad. European hedonism is at the root of white American culture today. "Wayward"? By attributing such behavior to women is to leave out the originator of the sickness of sexual perversity: the white male.

And extension of that perversity is the concept of and the blind allegiance to the concept of "monogamous marriage." That is why the divorce rate is so high: being married to one person no matter what? That is sick in itself. That is why people get married only to re-marry again. It is the white man's version of polygamy; since his system has outlawed having more than one spouse, he instead functions based on what could be called, "Serial monogamy" – one spouse after another, ala Elizabeth Burton, Jennifer Lopez or Mickey Rooney.

The article begins by informing us, *"Throughout history, women, both real and imagined, have shown that when it comes to infidelity, it's not solely a man's world. Here's a crash course."* What it should have said is "white women" because that's all they showed. In addition, don't forget that these women are married to someone else; their men create these "moral guidelines" and these women agree to them during their vows of marriage. And even in that, they STILL go out and screw around behind his back. This is not to infer that black women don't do it; but this secondary article, along with the main piece, is clearly directed toward and made up of information by provided by white women. And that is who is responsible for the contents of these articles and who this response is directed at. White women don't share anything else, I'll be damned if I'm going to allow them to "share the blame" and try to "sisterize" black, brown, red and yellow women so that they can alleviate the pain of being lascivious.

And if the writer call their examples of infidelity a "crash course," then we must make sure that they never teach in any school system in America! Their examples, as I will show, are flawed; these women are not good examples of being adulterous or unfaithful because, on varying levels, they were abandoned long before they decided to give up the ass to someone other than their husband! There are millions of white women who, during the course of everyday life, show how little they think of their husbands; why go through history and pick out eight to are more victims of circumstance than of the "easy booty" ilk that dominate white female history, both past and present?

So now let us look at each of the simplistic "examples" provided and we will be able to see more examples of how the writers – and white folks in general – distort facts in attempts to "prove their points." One man's "infidelity" is another man's "controlled and contrived situation." I'll prove it.

The article begins with Bathsheba (circa 1000 B.C.): "Spotted bathing by a voyeuristic King David, the married Bathsheba obliges his demands for a royal romp. Pregnant with David's child, Bathsheba stands by as he murders her husband; the child conceived with the king dies." There's more to it than that.

Bathsheba "obliged" David's demands the way a woman "obliges" a rapist wielding a butcher knife. First of all, David checked her out when she was bathing. Then he sent his flunkies to "fetch" her and because he was King, she felt she had no choice. He screws and gets her pregnant. Then, he sent his buddy, Joab after her husband, Uriah. He sent Joab a letter with instructions. As the Bible put it, "And he wrote in the letter, saying, Set ye Uriah in the forefront of the hottest battle, and retire ye from him, that he may be smitten, and die" (II Samuel, 11: 15).

So he had Bathsheba's husband killed and then she mourned and then turned around and married David – and got pregnant by him right away. Here's how the Bible describes it: "And when the mourning was past, David sent and fetched her to his house, and she became his wife, and bare him a son. But the thing that David had done displeased the Lord" (II Samuel, 11:27).

Where, in all this, do you see "infidelity" on Bathsheba's part? She was in a no-win situation, being ordered around and essentially RAPED by David. And when God got pissed off, was he angry at Bathsheba? No – he was angry at David. So this "example" of infidelity is grossly distorted and instead, "revised" the way white writers tend to do.

Next up is Guinevere, Fifth or Sixth Century. According to the Newsweek blurb, "Though accounts of the myth vary, one fact is almost indisputable: Guinevere, betrothed to King Arthur, fell for Sir Lancelot. In some versions, their first kiss ignited their undying love. In others, they united during a rescue." What difference should that make? She was married to King Arthur and she kissed and fell in love with another man.

Again, we have a man with power, an older man, securing a younger woman and calling it a "marriage." Arthur won the round table as a part of the dowry that Guinevere's father provided him, and it became a place where his main knights sat. This man found out about her affair with Sir Lancelot and turned around and sentenced her to death. He was the king – he had control over the laws and how those laws were administered. He could have come up with some option; but because she was a woman, he allowed his ego to come first. If he acted this way in public to appease his ego, can you imagine how screwed up he must have been at home and in bed?

There may be no justification for infidelity for women – if you're a man. But in strictly human terms, if a liar creates a culture where there are wedding vows, then violation of those vows should be expected. White folks have been lying, cheating and stealing as far back as the Fifth or Sixth Century; how can what

Guinevere did be seen as "adulterous" when men were invading villages and raping women (including her man, most likely) and had women only for the purposes of sex and, in Arthur's case, as trophies. Guinevere was no slut in and of itself; she was an impulsive victim.

Then, there's Catherine the Great, from the Eighteenth Century. Here's what these pseudo-intellectuals wrote about this woman and her sex life: "She needed to produce an heir to the Russian throne but her husband (and cousin), Peter III, was impotent, sterile and mad. Somehow, though, she conceived five children."

As you can see, white morality is relative. While questioning the sexual potency of Peter III, note that the issue of her being his cousin is overlooked or accepted. And that is what these white folks here in America are the products of: perverts, incest victims and homosexuals. What's the real story about Peter and Catherine?

This woman grew up labeled as "precocious." For instance, once when she was asked to kiss the hem of William I of Prussia, she refused and when asked why she said, "His coat is so short, I cannot reach it!." This pissed everybody off and her mother, Johanna, beat the shit out of her all evening long. Catherine was labeled "ill-mannered," and those around her figured to arrange a marriage for her. They came up with Peter – so at age 14 the two of them got married. Peter was ugly and had no charm at all – plus he played with dolls and toys!

Forced to marry at too early an age, Peter wasn't thinking about knocking boots, so the people around him made up a lie and attributed his limp penis tendencies to the fact that he drank too much! Catherine got tired of this ugly asshole following her everywhere, even if she was married to him. While Peter trained his hound dogs and chased them around the house from one room to another, and while they sat on the swing together and shared secrets, he was more of a boorish buddy than somebody that could be counted on to impregnate Catherine.

Even by the time he turned 25, Peter was playing with toy soldiers in bed and shouting orders to them. When people came by to check on the noise, he'd hide the toys under the sheets. Once, he executed a rat that had bitten into a couple of his wooden soldiers. When one of his pet dogs broke its back, Peter executed it by lynching it in public. But in order to make Catherine appear to be a slut – as if she was deviating from the white female norm – the writers of the article focus on her and not on the asshole she was forced to marry and live with.

They slept together eight years and no children were produced. Peter told people he was sleeping around to avoid the fact that he wasn't screwing Catherine. He was lying – which in my view, makes him worse than someone who WAS screwing around! Catherine got tired of his bullshit and started taking lovers, the first one a guardsman named Sergius Saltykov. He fucked her, got her pregnant and then when Peter was drunk, they set it up so he'd think he had sex with Catherine.

In September of 1754, Catherine gave birth to a son. Those who were conspiring rigged the sheets to make it appear as if Catherine was a virgin, but Peter always doubted and so did others. But we're talking about white folk here; their political aims were met because all they gave a shit about was making sure that the Empress finally had an heir. After several other children, Peter dies from "hemorrhoidal cholic."

The next woman incorrectly posed as a "wayward wife" is Hester Prynn of "Scarlet Letter" fame (1850). The blurb provided in Newsweek (next to a picture of Demi Moore's character rather than the real Prynn) states, "Assuming her husband is lost at sea, Hester takes up with the town's Puritanical preacher, and after giving birth to his child Pearl, Hester is forced to sew her guilt onto her garments."

The affair between Arthur Dimmesdale and Hester Prynne was the result of human nature. A proverb will serve to explain the thrust of why Prynne is miscast as being "unfaithful:"

> A young boy turns to his father after the father has completed reading a story to him and asks, "Father, you tell me that the lion is the king of the jungle, and yet in all of the stories that you read to me, the hunter is the winner. Why is that?" The father turns to his son and says, "That's the way it is always going to be – until the lion learns how to write!"

In like manner, the white woman will never get justice until she tells her own story. Not the re-created and revised lies like the ones that permeate the Newsweek article, but the historical reality. White women, with all their power, have adapted to and accepted the sexist norms imposed by the white male. They accepted his bullshit ideologies and aided and abetted him in oppressing others. Hester Prynne was not out looking for some beef; she thought her husband was killed and, as a result, fell in love with another man and gave that man the bootie. For that act, once the husband reappeared, she becomes the subject of ridicule and scorn. Not only punished, but degraded – ordered to stand for three hours on the platform of the pillory and then thereafter, for the rest of her life, to "wear the mark of shame upon her bosom" -- the scarlet letter – an "A" for adulteress.

But the man who screwed her, Dimmesdale, sits back and watches but is too spineless to admit his role in seducing her. Not only did he seduce her – he got her pregnant. And yet she bore the brunt.

In simpler terms, atrocities greater than a woman's seduction permeate this woman's life. You have the original deadbeat dad, you have a man who is a coward, you have a system that brands a woman with a stigma and who hypocritically persecute her. The very concept of "Puritanism," in the face of white folks' history, is a mythical joke. What could be pure about a people that has done what they, as a collective have done? What could be "pure" about people who treat their women in such an abominable manner? The same can be applied to other cultures as well. But other cultures are not the ones who are seeking to impose their views and values on the rest of the world. The white man is. Therefore, he is responsible for what he has created. And, the fact is, he must be made to pay for it.

He cannot pay, and in fact benefits, when the victim of his system is made to look "wayward." In much the same way that Dimmesdale – the man who impregnated Ms. Prynne – is viewed by the townspeople as a man of God and a man who can do no wrong; much the same way that today's preachers are viewed. And while being viewed this way, many of them are raping under aged boys and girls, having affairs with members of their congregations, and involving themselves in sordid perversions behind closed doors. In a culture of "waywardness," the wayward person is therefore normal.

Yet another contorted example of someone who is "wayward" is Emma Bovary (1857). As the Newsweek article posits, "The 19th century's material girl, Emma is more interested in couture and cash than in her husband. But the debts and suspicions mount, and rather than swallow her pride, she swallows arsenic." Once again, not quite the whole story.

Madame Bouvary is the title character of a novel by Gustav Flaubert. She was a beautiful woman married to a small time doctor, Charles. Dissatisfied with her marriage, Emma has a series of love affairs which eventually lead her to social disgrace, financial ruin and suicide. Again, we find the double-standard and as a result of women complying with it (or having it imposed on them, take your pick), the woman is labeled "wayward" by people like Newsweek reporters when, in reality, the situation that they inherited was "wayward" from the get-go.

First of all, a man wrote this novel. Secondly, he writes of a woman, Emmy Bovary, who has affairs behind her husband's back. But why? Because she is not satisfied with her marriage. Is that her fault? No. Therefore if the husband is failing, is seeking an alternative like an affair a big enough deal to qualify it as a crime? The white man's system of morality says yes. Meanwhile, in the name of war, "spoils theory," "boys will be boys" and other excuses, he can rape and have sex whenever he wants to, married or not.

In this novel, based on the numerous reviews I read, Flaubert took the female character and used her death as way of upholding morality and illustrating the consequences of sin. Again, we find the white woman as a martyr because she sought to do something other than allow the white male in her life to be his usual, inattentive self. She is punished, in other words, for being independent.

Then there's Anna Karenina (1878). Of this, the Newsweek "journalists" write, "Vronsky loves Anna. Anna loves Vronsky. Anna is married. What to do? She begins seeing Vronsky, and seeks divorce from her husband to no avail. Trapped, she throws herself under a train." In this novel, the key is how adultery looks to other people. The husband doesn't care about the affair, as long as Anna doesn't file for divorce or separation. As one reviewer put it, "He does not care so much about the fact that his wife loves another man; he cares only that she continue to appear to be a good wife."

How can she be "wayward" if she has her husband's blessing and is carrying on with the man she loves? She might want more, but the fact is, she is not "wayward" as the Newsweek people imply. And their selections get sicker as they travel ever closer to the present day.

Next on the list is none other than Ingrid Bergman (1949), of which the following is written: "The cold war had started, but this Swedish star's affair with director Roberto Rossellini had Americans steaming mad. After leaving her family, she retreated into a seven-year acting hiatus." Is that really what happened – or did Jewish-controlled Hollywood "whitelist" her? After all, she was a Jew, was she not? Did she not win an Emmy for her portrayal of Jewish leader, Golda Meier in the 1982 flick, A Woman Called Golda?

Why was she listed as "wayward" when, indeed, her relationship with Rossellini was a case of two people who were, at best, more than willing to violate any marriage vows that were taken. As the "Official Ingrid Bergman Web Site" informs us,

> In 1949, Ingrid wrote a fan letter to Italian director Roberto Rossellini, expressing her desire to working one of his films. He responded by writing a part for her in his 1949 film Stromboli. During the production of this film, Ingrid and Rossellini began an affair that would change her previous wholesome image forever and cause her to lose many fans in America. Ingrid was still married to Peter Lindstrom at the time, although their marriage had not been happy for many ears. Rossellini was still married to another woman as well, although they were separated. Ingrid became pregnant, and she and Rossellini sought divorces from their respective spouses so they could marry each other. Ingrid gave birth to a son, Roberto, before the couple were married in 1950 ….

Now, the stroke that kills:

> Moralists and fans in America expressed outrage at this seeming downfall of their former idol and denounced her as immoral.

> Although her marriage had been unhappy for quite some time the public had only seen Ingrid's saintly image before, and balked at the revelation of the affair. United states Senator Edwin C. Johnson of Colorado even criticized Ingrid, condemning her publicly as "a powerful influence for evil.

You see? Rossellini was just as licentious as Bergman was, but she was held to a different standard. Where is the castigation of the Italian? America held her to a different standard while, at the same time, practicing racial segregation against people of color. Hypocrites, all. How can a white woman be viewed as wayward when she was only doing what white women have done throughout history? The key is the wedding vow, which is taken much too seriously. Just because people say words, words that include predictions and projections far into the future (e.g., "for as long as you both shall live," "from this day forth," etc.), doesn't mean these words are somehow sacred because they are stated in front of some cracker in a robe or a collar!

The fact is, what Bergman did is hardly different from any other "starlet" of her time; the concept of the "casting couch" is a well-known norm in Hollywood and therefore these women are willing to do what it takes to "break into" the business. Does that make them "wayward" because they are married to someone else, someone who in most cases is out screwing anything that has a pulse? The fact is, Bergman would return to Hollywood in 19546 and her marriage to Rossellini ended in 1957. She went on to win her second Oscar (Best Actress for Anastasia), she won an Emmy in 1959, and in 1974 won another best actress Oscar for Murder on the Orient Express. During this time she was married to Lars Schmidt. Tell me: you don't think she screwed somebody to get those awards? She's as Jew in Jewish-controlled Hollywood. You do the math.

The fact is, *Newsweek* buys into a double-standard with the article and these so-called examples and, in doing so, misses an essential point: you can't make a whore into a housewife. Bergman was wayward because basically, white women in general are wayward. Look around: who is the biggest whore in the world? Who is the biggest slut parading around for all to see? Who is on screen but naked, fucking and sucking like there's no tomorrow? The first naked woman most black children will see will be on television. Other women follow suit, but is there any doubt that white women are weak-minded? That is why they fall in line with a moral doctrine that they full well KNOW they cannot comply with. Their pretend, fake it and go through the motions so that they can find a white man to adopt them. That is what all these "examples" have in common. And we still have one more to go: Elizabeth Taylor.

Of this "example," the article asserts, "Talk about a serial spouse. While filming the 1963 movie "Cleopatra," Taylor – then with hubby number four, Eddie Fisher –fell for her costar Richard Burton. She ran off with Burton soon after." If a woman is a whore, if a man is a cockhound, it matters not that she takes some vows and says, "I do." For Newsweek to claim that these women are wayward is to imply that they were, at some time, highly moral. They were not. These women did what they did because they were acting in accordance with their nature. The man initiates the affairs by acting in accordance with HIS nature – he fucks around. The woman sees it and is not getting attention so she feels she can do it. What is "wayward" about that? ***It is the institution of marriage that is fucked up, not the people who deviate from it.***

In the case of Elizabeth Taylor, we clearly have a woman that has "game." Even with her reputation as an easy piece, she still attracted man after man and even got married to one of her husbands – Richard Burton -- twice!

Ever since the white man came across film and movies, he has been projecting his woman as a whore who lusted after him. Elizabeth Taylor contributed mightily to this image; in fact, her first on-screen kiss came in the movie called "A Place in the Sun" with Montgomery Clift. Here is what Bruce Kirkland of the Toronto Sun newspaper wrote about Ms. Taylor back in August of 2001:

> Elizabeth Taylor still remembers her first real on-screen kiss, a sizzling, sensual encounter with Montgomery Clift in 1950 … "The timing was particularly fortuitous for me because I'd only receive my first real kiss in real life two weeks before," Taylor says in an interview … She was 17 years old when [she] co-starred for director Stevens in his classic romantic tragedy (Kirkland, 2001).

Seventeen years old. And yet she was hired by men who knew better. Hired to do what? Seduce and titillate – something that the white female has always been forced to do and has done with a smile. She might complain, but she accepts the roles; she might bicker, but she does it anyway; she might raise concerns, but she stands by while black people get discriminated against, maimed and murdered. This is not "wayward" behavior; it is inextricably bound to the white supremacist structure. ***"The hand that rules the cradle rules the throne."***

Taylor was no victim. In fact, according to one source, "In the early '60s, Taylor had past-life therapy and discovered she used to be Cleopatra. She was then paid the unheard-of-sum of $1,000,000 to star in the film" (Kirkland, 2001). First of all, Cleopatra – despite the white man's efforts to claim otherwise – was a black woman. So how can this racist white woman make such a claim? She made it at a time when black power and civil rights were laying claim to black history and she boldly jumped on the bandwagon. But only did so to land a part in a movie. Is this "wayward" activity or the calculated and shrewd actions of a white woman who is subtly slithering away up and around Hollywood?

Look at the husband's list of this so-called "wayward" woman: Nicky Hilton, the hotel heir; Michael Wilding, Mike Todd, Eddie Fisher, Richard Burton (twice), Senator John Warner and Larry Fortensky. Furthermore, she has never received alimony or child support payments from any of her husbands, and she's been widowed once and divorced seven times. This woman once had a boyfriend named Henry Wynberg, a used-car salesman with a police record!

Wayward? No. Elizabeth Taylor is right in line with the norms of white women. That's why they are committing adultery – when they take those vows they are forced to act out of their nature! She only has a high school education and that came from some place called Metro-Goldwyn-Mayor School! One of her husbands, Larry Fortensky, was a 10th grade dropout! Wayward? In addition to all those husbands, she was "romantically linked" (that's what they call it when its white women) to Frank Sinatra, Peter Lawford, Joseph Mankiewicz, Victor Mature, Michael Jackson, Rock Hudson, George Hamilton, Malcolm Forbes, Vic Damone, Carl Bernstein and Montgomery Clift.

Already having grasped at straws (and obviously failed to secure any), the writers continue delving into examples of "wayward" women and the best they can come up with for the 1960s is Mrs. Robinson from the movie, "The Graduate" (1967). Here's how the writers describe it: "A restless housewife, Mrs. Robinson (Anne Bancroft) seduces Ben (Dustin Hoffman) shortly after his college graduation. When he begins dating her daughter, the middle-paged ice queen exacts revenge by sabotaging their relationship."

Wayward vis-à-vis wedding vows, or just plain sluttish? Again, we must recall how shallow the vows of marriage and what the mean in a capitalist society. ***Just because one submits to the law and to protocol doesn't means that one's inherent moral compass and values will change.*** Rather than adapt the concept of marriage to fit the hedonistic and lascivious realities of a white society, those in power instead opt to force-fit marriage onto people who don't have the slightest intention of remaining monogamous. Such is the case with Mrs. Robinson, with Elizabeth Taylor and the rest.

Mrs. Robinson, the older woman in "The Graduate," was not a happy woman – so she seduces a younger man. As most reviewers will note, Mrs. Robinson is not only bored by her husband, but she drinks too much and she seduces Benjamin, not so much out of lust, but because she is alone and desperate for some kind of kinship. Again, what do we find -- women who finally see the vows for what they are: mere words. Either that, or we find women who are out for something else (money, status) and as a result, repeat those vows so that they can get something material or tangible, but certainly not out of any abiding believe in "til death do us part." Again: what is "wayward" is a system that would promote monogamous marriage when its hedonistic, individualistic and selfish value system is diametrically opposed to such a union being successful for the long term. The fact that one out of every two such unions fails should be a wakeup call for this system.

Finally, desperate for someone to fill the final slot no doubt, the two writers come up with Francesca Johnson from the movie, "The Bridges of Madison County" (1959). They describe Francesca thusly: "A lonely Iowa farm wife (Meryl Streep) plays tour guide to a rugged National Geographic photographer (Clint Eastwood). They begin looking at bridges but have eyes only for each other." Really?

First of all, the character of Francesca Johnson is an Italian woman, a woman who has ended up living on a farm in hick-ass Iowa someplace. Life on the farm is boring and it is clear she is unhappy. Even when Clint's character asks her to leave with him, she is tempted to the utmost – she wants to get the hell out of Dodge – in much the same way these white woman want out of their marriages to these corporate types, want to get away from the dinners and lunches and vacations. Clint's character represents freedom in much the same way that these white women go "slumming" into black communities and barrios (something almost every single brother or sister has seen) and even with all their wealth, they seek people of color to make them feel "alive." Black men are to these white women what Clint Eastwood's character is to Meryl Streep's.

It is not that Streep's husband is a bad man – it is simply that she is bored to death, having taken care of children and a home all these years. She says at one point, "We are the choices that we have made …" But not really; these women are not going to be forced to live a life where they are nothing more than a set of reactions to some white man. And so they have affairs, and the live, even for the most fleeting of moments, in the present. Some risk a great deal, some risk nothing. But the fact is, "The Secret Lives of Wives" is a piece of drivel that touches upon issues but bails out these white women by making it appear as if they are "deviating from the norm." There is nothing normal about the monogamous system of marriage concocted by the white man, just as there is nothing logical about the four- and five-inch stiletto heels that he makes for her to wear and, in the process, he destroys her feet and posture just as his marital "rules" destroy her chance to live and breathe.

With this preliminary junk out of the way, and having made clear my thesis and views on white women in general and the system of marriage that they have imposed on them as a "norm," let us now look at the article itself and address what I view as the inadequacies within.

White Women, the American Dream and "New Gomorrah: "A Response to "The Secret Lives of Wives"

Thus far we've had some background and some case studies on how these white women carry on when they think no one is looking. And much of what is taking place is taking place with black men. Therefore, it was a shock to believe that what is obvious to most people who live in the black community or those who have attended college and have seen how these women make themselves available to black athletes, could be deemed a "secret."

Information on how and what women think is always indispensable. The only problem is that the women who are usually interviewed, analyzed, observed or monitored are usually white women. And so it is with this article – although one of the authors' names is Ali, I doubt very much if she is black; more than likely an assimilated former middle eastern academic. At any rate, the articles begins, thusly:

> When groups of women get together, especially if they're mothers and have been married for more than six or seven years, and especially if there's alcohol involved, the conversation is usually the same. They talk about the kids and work – how stressed they are, how busy and bone tired. They gripe about their husbands and, if they're being perfectly honest and the wine kicks in, they talk about the disappointments in their marriages (Ali & Miller, 2004: 47).

Sure women do this. But these white women – the numerical majority in the nation – have duping their man down to a science. His immense ego, combined with his obvious density when it comes to caring about or understanding her, makes him the perfect "mark." No one will write words like these or express thoughts like this because they fly in the face of the white supremacist bullshit that every single one of us has been force-fed; From Batman, Green Hornet and Wonder Woman to the president of the United States, James Bond and Farrah Fawcett, we are told that the white man and his woman are ideals worth emulating, that they are infallible and super-sexy.

But when these women get together, they share the truth. They talk about getting beaten up, about the alcohol abuse and about how he sits in front of the television calling people of color niggers, spics and wetbacks. She hears all this and in many cases, she has no respect for him. But she sticks around because she wants security, she wants respect from her peers, and she wants to take care of the children. But Newsweek should take one of those assimilated reporters they've got (they can start with the twisted Ms. Ali) and send them to the black bars and the black communities and ask those white women why they are cruising the ghetto and the barrio. If they did, there would be less shock at findings such as those described in the following excerpt:

> Not long ago over lunch in Los Angeles, this conversation took a surprising turn, when Erin, who is in her early 40s and has been married for more than a decade, spilled it. She was seeing someone else. Actually, more than one person. It started with an old friend, whom she began meeting every several months for long dinners and some heavy petting. Then she began giving herself permission to flirt with, kiss –well actually, make out with – men she met on business trips. She understands it's a "Clintonian" distinction, but she won't have sex with anyone except her husband, whom she loves. But she also loves the unexpected thrill of meeting someone new. "Do you remember?" She pauses. "I don't know how long you've been married, but do you remember the kiss that would just launch a thousand kisses?" (Ali & Miller, 2004: 47).

The concept of "making out" is the white woman's way of saying that she sucked a dick. How do I know? Because, like most high school guys, I listened to white boys talk about what these white girls do. They might remain virgins throughout high school, but in order for many of them to save face and be considered "hip," what they do is masturbate these white boys off into a handkerchief or give up head. Reliable sex studies clearly show that white women engage in fellatio before black girls do. Many a black-on-black relationship has been divided because the white girl comes in and performs any number of acts that "the sisters" may nor or will not do – until after marriage or until the relationship becomes more serious. If these writers got out on the streets and asked around, they would know that what I say is true.

This leads to the issue of "innocent flirting" and "the thrill of meeting someone new." You can meet someone without seeing that person as a sexual alternative. And if what I write about these white women is not true, then why do they allow these white men to portray them as whores and sluts and women who you can tongue kiss after only knowing them for a few minutes? It's because they enjoy being painted that way, that's why. These white women have come to link romantic love to premarital sex.

This mindset, this lascivious tendency on a great many white women (which admittedly, many women of color have come to emulate as time passes on), is at the basis of their willingness to rationalize their extramarital affairs. Not only is the institution of marriage itself constricting on even the most conservative of human beings, but a woman who is suppressing her sluttishness is truly at odds with herself psychologically. Flirting, "dick-teasing" (as we call it in the 'hood) and screwing around can be viewed in this context as therapeutic.

Moving on:

> Erin started seeing other men when she went back to work after her youngest child entered preschool. All of a sudden she was ***out there.*** Wearing great clothes meeting new people, alive for the firs time in years to the idea that she was interesting beyond her contributions at PTA meetings (Ali & Miller, 2004: 47).

The company line is that Erin was frustrated with her husband not paying any attention to her. But if we accept my position, these white girls are not "monogamous" in their thinking once they graduate from high school or college. In the case of college, more than a few have had affairs with black men and have been turned out. Some have give their money to men, buying friendship and sex. By the time they get married, they do not forget these experiences, and more importantly, these women are under pressure to marry – as are most women. But the white woman, falling for the dupe that she is some kind of "ideal" and is "entitled" to much of what life has to offer, marries and finds it's not all it's cracked up to be. Again, you can't turn a whore into a housewife.

The case studies continue:

> Veronica, on the other hand, fell in love with a man who was not her husband while she was safely at home in the Dallas suburbs looking after her two children. Hers is the most familiar story: isolated and lonely, married to an airline pilot, Veronica, now 35, took up with a wealthy businessman she met at a Dallas nightclub (Ali & Miller, 2004: 47-48—emphasis original).

The very fact that she as out at a Dallas nightclub despite having two children and a suburban lifestyle lends more credence to my earlier point: you can't turn a whore into a housewife. She went to that club and met someone ***by design***. That was her purpose. She was hot to trot and her husband was probably having affairs in other cities as many pilots are prone to do. This is what white women do and it doesn't get reported because their husbands are "pals" with the newspaper editor or the television station manager; golfing buddies with the cops and drinking pals with the local attorneys and judges. But it's far more pervasive than we are led to believe.

Continuing with Veronica's story:

> Her lover gave her everything her husband didn't: compliments, Tiffany jewelry, flowers and love notes. It was, in fact, the flowers that did her in. Veronica's lover sent a bouquet to her home one afternoon, her husband answered the door and, in one made-for Hollywood moment, the marriage was over. Now remarried (to a new man), Veronica says she and her friends half jokingly talk about starting a Web site for married women who want to date. "I think there might be a market in it," she says. There is. Wives who want extramarital sex – or are just dreaming about it – can find what they seek on Yahoo!, MSN or AOL (Ali & Miller, 2004: 48).

See? She screws around behind her husband's back and then goes right out and does what? Gets married again! Why? She's obviously not happy in a relationship where there are boundaries. She claims her husband wasn't making her happy, but she didn't use that as a reason for divorce, did she? No, she stuck around and spent the money, drove the cars and lived in the house. Just like a prostitute would do. She allowed herself to get pimped. Then, once busted, like a prostitute that wants out, she goes out and "chooses" someone else to take care of her – someone else to "turn a trick" with. Then she says, while still married, "Three might be a market in" wives who want to have affairs. I wonder what her current husband has to say about that? Her mentality or outlook has not changed one bit; the only thing that's changed is the man that she's living with.

The article then shifts into a legal information regarding adultery:

> Much has changed since Emma Bovary chose suicide with arsenic over living her life branded an adulteress – humiliated, impoverished and stripped of her romantic ideals. In the past, U.S. laws used to punish women who cheated; in a divorce, an unfaithful wife could lose everything, even the property she owned before marriage. Newer laws have been designed to protect these women (Ali & Miller, 2004: 48).

The fact that U.S. laws punished women and not men shows that the basis of the rule of law – the white male and his chauvinism – is the problem, not the women. The creator of monogamous marriage, which must be recognized by the state (so you can pay money for a piece of paper" validating" your commitment) is another part of the problem. And yet women were put to death, ridiculed and scorned. That same mentality exists today because the same person who created all this hell and heartache and transported it to these shores is still in power. Now, his system has created a slingshot effect, and his women are rebelling against him. As the authors of the article explain,

> The reality is this: American women today have more opportunity to fool around than ever: when they do fool around, they're more likely to tell their friends about it, and those friends are more likely to lend them a sympathetic ear (Ali & Miller, 2004: 48).

The preceding comments, apparently the thesis of the article, is rife with bullshit assumptions and contortions of reality. As an African-American male who has been around white women all my life (not as a boyfriend, but as an observer), and as someone who has studied their behavior as a part of my expertise in the area of black history, these women seize and have seized, opportunities whenever they could. They seize them because they are desperate for human attention. And they will take it from anybody they can get – even while sitting back and allowing it to be denied to other groups.

For instance, take slavery. Those "rapes" of white women that were reported was the white man protecting his woman's reputation. She was advancing on enslaved men, forcing them to screw her or she would report them. If she got caught, she simply said she was being raped or, worse, the white man would ASSUME that this was what was taking place. This situation is most graphically depicted in the movie, "The Affair," where a black GI is "caught" having sex with a white women he loved and who loved him, and yet is convicted in the military courts for rape. He was lynched.

Black people know white people better than white people know black people. We laugh at some of what they do but we analyze all that they do. We talk about it, among ourselves at the barber shops, the beauty salons, over the poker table and at church. We see white folks for what they really are, not the manipulated manifestations of what they want the world to believe. And it is not a pretty picture.

The excerpt claims that these women, who have "more opportunity to fool around" are making light of a situation that is really pitiable. This "Sex and the City" slut-for-a night perception of the white woman is not a fair depiction of white women in my view. These women are horny but even more than that, they are lonely and desperate. And this desperation is why they will allow themselves to be approached by a man of any race or, for that matter, even by another women. Look how many of them "discover," at a late age, that they were lesbians all along.

The "friends" that lend the sympathetic ear do so because they, too, have issues. But these friends know more than just the fact that she's fucking around behind her husband's back. They know that the husband is, in many cases, beating the shit out of her, having an affair on his own, or is so drunk and drugged up, he cannot perform sexually. These white women are observant, too. And with the advent of the feminist movement, they interpret all this new-found "liberation" as a chance to get "payback." And what better way than to screw someone else, perhaps even a close friend of the family, but better yet, the bane of the white man's existence: the "nigger," the "spic" or some other man of color?

More half-truths about the white woman's so-called "infidelity" continues in the following passage:

> They probably use technology to facilitate their affairs, and if they get caught, they're almost as likely to wind up in a wing chair in a marriage counselor's office as in divorce court. Finally, if they do separate from their husbands, women, especially if they're college educated, are better able to make a go of it – pay the bills, keep at least partial custody of the children, remarry if they want to – than their philandering foremothers. "It was just so ruinous for a woman to be caught in adultery in past times, you had to be really drive or motivated to do it," says Peter D. Kramer, clinical professor of psychiatry at Brown University and the author of "Should You Leave?" "Now you can get away with it, there's a social role that fits you" (Ali & Miller, 2004: 48).

The preceding paragraph omits one key point: that being that white women are in a society that rewards whiteness. They are also the beneficiaries of what a number of scholars recognize as "white privilege." In light of these two facts, the white woman can "get away with it" because she has a wide variety of options. With the media painting her as the standard of beauty, she has no problem being accepted (and even sought after) by men of color, which is another reason why so many women of color despise the very presence of any white females. These women of color know that this white woman is always on the prowl and that there are no boundaries for her.

As a result of all this, the information provided in the article is really moot. The white woman is going to make it, one way or the other. She's white in a society that is majority white, and as a result, she can always find someone who is as lonely as she is (the white man's quest for prostitutes in black communities clearly shows he's not happy, either). So when Dr. Kramer claims that "Now you can get away with it, there's a social role that fits you," she is describing the way it has always been for the white woman. While she might have been caught and sentenced legally, when it comes to her morality (or lack thereof), she has ALWAYS been able to "get away with it."

On with the *Newsweek* piece:

> Just how many married women have had sex with people who are not their husbands? It's hard to say for sure, because people lie to pollsters when they talk about sex, and studies vary wildly. (Men, not surprisingly, amplify their sexual experience, while women diminish it). Couples therapists estimate that among their clientele, the number is close to 30 to 40 percent, compared with 50 percent of men, and the gap is almost certainly closing. In 1991, the National Opinion Research Center at the University of Chicago asked married women if they'd ever had sex outside their marriage, and 10 percent said yes. When the same pollsters asked the same question in 2002, the "yes" responses rose to 15 percent, while the number of men stayed flat at about 22 percent (Ali & Miller, 2004: 48).

The statement is that men amplify their sexual experience, while women diminish theirs. That doesn't mean that the women are not lying; they diminish theirs because they know men have fragile egos and furthermore, in a sexist system, a woman with a lot of lovers is viewed as a slut. My proposition is somewhat different when it comes to white women: I view them as being sluttish whether they have a lot of lovers or not, because I believe they possess a mindset that is slut-like from the get-go. I believe that the moral compass of white women is broken, and that the majority of them would take a dick over a smile any day.

Furthermore, if half of men are having sex with people who are not their spouses, then why would the figure be lower for women, especially when women tend to diminish their numbers? The fact is, I believe that all men cheat if given the chance. And I also believe that most of the men who cheat get caught. And if that is the case, then I further advance that the men who get caught cheating have wives who will, one way or another, get revenge. And the best revenge is fucking someone that the husband knows or the husband hates.

"Couples therapists." Get the fuck outta here! White people continually pawn themselves off as experts in human nature but for some reason, they haven't found the cure for the world's number one disease: racism! And yet here they sit trying to solve other people's problems when they sit in segregated living rooms, living away from people who they both hate and fear. In simpler terms, psychotics giving out advice to neurotics!

And as for those polls, these social scientists want to study everything except for the one thing that is most relevant: why do white men buy pussy from black women while all the while hating black people? Why do white women give black men head and then refuse to hire or promote any? These are questions that get to the core of the mental state of the people who control and make decisions in this society. Figure THEM out, and you've figured out the "key to the colors."

More information on "data" is provided by the authors:

> The best interpretation of the data: the cheating rate for women is approaching that of men, says Tom Smith, author of the NORC's reports on sexual behavior. When Michele Weiner-Davis, a marriage counselor and founder of the Divorce Busting Center in Woodstock, Ill., started practicing 20 years ago, just 10 percent of the infidelity she knew of was committed by women. Now, she believes, it's closer to 50 percent. "Women have suddenly begun to give themselves the same permission to step over the boundary the men have" (Ali & Miller, 2004: 48).

Again, I was right; but if these white people are saying "closer to fifty percent," then that means it must be around 70%. Again, in day-late-dollar-short fashion, and in a defensive statement, the claim is made that, "women have suddenly begun to give themselves the same permission to step over the boundary the men have." Suddenly? As I have stated, these white women have been doing it, but the social scientists – most of whom are married men – didn't want to admit it, and the women were lying by telling their husbands what they wanted to hear. The reason they are just now coming up with figures like those quoted is because social scientists are running out of issues to study, so they've turned to taboo issues: interracial sexuality, penis studies, homoerotic tendencies and, of course, female infidelity.

Now comes anecdotal research and additional evidence that mythology is still at work. Ali and Miller write,

> A rise in female infidelity, though titillating, does not do much to clarify the paradoxes in American culture surrounding sex. Taboos about female sexuality are falling away; together, Dr. Phil and "Sex and the City" have made very imaginable sex act fodder for cocktail-party conversation. At the same time, Americans developed a lower tolerance for infidelity: 80 percent of Americans says infidelity is "always wrong," according to NORC, up from 70 –percent in 1970. Popular opinion is on to something: infidelity can be devastating. If discovered, it can upend a marriage and create chaos in a family (Ali & Miller, 2004: 49).

What the authors pose as "paradoxes" are really overlapping realities, not separate moral modalities. The "rise in female infidelity," as I pose in this paper, is in actuality a mis-representation of the facts. What they mean is "the rise in the REPORTS OF female infidelity." The white woman, like her man, have a history of being able to sweep their immorality and dirty linen under the proverbial rug. They use their power of the media to hide what they really stand for. Any "rise" that exists can be attributed to more investigative reporting by the media, more serious-minded social science research and of course, the overt actions of a woman who was at one time a slut who preferred clandestine methods.

The fact that 80 percent of Americans say infidelity means nothing when you also understand that more than 80 percent of Americans have stated, in surveys, that they would lie and cheat if they believed they could get away with it. You can't trust white folks to tell the truth about much of anything if they don't see any personal benefit in it. The concept of "female infidelity" is a secret that the white man wanted to keep and that the white female wants to openly flaunt. She allows his media to show her for what she really is. And being the immoral person she is, she considers those sluttish images as flattering.

For instance, ask a Hollywood actress what role she truly wants to play. Know what it is? The role of a hooker, prostitute, or call girl. In the article in question, Diane Lane, who starred in the movie, "Unfaithful," tells the writers that, . "Women always say 'thank you' for that role, and at first I wasn't sure how to take that," says Lane. What was the role? A happy woman with a child, a rich husband who loves her – who nevertheless fucks around behind her husband's back! This then, is the role that day-to-day white women are "thanking" Diane for. What does that say about the morality of these people?

However, there is something she should be thanked for. She acted out a response to the misconception that permeated American society for centuries. That misconception is the belief that only women who are unmarried can be whores and sluts. Another myth that she overturned in her role was that only ignored, neglected or abused wives sneak out on their husbands. Her role showed, straight out, that a white woman is going to screw around if she gets the opportunity. And she can have the greatest marriage that there is going. The fact is, ANY woman will do it and so will ANY man. The issue isn't the character of the people involved in the marriage (although this plays a major part), it is the concept of "monogamous marriage" itself!

Even as these words are being written, the ABC television network is about to air two new television programs that will show the reality of the white woman and what she's been getting away with all along. The first one is called, "Desperate Wives," and the promo says that "every family has a secret it wants to bury." This show became a hit right away, as it is rooted in the false premise that, "These women aren't like the women in our neighborhood." That is a lie. The white woman knows what she is and what she likes. The white man ALSO knows what she's about, that's why whoever wrote the script for "Desperate Wives" knew that it would catch on. It was no "fantasy;" it is rooted in the lives of white women in general and suburban white housewives, in particular. The more they are ignored and neglected, the greater the tendency to fuck around behind her golf-playing husband's back.

The second one is called "Wife Swap," and I think it is self-explanatory. The point here is that these white producers and writers are not speaking for black people because they don't know any. They're talking about their own race members.

So the concept of sluttishness is a white female norm, with women of color emulating her in some respects. But with women of color, the sluttishness starts on the outside and goes in; they see it as a fad, a trend or a way to appeal to men's sick fantasies. But the white woman, I believe she is a slut from inside out, almost to the point of being genetically predisposed to be a whore. And that is the way the world perceives her – ask any foreign student about white girls and watch the look on his face. They come here lusting after them because the word is out: the American white women is a whore.

If infidelity is "always wrong," then why do Americans reward it and pay so much attention to the practice of it? There's no scarlet letter here; there's only kudos and exposure. Look at how married women, in the name of "celebrity" or being "stars" do in front of movie cameras? Look at how they cavort openly with other men, and how the moviemakers and image makers play them up for doing so? The looser the woman, the more slutty, the more fame: names like Gypsy Rose Lee, Marilyn Monroe, Sharon Stone, Britney Spears, Nicole Kidman and others, immediately come to mind. From the ranks of black women add Millie Jackson, Ola Ray, Cheryl Underwood, Halle Berry and Li'l Kim. Latinas who rank high on the skankometer are Jennifer Lopez, Eva Longoria, Eva Mendes, Charo, and Maria Conchita Alonso.

So they say that infidelity can be devastating. And yet the women above either became famous by being linked to being unfaithful or they portrayed roles where infidelity was promoted. In sum, there is no paradox, only lies used to make the reality all the more tempting, tantalizing and titillating.

And yet naïve people who don't understand the nature and history of human beings continue to argue otherwise – such as in the following passage:

> Nevertheless, in America, as in other parts of the world, a double
> standard continues to thrive: boys will be boys, but girls are
> supposed to be good. Even though women are narrowing the gap,
> men still do the bulk of the domestic damage. "Bill Clinton, ho
> we're all loving on TV – he's a charmer. The poor, weak,
> wandering guy is kind of a cultural norm," says Elizabeth

Berger, a psychiatrist in Elkins Park, Pa., and author of "Raising Children With Character." A weak or wandering mother is s scarier image, she adds (Ali & Miller, 2004: 49).

There is no doubt that much of the world holds a gender bias. But within that gender bias is major acceptance on the part of the gender that is discriminated against. This is not like white racism, where blacks understand it and adapt to it while fighting it all along. These white women accepted sexism and the concept of "boys will be boys" was accepted by them, from the sororities on college campuses to the workplace. In fact, much of what their "movement" is about is joining those "boys" in power to work to oppress others. That is why the feminist movement was about white women, not black women. As Fanon taught long ago, "a racist in a culture of racism, is therefore normal."

In today's ultra-modern society, these white women continue to accept sexism in exchange for certain perks. Much like the black Uncle Tom who skins and grins, smiles and shuffles, she also "went along to get along." But that Uncle Tom sees the white man for what he is and hates him. But feeling powerless, the Tom continues to feign docility so that he can support his family. Not the white woman.

She has aided and abetted the white man in his crimes against humanity, pure and simple. She and her children cheered when he lynched and castrated black men. She listened to the tales of the white "boys" as they talked about how they caught and raped a "lively nigger gal." They were among those who jeered and spat on young black children in Arkansas during the Central High School integration days. And the list goes on and on.

In fact, the article lends credence to my assertions. One quote talks of Bill Clinton being a "Charmer." Then an author claims that, "the poor, weak, wandering guy is a kind of cultural norm." But that norm was created by the white woman ALONG WITH the white male. Let me explain.

The wandering guy, like the lonesome stranger, are both created for the purpose of attracting women. The reason the man wandered? He hadn't quite yet found himself a woman that "was to his liking" or who could "tie him down." During that "search" there were women all along the way who accepted whatever he offered. In most cases, that was money. He got what he wanted and then moved on. In other words, the white woman's acquiescence and submissiveness helped perpetuate the image of the "wandering guy." He was only weak when it came to morality, and was poor because of that same lack of morals. In the Christian ethic, work and character are closely linked; the concept of this man "wandering and being poor, then, was a reflection of his lack of ethics and morals. And yet he found a woman whenever he needed one.

In clearer terms, the ideology of gender bias was rarely resisted. Like the old-time brothers and sisters who towed the line, white women stayed out of the white man's way and allowed him to do his thing. But when it came to black people, while the line might have been towed to an extent, there was also always *a line that the white man could not cross and was not allowed to cross.* The white history books omit this fact, but even with their abuse of black history, there are still over 1,500 recorded "insurrections" against the system. That means there must have been more than 3,000.

When has the white woman ever revolted against the white man? When has she called a press conference and challenged his system? Were it not for the black-led Civil Rights and Black Power Movements, that white woman would still be wearing her hair in a bun, skirts to the ground and button-up blouses!

What does this have to do with the "secret lives of wives"? My thesis is that what these white women are doing is no secret to those they are doing it with! The reason it has been kept "on the down low" is because of the American taboo against interracial sex, the myth of sacred white womanhood, and the almost psychotic tendencies of her man to go out of his fuckin' mind at even the THOUGHT of her experiencing sexual satisfaction with anyone but HIM! And now, we have the rubber-band affect, or what could be called "the principle of the boomerang." Here is how Ali and Miller describe the situation:

> Popular culture has always been full of unfaithful wives, but even today's fictional cheaters share something that sets them apart from the tragic Anna Karenina or the calculating Mrs. Robinson. Their actions may cause their lives to unravel, but the new philanderers aren't victims. When, on the HOB series "The Sopranos," Carmella finally took a lover after putting up with her mob-boss husband's extracurricular antics for yeas, audiences cheered. (Her lover was a cad in the end, but the dalliance gave Carmella a secret source of strength.) Sarah, the heroine of this year's best-selling novel "Little Children," falls in love with a handsome stay-at-home dad she meets at the playground; the affair doesn't last, but it gives her the impetus she needs to leave her husband, a weaselly man with a fetish for the underpants of a swinger he met online.

Because their thesis about these "secrets" don't really hold muster when we apply serious historical analysis, the authors shift into the popular culture mode. They write that "popular culture has always been full of unfaithful wives" as if the mass culture is not! Popular culture is a reflection and reinforcement of the values of those who live in the general culture. Popular culture simply exaggerates what already exists. White women have been unfaithful because monogamy almost forces them to be. But technology and media sophistication have not always been what they are today. As more advances in these areas takes place, the more we will be likely to find out even more about what takes place in the white man's personal life and how the white woman deals with what takes place.

Fictional versions of female infidelity are addressed elsewhere in this paper. Let it suffice to say that those versions were the authors' ways of reaching out and expressing their resistance to monogamy. But they were far too few of them because the majority was smugly satisfied with sharing the throne of oppression with the Caucasian male.

The new popular culture roles are simply reflections of the white woman's new-found feelings of "liberation." Ali & Miller assert,

> … with her role in the 2002 movie "Unfaithful," Diane Lane created an iconic new image of a sexually adventurous wife. Beautiful and well dressed, Connie Sumner has what looks like a perfect life, and she fools around not because she's miserable but simply because she can (a decision that soon makes her life a lot less perfect). "Women always say 'thank you' for that role, and at first I wasn't sure how to take that," says Lane, who adds that the character was capable of far more denial than she could ever be. "I mean, she was cheating and lying. Then I realized it was because she wasn't a victim. She made a choice to have an affair. It's not something you often see" (Ali & Miller, 2004: 49).

Diane Lane didn't create anything. She was a woman who played a woman who went to bed with a handsome stranger from the other side of the tracks. Sound familiar? Those who controlled what her character did, from the writers (Alvin Lyne and William Broyles, Jr.) to the director (Adrian Lyne) to the guy (Claude Chabrol) who made the original film, "La Femme Infidele," put Lane right where they put all women: on her back. Then, the males who run Hollywood gave her their highest award because she expressed herself in a way that these men view women: traveling across town, taking risks, turning their backs on children and family, buying presents and fantasizing – ***just for some dick***. That's a male fantasy, one that is made possible by these fictitious characters who, in turn, are based on what the white woman's been doing all along – but has rarely been caught doing.

The "secret" affairs are not so secret then. These white women talk to their friends and their friends talk to other people and relatives. The key to making it a secret is that the white man controls the major media outlets. But even as he suppresses the general lack of morals among his race members, he nevertheless promotes it in a kind of "vicarious fantasy" mode; he wants the world to believe that he is the ultimate stud and that his woman is the paragon of beauty and sexuality. When it comes to the white woman, Karenga (1978) wrote that when it comes to the "flesh connection," these men want their women to be pristine in life and machines in bed, a paradox that he referred to as "whore-high priestess."

Even as the authors write about the Lane character in "Unfaithful" making a choice to have an affair, they then claim that "it's not something you often see." You don't see the wind either – but you know it's there. Today, we are not witnesses of the countless hundreds of thousands of rapes of Black women during slavery, but we can see the results. And so it is with the white woman; you don't see her affairs because she has the protection of the police department (many of their wives are divorcing them because of spousal abuse), the media (they protect their friends even as they focus attention on crime in black and Latinos communities), the church (which degrades her even as the white man engages in sexual perversions and child molestation in the "name of God") and most other institutions. But, as the old folks taught us, "what's done in the dark eventually comes to the light," no matter how well suppressed.

Although poorly researched from the sexual and moral standpoint, some good data was provided in the Newsweek piece. The following passage contains some relevant, though debatable, information:

> Where do married women find their boyfriends? At work,
> mostly. Nearly 60 percent of American women work outside the
> home, up from about 40 percent in 1964. Quite simply, women
> intersect with many people during the day than they used to.
> They go to more meetings, take more business trips and,
> presumably, participate more in flirtatious water-cooler chatter.
> If infidelity is an odds game, then the odds are better now than
> they used to be that a woman will accidentally bump into
> someone during the workday who, at least momentarily, interests
> her more than her husband does (Ali & Miller, 2004: 49).

And when the variable of race is interjected, we find that the concept of a "secret life" is laughable. Secret? In the citadel of gossip, the American corporation? Please. And since more than 80% of all jobs are created by small business, this makes the likelihood of an "affair" being secret all the more ludicrous. And then there is the actual "office affair," a definite no-no in the corporate world, but a reality that permeates the workplace.

So interjecting the variable of race, let us now examine the preceding claim that, "If infidelity is an odds game, then the odds are better now than they used to be that a woman will accidentally bump into someone during the workday who, at least momentarily, interests her more than her husband does." This, in my view, was one of the reasons why racial segregation in the workplace was so stringently enforced: access to black men by white women – what could happen? What happens when the crowd near the cooler includes those gossipy white women and some young brother who is well-dressed and single? I offer that when a white woman thinks of her ultimate lover, that image is not a white one; that it is a man of color on some level. And in the workplace, the people who occupy the middle positions are not white men for the most part. And the ones that do are headed upstairs via promotions. The glass ceiling, the concrete ceiling and racial discrimination keep blacks and women locked into a certain sector. And that fact increases contact and it does one more thing that could lead to an affair.

It breeds similarity of consciousness. Both groups know they are being bypassed by inferior white men, or that their boss doesn't know his ass from a hole in the ground. They know that were they white and/or male, that they would have a higher status within the corporation and more decision-making power. They would, of course, be making more money. And since, "misery loves company," one thing leads to another. These white women that Ali and Miller interviewed and talked to didn't tell everything; an affair is one thing, but an affair with a man of color is one thing that the white man simply will not tolerate.

The authors provide even more evidence that what I charge has validity when they assert,

> There's a more subtle point embedded in here as well: women and men bring their best selves to work, leaving their bad behavior and marital resentments at home with their dirty sweatpants. At work, "We dress nicely. We think before we speak. We're poised," says Elana Katz, a therapist in private practice and a divorce mediator at the Ackerman Institute for the Family in New York City. "And many people spend more time out in the world than with their families. I think sometimes people have the idea that [an affair] will protect their marriage." They get a self-esteem boost during work hours and don't rock the boat at home. "In some paradoxical sense this may be a respite, a little break from the marriage" (Ali & Miller, 2004: 49).

What is written above about speaking nice, dressing nice and leaving bad behavior at home applies doubly when it comes to black men and women in the workplace. We know we have to be "extra special" in order to compete with just average white folks. And that is the black person these white folks see: their version of the paragon, the "good black." This goes for both black men and women. And they like what they see – the feel comfortable because they don't have to fear these kinds of blacks. These are "the good ones." The white man may not feel that comfortable because he knows an Uncle Tom when he sees one. But when it comes to white women, such is not the case: they can worm their way up the ladder, sleep with the right person and in most cases, simply get cut some slack because they are white.

That is why the office affair or the rumor of one spreads so quickly. It is not because the workplace feels that it is an anomaly or quirk; it is because it is he attitudinal norm and is just a matter of degree. White women will perform oral sex much sooner in a relationship than black women will; and many of them have more courage when it comes to public displays of affection and the public "nooner" than the sister. While statistics are not yet available, there are studies that can bear out what I allege but, for the most part, the word on the street will confirm this as fact. Again, black folks know white folks better than white folks know each other.

Anecdotally speaking, a large number of black men would agree with the fact that, for the most part, the white woman is not getting the attention at home that she should be getting. In order to maintain power and position, these white men stay at the job upward of 18 hours a day, and weekends. What time they don't spend planning setbacks for those they oppress they spend working their way up the ladder to acquire more power. The white woman, held up as some kind of ideal for the world, is not the "happy camper" that she is portrayed as being. She is much more like the character on "Mary Hartman, Mary Hartman," than many ever cared to admit.

So here she is, held up as the ultimate female, the soccer mom and he Miss Universe. But she's sad and lonely because there are so many of them. After all, whites are the numerical majority in this country. They are pale and bland and the white man sees them, but he also sees the black woman. Not only is she nattily clad, but he sees the voluptuousness that accompanies those nice clothes. And don't forget this: the prostitution racket is billion dollar a year industry and it is because of the white man's lust and loneliness. This is the contemporary version of the same thing he did back on the plantation: leave his wife alone and go out and get laid elsewhere. Prostitutes from all racial and socioeconomic backgrounds are, today, what the vulnerable and powerless black enslaved woman was in the antebellum South: sexual fodder for the white man; nothing more than a sperm spittoon.

Ali and Miller offer that affairs, in some cases, provide a respite, a little break from the marriage. The white woman has a history of such "respites." In America, many of those began with her beginning to take a trip "out back" herself. The only problem with her lust for black men was that she could end up pregnant. But that didn't stop her. The history books are jammed with examples of not only the white male preying on black women to satisfy his urges, but also of the white woman having sex with black men. That is why "anti-miscegenation laws" had to be passed by the upper class white folks: they tired of seeing mulatto children running around plantations and white lust was blurring the racial hierarchy. Today, we have much the same concerns, and the same taboos still exist. But these taboos don't exist because black men are after white women or black women cannot resist the Caucasian male; it is the other way around.

Moving on to the next excerpt:

> "I wasn't out there looking for someone else," says Jodie, 34, a marketing professional in Texas and mother of two. (NEWSWEEK talked at lengthy to more thank a dozen women who cheated, and none of them wanted her real name used.) Her continuing affair with a co-worker started innocently enough. She liked his company. "We would go to lunch together and gradually it started feeling like we were dating." At Christmas, Jodie asked her husband of 10 years to join her at the office party, and when he declined, the co-worker stepped in. "We just had so much fun together and we laughed together and it just grew and grew until … he kissed me. And I loved it" (Ali & Miller, 2004: 49-50).

The problem with the methodology, interviewing only twelve women who claim to have cheated, is that all of them have every reason to watch what they say, even though they are anonymous. For example, Jodie claims that she wasn't out there looking for someone else. Can that be true? Although "not looking," she certainly lacked the moral character to resist looking indirectly, did she not? For the sake of her own sense of self-worth, she HAS to say that she was not out there looking, because to be married and to be out looking is tantamount to being a whore or a slut. No married white woman worth her salt would want to succumb to such a label.

The article attempts to rationalize or justify the relationships of these women. Notice above where after telling us that the affair "started innocently enough," there is a description of Jodie going to lunch with the man. Did she tell her husband about those lunches? Of course not. So this was the beginning of the deception, not the actual sex that took place.

Another point: Jodie asked her husband to attend a holiday party and he turned her down. After ten years of marriage, didn't she know her husband wouldn't be interested? So the request was just a matter of social courtesy, a way of letting him know that indeed, she would be going out. If she really wanted him to go she could have purchased him a shirt, a suit or used her feminine wiles to let him know she REALLY needed him there. She did none of these things; the request was for appearances only.

So she gets to the party. And the article says that, "The co-worker stepped in." Did she inform her husband that there was someone else who would accompany her? No. Did the husband care? Evidently not. How did the worker know she'd be available? Did she phone him? How did she get his home phone number? Was the co-worker married? If not, why was she going out with him in the first place? These are the issues that the article intentionally avoids to ensure that the reader won't see the white female for what she really is. Not only is she lascivious, she is also conniving and manipulative.

They had fun together and "it just grew and grew until …" It grew because she allowed it to. These relationships can only go as far as the woman allows it because, in American culture, it is the woman who does the "choosing." She is the one who has to agree to go out on the date, she determines what kind of date it will be and she is the one who decides when there will sex. Oh sure, they can make it APPEAR as if it is the man who is calling the shots, but that is only because women know men have frail egos. But in reality, she is setting the table and determining what takes place, when and where.

By the time she tells the writers that "she loved" his kiss, she was really in love with him. The way she describes what happens proves that. The kiss was just her way of allowing him to know that it was time to move to the next level. This woman was tired of her husband and was simply acting on her real feelings. Monogamy, once again, is not a marital system that is conducive to human nature.

Ali and Miller continue:

> It's not just opportunity that fuels the impulse to be unfaithful; it's money and power as well. American women are better educated than they've ever been. A quarter of tem earn more money than their husbands. A paycheck and a 401(k) don't guarantee that a woman will stray, but if she does, they minimize the fallout both for her and for her children. The feminist Gloria Steinem once said, "Most women are one man away from welfare," but she recently amplified her views to NEWSWEEK: "Being able to support one-self allows one to choose a marriage out of love and not just economic dependence. It also allows one to risk that marriage." In other words, as women grow more powerful, they're more likely to feel, as men traditionally have, that they deserve a little bit of nooky at the end (or in the middle) of a long, busy day (Ali & Miller, 2004: 50).

The writers say that not only does opportunity fuel the impulse to be unfaithful, but money and power as well. The fact is, the writers have not established that being unfaithful is an "impulse" at all; they have shown, on the contrary, that most of them begin as being an attraction and then, after some time, the sex takes place. Is that what being "impulsive" means? No, it is not. An "impulse" is defined as, "an instinctive motive," or, "a sudden desire." If it takes time for something to be "fueled" by money, opportunity and power, that is not something that is "impulsive." Women who have affairs in closets at the spur of the moment, or who end up in a hotel room with someone they just met, THAT's impulse. But for the most part, these white women like that idea, but it is not the approach that brings them the kind of emotional security they crave.

For the most part, they plan. As stated earlier, women CHOOSE men, not the reverse. She might have an initial desire for a man based on physical attraction, and that may lead to sex, but the authors trivialize and down play how manipulative these white women are when they frame what takes place in such a way. For instance, greed and lust are at the base of the decisions these women make. So no matter how they act, the impulse for acquire money or sex is already there. The attitude precedes the act. There is nothing impulsive about the behaviors of a woman who has fantasized about having sex with someone she is not married to; her husband is a constant reminder that she needs some "outside lovin'." And that's the name of that tune.

Ali and Miller write that of their small and non-representative sample, "a quarter of them earn more money than their husbands. A paycheck and a 401(k) don't guarantee that a woman will stray, but if she does, they minimize the fallout both for her and for her children." The preceding statement says a great deal about the perceptions that these writers have about marriage. And, in fact, they might have a point. The white man and white woman, even as they point the fingers at other races of people, have always had issues with one another. And, in realizing that, it makes sense that a paycheck and a 401(k) would play a role in keeping them together. For far too many of them, it's all about the money.

And why shouldn't it be? Have many of them ever had to struggle the way people of color have? Have any of them ever faced the stigma of isolation and neglect based on a physical characteristic that they were born with? The fat white person, the handicapped white person or the physically deformed white person is still white in a majority white society. And in that context, skin color trumps ANY other physical variable.

And in regard to Gloria Steinem's statement that, "Most women are one man away from welfare," she stole that saying from black people and modified it to fit her racist needs. This woman, a key cog in the Feminist movement, was as racist as any white man; when she used the word "women," she was speaking about white women. What Bell Hooks says about Betty Friedan also applies to Steinem:

> It appears that Friedan never wondered whether or not the plight
> of college-educated, white housewives was an adequate

reference point by which to gauge the impact of sexism or sexist oppression on the lives of women in American society. Nor did she move beyond her own life experience to acquire an expanded perspective on the lives of women in the United States (Hooks, 1984).

The Women's Liberation movement then, was about white women. Once again, the sisters were left out but indeed, had been involved in a liberation movement of their own for decades. The point being made here is simple enough: when these people write articles about "women," they are essentially writing about polls, surveys and interviews about and of white women. They then believe that what applies to white women is generalizable and fits ALL women. Nothing could be further from the truth.

`The article then deals with the power of being able to support one's self and how that enables one to choose a marriage out of love and not just economic dependence, and it allows one to risk that marriage. Two points of clarification are in order.

First of all, money gives someone options and the more options one has, the more choices, the more freedom. Bell Hooks defines oppression as, "the absence of choices." In the case of these women having affairs, the writers are saying that the more money they have gives one the option of marrying for love, not just economic dependence. As if this culture differentiates between the two.

For instance, look how they define love. You meet someone and the first thing the woman expects the man to do is shell out money for what they call a "date." It may be in the day or night, but during the second date, even MORE money is spent. These white women, even when they do have money, still fall prey to this whole "romantic love" myth. In other words, they have free sexual choice: they can date any man of color, the white man, or play the bisexual game. Or they go the lesbian route. Because of the pervasiveness of white privilege, a reality that even the most least talented white woman has taken advantage of, they don't go into dating situations at a disadvantage no matter what their socioeconomic status. Most of them CAN support themselves and their greed still puts them in positions of FAKING dependency.

Choosing a marriage out of "love"? What is that? That is a Eurocentric invention. Most of the world deals with economic realities, arranged marriages and the like. These white people want to talk about emotion and love and what they are really talking about is sex. This is a point the Newsweek writers overlooked.

Secondly, the statement about economic independence being able to allow one to risk their marriage. If these women are risking their marriages, then their problem is not one of how much economic independence they have or are willing to risk. It is a matter of them attempting to break away from and out of a monogamous marital system that is restrictive and harmful. Again, the writers view monogamous marriage as a "universal norm" and then define infidelity as a deviation from that norm. In reality, monogamous marriage is the problem and deviation from it is seen, at least by me, as a sign of good mental health.

So the white woman, who is working alongside her man in the workplace, is seeking to be free from the constricting bonds of monogamous marriage. So she – and this culture – are being disingenuous when they call deviation from this marriage form "infidelity." The white woman is simply acting in accord with her nature. Among all the world's women, she is easily the most lascivious, even when her "man" imposes ideological and societal constraints on her. She will find a way to achieve orgasm in some way and with some creature.

And yet the authors don't investigate the possibility that my statements could be correct. Instead, to them, it's a matter of "entitlement." Ali and Miller posit make the following observations:

> And like their fathers before them, these powerful women are learning to savor the attentions of companion who is physically attractive but not as rich, successful – or as old –as they are. In his practice in Palo Alto, Calif., family therapist Marty Klein sees a rise in sexual activity between middle-paged women and younger men. "Forty-year women have more of a sense of entitlement to their sexuality than they did before the 'Hite Report,' the feminist movement and 'Sex and the City,'" he says (Ali & Miller, 2004: 50).

Before moving on, let us deal briefly with the preceding comments regarding these 40 year old white women and the so-called "feminist movement."

The authors say that, like their fathers before them, these women are learning to savor the attentions of men who are younger than they are. But in order truly understand why this is taking place, the authors should have documented OTHER ways that these women are like their fathers. For instance, the fact that they buy into their father's racist ways, and how they refuse to fight against the glass ceiling as long as they have personal wealth. The way that they see themselves as the center of the universe and the rest of the world, no matter how impoverished, be damned. These are the attributes that create the attitude that Ali and Miller are describing. An attitude of what Haki Madhubuti once referred to as "mefirstness." And as Karenga (1967) once said, "individualism is a white desire; cooperation is a black need."

The "rise in sexual activity between middle-aged women and younger men" that Ali and Miller refer to is no "rise" in my book. It is an extension of what has taken place all along. After all, those white women have been going to bed with black men, behind their husbands' backs, for centuries. They just didn't get caught. But the fact is, these women can be found in black bars, black lounges and black events more than the public thinks. And here's something else: show me a white woman who has a black friend or best friend, and I'll show you a white woman who will, sooner or later, screw a friend or relative of that black woman. In many cases, that's how it works.

And today, the young white girl is at it at an even great pace. One 2003 movie titled, "Thirteen" deals with a hard-headed teenager, her friend, and how the yearn to be cool by being around those deemed cool: young black males. Let me take a minute to deal with this movie and show the impact that the young white girl's activities with black boys is having on society, in general.

In this movie, a young girl, Tracy, is lead astray by another, more wayward teen by the name of Evie. Evie smokes dope, drinks, has sexual experience with boys and influences Tracy. They become close and Evie moves in with Tracy whose mother, Melanie, is one of those "cool moms" who smokes weed, tries to act as young as her daughter, and is not paying attention to the way that Evie is changing Tracy. Behind the close door of their bedroom, these girls perform a number of wayward acts as their mother and her boyfriend have sex in other parts of the house; they experiment with tongue kissing each other, they smoke cigarettes, sneak out of the window to meet black boys in other parts of the city, get drunk – just about the gamut.

The point that is most pertinent here is that the boys that these white girls were meeting were black. In fact, Evie was "going with" one of them and in one scene, she and her boyfriend are making out while Tracy and her black acquaintance do the same. What Tracy sees Evie do, she does. In other scenes in the movie, they get high with these black boys, Tracy goes ballistic when one black boy asks for her phone number, and in another scene, they lay back, getting high in some park, making out with these same brothers.

Heres' the point: white society would be ashamed of these girls. Black parents would be ashamed of the black boys as well, but we're not talking about the "infidelity" of black boys or their sexual behaviors. For better or for worse, it's not the same for boys as it is for girls. When you're talking about white girls however, you're talking about the genetic future of a white society. If they don't have babies for the white man, all is lost. That is why these white parents want to control, to as great an extent as possible, the sexual activities of these miniature snow bunnies.

As evidence of this, look at the words of my favorite movie reviewer, Roger Ebert. No one is more honest or observant than Ebert, who has reviewed movies for decades. Following is how he describes the scenes where the girls are dating, making out and getting high with young black dudes:

> There are moments when you want to cringe at the danger these girls are in. They slip through the bedroom window and hang out on Hollywood Boulevard, they experiment sexually with kids older and tougher than they are, they all but rape "Luke the lifeguard boy" (Kip Pardue), a neighbor who accuses them, accurately, of being jail bait. They want to fly close to danger without getting hurt, and we wait for them to learn how hard and cruel the world can be (Ebert, 2003).

Take note of how the kid "Luke" is mentioned. That scene only lasts a few minutes, and Kip is a white boy. But when it comes to the black guys that these girls are making out and getting high with, their names are not mentioned and there is no mention of their racial background. Why? Because Roger Ebert knows that if those reading his reviews know that this movie includes interracial dating and implied sex, they will not go see it. So he leaves something to the imagination by writing that the white girls, "experiment sexually with kids older and tougher than they are." What makes these guys so tough when all they were shown doing was standing on street corners "rapping" and singing?

The fact that they were black teens, that's what. Ebert does what society in general does: puts a positive spin on a known taboo. As Richard Pryor's junkie character says to the wino in one skit, "Tell me some more of them lies of yours so I can stop thinkin' about the truth!"

The fact is, today's white girls are meeting young black men at this urban malls because their parents don't like black people. Young black men are cruising all over the community in these white girls' sports cars. These young men are sneaking out into their homes while the white girls' parents are at work or "on vacation." And this isn't just "white trash;" it's these well-to-do suburban girls that are turned on by black culture.

These white girls know white boys are squares, and they know that they like the way black people dance and carry themselves. They want to be a part of that. This may sound simplistic, but most of what is taking place in society is just that – simple. It is only when the white man comes along to "complicate" things and make things complex with his statistics and social scientists, that the problems are able to persist and remain unsolved.

A "rise." If my back is turned and someone is raping a woman behind my back, five or six times a day, then I turn around and look, and he continues at the same pace, there has been no "rise" in the numbers of times he raped her. *It's just that for the first time, I'm taking notice.* Same thing with the white woman and her sexual appetite, her so-called "feminist liberation" and her long-time lust for someone "tall, dark and handsome."

The doctor quoted in the preceding passage offers up a story that he heard regarding the infidelity of one woman:

> A story currently circulating in Manhattan underscores his point. It seems that a group of 6-year-old girls from an elite private school were at a birthday party, and the conversation turned to their mommies' trainers. As the proud mothers listened nearby, one youngster piped up: "My mommy has a trainer, and every time he comes over, they take a nap." The wicked laughter this story elicits illustrates at least what is dreamed of, if not actually consummated (Ali & Miller, 2004: 50).

Again, this information falls short of linking what took place to the reality of the situation. As Jesse Jackson once said, "a text out of context is a pretext."

In the first place, the fact that these women have "trainers" and the white man allows this says something in itself. These women have idle time, are at the house and have money. Then they go out and hire male trainers. Does this sound as if the white man really cares? At this point, the marriage is probably nothing more than a façade, anyway. Why is she working out? So she can maintain her "trophy wife" image for someone who she probably is not even sleeping with. So the idea of this being an "affair" is, at best, ambiguous.

Secondly, the fact that these women would allow the children to be around when the carried on with these trainers, and that the trainers would be present while the child was home. This shows, again, the white woman's own carelessness and lack of commitment to the institution of marriage. A related factor is that the child knows that the mother and the trainer are "taking a nap" – this means she observed them going into the bedroom. Who was watching the child during that time? So this woman, whoever she is, is not only a whore, but she's also guilty of child neglect. Far too often, the two work hand-in-hand as the gigolo, who doesn't give a shit anyway, views the children as an obstruction and has little problem convincing the horny housewife to just "leave him/her out here with some toys."

Third and finally, this marriage is over so no real "affair" is taking place. If that child is sharing observations with other children, in the presence of adults, it is only a matter of time before one of those children – or one of those adults – shares that information with someone else. The key to being "unfaithful" is keeping it quiet; it's not infidelity if everybody, including the husband knows about it. And is sho' ain't no affair if the husband knows and just don't give a shit. That means HE'S out messing around, too!

But on the subject of "trainers" and getting in shape, one article makes it clear that, "it seems that fitness centers themselves are becoming more than just a place to get in shape as busy people seek social and entertainment value, too (Aksamit, 2004: 1E). Continuing:

> Randy McGlothlin, a 48-year-old from Honey Creek, Iowa, loves the social part of is daily workouts, which he says involve about one hour of exercise and a half hour of gabbing. In the fie years he's been a member of Gold's Gym near 108th and Maple Streets, diner engagements and other social events have evolved from chatting with regulars. "You begin to see people on a regular basis, you introduce yourself, and you just get a chance to socialize," McGlothlin says. "This is one of the few places to do that, except for the bars. In fact, I'd say some people come here and don't really work out that much" (Aksamit, 2004: 1E).

The setting is not really the issue. If someone doesn't want to sit around with or be faithful to someone, then that's a secondary fact as well. It's a matter of "love the one you're with" in far too many cases. And the reason for this is, once again, that the concept of monogamous marriage is not healthy. And when you try to force-fit it onto the values of a nation of sluts and man-whores, what you get is "fuckfest 2004." And these values mean that affairs are going to take place in bars, in the gym, in the back seat of a car, on elevators or in the bathrooms of airplanes.

And yet, despite my street logic and grass roots common sense about these white women and how they manipulate their marriages, the authors want to use anecdotal evidence, wild conjecture, and bullshit in their attempts to justify their claims. For instance, take note of the following excerpt:

> The road to infidelity is paved with unmet expectations about sex, love and marriage. A woman who is 40 today grew up during the permissive 1970s and went to college when the dangers of AIDS were just beginning to dawn. She was sexually experienced before she was married and waited five years longer than her mother to settle down;. She lives in a culture that constantly flaunts the possibility of great sex and fitness well after menopause. "Great Lovers Are Made, Not Born!" read the ads for sex videos in her favorite magazines; "What if the only night seats you had came from a good workout?" ask the ads for estrogen therapy (Ali & Miller, 2004: 50-51).

The preceding excerpt clearly shows that the conclusions of the 1968 Kerner Report – the part about us living in "two societies, one black, one white, separate and unequal" -- also applies today in the areas of social analysis and personal perceptions of reality. Let's check out the preceding and I'll show you why this is the case.

The writers say that the expectations about sex, love and marriage are "unmet;" the fact, is, these expectations are "unrealistic." And because they are unrealistic, they cannot be achieved on a long-term level, hence the on-going instances of infidelity and adultery.

The writers talk of a woman who grew up during the "permissive 1970s." The fact is, white women were licentious even during the most conservative of periods, dating at very least back to the days of England the so-called "chastity belt." These white folks bought those so-called "puritanical" values over here, but that didn't stop the white woman. And she continued on, accepting the sexism but still sneaking and skulking around in order to gain some semblance of sexual satisfaction. She might have worn the long dress, the petticoat and all of that clothing – even on the hottest of days – but she found ways to pass her time when her husband ignored her.

But she is spared the TRUE reports on her licentiousness because her man is the one who writes the psychology, history and sexuality texts. He spares her because he is too busy propping up himself; if he divulges the truth about what she's done behind closed doors or how she's violated so-called wedding vows, he would be exposing his own inadequacies. So it's a trade-off, much like the homosexual who marries a lesbian so they can appear to be a couple in public while actually indulging in their true desires on "the downlow." The white man has been on the downlow for centuries. And now, thanks to the media, we see that the white woman has, as well.

The writers mention attending college and how this woman of the 1970s was "sexually experienced before she was married." That's where the black men come in! Disproportionately high numbers of these white coeds are using college, not only as a "marriage market," but also as a time to experiment with the black penis. Look at all these white girls who are latching onto black star athletes. The list is longer than Yao Ming's arm. They are on these campuses and they are going to parties and leaving those parties with black men. They do these brothers' homework, loan out their cars and allow them to use their credit cards. All of this behind their parents' backs. This has taken place on every single college campus of any merit in this country. But Ali and Miller don't want the truth: they are too busy documenting some fantasy-oriented anecdotes from the TWELVE women they interviewed!

These writers concentrate on the "married mother," the soccer mom who may be sneaking around. These writers paint the role of a victim who has few options. For instance, read the following

> At the same time, she's so busy she feels constantly out of
> breath. If she's a professional, she's working more hours than her
> counterpart of 20 years ago – and trying to rush home in time to
> give the baby a bath. If she's a stay-at-home mom, she's driving
> the kids to more classes, more games, more play-dates than her
> mother did, not to mention trying to live up to society's demands
> of perfect momhood: Buy organic? Be supportive, not
> permissive! Lose five pounds (Ali & Miller, 2004: 51).

The white woman is busy doing the work that has to be done to maintain what is essentially a suburban/segregated lifestyle. She is contributing to the white supremacy structure. She is supporting the man who is the most domineering and racist man on the planet. And she knows full well what she is doing. She cannot, on any level, compare with the black woman or the Latina who goes to work every day, does the things the white woman does and much more, and THEN go to community meetings to offset some of the problems created by the husband of this white female.

She feels constantly out of breath? From doing what? Riding around in a new car, perhaps cleaning a large house in the suburbs while the kids play in a huge back yard? Please. These white women don't have a CLUE as to what it is to be out of breath. These two writers, Ali and Miller, need to follow some of these sisters around and watch what they have to do around the house, oftentimes WITHOUT the aid of a husband. And then, on top of that, they have to go to work and deal with the finicky and racist attitudes of their bosses. And it gets worse:

> As difficult as the employment prospects are for African
> American males, they are less severe in many ways to the
> challenges that confront women of color. According to the
> research of the Women's Action coalition, an alliance
> representing thousands of women founded in 1992, gender
> discrimination especially affects black women and other women
> of color in the workplace at all levels. About three-fourths of all
> U.S. women who work full-time earn under $20,000 annually,
> compared to only one-third of all U.S. male workers. The
> Women's Action Coalition notes that "the average salary of an
> African American female college graduate in a full-time position
> is less than that of a white male high school dropout (Marable,
> 2004: 9).

The white woman's condition, as emotionally pitiful as it might be, doesn't even come close to comparing to the drudgery and denial that the black woman is experiencing – and the white woman knows it. That's why the sisters were excluded from the feminist movement: these white women knew well that there was nothing they could tell black women, women who had to watch while white women swooped on black men!

Check out the reality that Bell Hooks paints about these liberated white women, these "poor witto white soccer moms" and how racist they really are when stripped of all the pomp and impious ceremony:

> …. Frequently, white feminists act as if black women did not know sexist oppression existed until they voiced feminist sentiment. They believe they are providing black women with "the" analysis and "the ' program for liberation. They do not understand, cannot even imagine that black women, as well as other groups of women who live daily in oppressive situations, often acquire an awareness of patriarchal politics from their lived experience just as they develop strategies of resistance (even though they may not resist on a sustained or organized basis) (p. 140).

Is this white woman, or is she not, an ideological clone of her man? But the key to remember is this: these white women and their adulterous affairs are nothing new. Black women, who have cleaned more than their share of these women's homes, have seen the white woman for what she really is. Nobody knows the slave master better than the enslaved. The authors, blinded by their commitment to sensationalism and a paycheck, seem to have ignored this fact.

Moving on:

> Her husband isn't a gad guy, but he's busier than ever, too, working harder just to stay afloat. And (this is practically unmentionable) therapists say they're seeing more cases of depressed male libido. It turns out HE'S too tired and stressed to have sex. An affair is a logical outcome of this scenario, therapists say: women think they should be having great sex and romantic dates decades into their marriage, and at the same time, they're pragmatic enough to see how impossible that is. Couples begin to live parallel lives instead of intersecting ones, and that's when the loneliness and resentment set in (Ali & Miller, 2004: 51).

The key to depressed male libido is the motivation BEHIND working more than ever before: the inability to deal with women who are breaking away from the traditional sex role socialization! There is nothing secret or complex about the fact that women are physically and sexually superior to men. That is why the white man spends billions every year creating mythical images of the "white male stud" even as he is losing contact with the female gender more and more with each passing day. Black men are not much better, but we HAVE no jobs to run to! And one reason could be that because this European eunuch is so angry at his feelings of inadequacy that he takes that frustration out on us at the workplace!

The reason why "couples begin to live parallel lives instead of intersecting ones" is simple: the institution of marriage is just that – an institution! Other than for the reasons of giving kids a name, I don't see any value in monogamous marriage. These expectations of romantic love lasting forever is the reason why so many people get disappointed. That is why these white women are on the prowl, lounging in bars, going to clubs with their faces all painted off, and that is who this expensive underwear is being made (Victoria's Secret, Frederick's of Hollywood). She's hanging out with her friends in the name of "girls night out," he's hanging out with the guys in the name of "boys night out" and both are out to do essentially the same thing: re-establish their feelings of attractiveness and sexuality by flirting with – and having sex with – people outside of the marriage.

But even in all that, this woman is made out to be a victim, not of a narrow minded social institution called "marriage," but of the man that she took a vow to "love and honor." The following passage is yet another example of the authors missing the proverbial boat:

> Marisol can't remember the last time her husband paid her a compliment. That's why the 38-year-old grandmother, who was pregnant and married at 15, looks forward to meeting with her boyfriend of five years during lunch breaks and after work. "There is so much passion between us," she says. "He tells me my skin is soft and that my hair smells good. I know it sounds stupid, but that stuff matters. It makes me feel sexy again" (Ali & Miller, 2004: 51).

Marisol's situation is more understandable: she was a slut from the get-go. She got married and then her daughter, borrowing from the mother, becomes a teen mother as well. So she's a 38 year old grandmother and she's not getting the attention she feels she deserves from her husband. But it is clear that the need for this attention from her husband, and probably the reason why she got married in the first place, was to make up for the attention she evidently didn't get from HER mother. So it only stands to reason that as the husband is out working, she's going to be overwhelmed by somebody telling her how good her hair smells. She was out of control as a child and got talked out her panties by someone probably older. As they say, like mother, like daughter.

The fact is, she never experienced true teenaged life. She didn't get to have all the fun the other white girls had because she was taking care of a child. Now, as an adult about to enter her '40s, she wants to make up for what she lost. She probably feels the inbred restrictions that monogamous marriage carries with it, and she wants to be free; so free that there is no doubt her daughter will carry on the tradition. What she calls "passion" is just that: not love, not concern – just animal lust. As she says, "it makes me feel sexy again." She's reduced herself to its lowest denominator possible: raw animal instinct. And since she's been at it for five years, it's clear that she doesn't give a shit about her daughter or her husband. Why didn't the writers entertain THESE core issues?

The "strategy and tactics" that the writers proceed to provide are nothing but smokescreens for the real issues; the constraints of monogamous marriage, the fact that white women have been getting away with this for centuries, and the reality that the white man – the husband – is either doing the same thing or just doesn't give a shit. Their thesis seems to be that the husband doesn't know what is going on. The white man may be dense, but even he can sense when his wife's had another man's dick in her mouth.

Here is what Ali and Miller had to say:

> Ironically, the realities of the over-programmed life make it easier, not harder, to fool around. When day are planned to the minute, it's a cinch to pencil in a midday tryst – and remember to wear the lace-edged underwear – at least compared with trying to stay awake an in the mood through "Law and order." And as any guileless teenager knows, nothing obscures your whereabouts better than an Internet connection and a reliable cell phone. Amanda's husband has no idea she has six e-mail addresses, in addition to an account specifically for messages from her boyfriend Ron. Amanda, a customer-service rep in L.A., uses e-mail to flirt with Ron, then turns to her instant messenger or cell phone when it comes to setting up a rendezvous. "Text messaging is safer than e-mailing," says Amanda, 36, who's been married for eight years. What would she do without her mobile or computer? "No cell phone? I can't even imagine" (Ali & Miller, 2004: 51).

The thesis that, "the realities of the over-programmed life make it easier, not harder, to fool around" is sheer conjecture. Not only that, but for everybody who is playing around, there is somebody who is being played around ON. That person can take the technology that these women are talking about and use it to trap the person who is committing adultery. The hotels that the people meet at have video cameras; they have to sign documents in order to meet at such places. The advent of the computer and the credit card can trace wherever people eat, sleep and socialize. The resources that the present-day detective and private eye have at their disposal, if called, to "follow" a spouse or a girl friend. I believe that these women might be playing around, but I believe most of them don't care if they get caught. If this were not the case, they would be considering the kinds of facts that I am discussing.

Ali and Miller claim that it's a cinch to pencil in a midday tryst. Again, it's not the tryst that is the issue or the penciling in of a fake appointment to cover up behind it; it's the overriding ideology of "one mate for all time" that scares the hell out of some people and dupes the rest into believing that marriage is some kind of cure-all for society's ills. Even as I write these words, the Republican Convention is taking place and these white folks are talking about "values" and about "family." These are the descendants of a race of people that made slavery legal, that made separation of the races a matter of public policy. In other words, they have no credibility; they are, in turn, the progeny of people who denied women basic human rights and maintained a double standard for over two centuries.

And look what all that white male domination has wrought: a system where grownups feel the need to take vows of marriage and have to swear to stick with each other no matter how sick one mate gets. This is a society where human beings – in this case women – have to "pencil in" fake appointments (translation: lie) in order to "keep whole" their obviously deteriorating "commitments" to someone else. Women being unfaithful is not the problem – the problem is monogamous marriage. Don't hate the player – hate the game!

Some woman named Amanda uses her emails to flirt with Ron and makes dates using her cell phone. Why all the bother? Take that email and locate a good attorney. Use that phone and tell your husband you don't love him and that he can have the kids. Why all the game-playing? In the first place, it is clear she no longer respects her husband because she is keeping a secret from him. Secondly, it is clear that she prefers the company of someone else. Why then live a lie? Why pretend and hurt someone in the process? Why not be an adult, sit down, tell your husband how inadequate he is, and then divide up the assets?

The problem with Amanda, age 36, is that she loves her text messaging and her phone more than she loves her husband. Her "boyfriend" Ron is getting the best of both worlds: he has her in his bed only when he bothers to respond to the text messages and phone calls. She then takes his semen back to her husband, who is left out in the cold. In a manner of speaking, Ron is screwing them BOTH. Is that any way to be?

More information on the "technology of adultery," as it should be called, is provided in the following assertions:

> Along with its 4 million porn sites, the Internet has exploded
> with sites specifically for people who want to cheat on their

spouses – sites like "Married and Flirting" at Yahoo, "a chat room dedicated to those who are married but curious, bored or both!!" These sites contain all the predictable pornographic overtures, but also such poignant notes as this: "Ok, I know it is late almost 11:30 my time, and I am still up on this pitiful Friday night. Hubby STILL at work" (Ali & Miller, 2004: 51—emphasis original).

Racist is what racist does. The problem is not the porn sight, but the mentality and attitude that gave rise to the porn sights. What you find is what the white man has concocted. While people of color might emulate it, can there be any doubt that this society's number one pervert is the white male? Can there also be any doubt that this society's number one slut, in sheer numbers alone, is the white female? And on the college campus, known as "higher education" just visit one and observe who you see acting like some barroom floozie from days gone by: its that white suburban coed who is away from home for the first time and who can now literally and figuratively, "let it all hang out."

The Yahoo chat room mentioned in the poorly researched article quoted from above is but the tip of an iceberg, a reflection of a society that is rooted in hedonism and perversity. All that the white race was in England is what you see now: land-obsessed, money hungry and perverted. Sure, they point the finger and attempt to blame their mythical creations such as Suzy Wong, black Sapphire, Pocahontas or Charo. But these women of color do not come close to approximating the numbers of white women who are making a living selling sexual favors. Many of them are prostitutes. Most of then, however, can be found under the heading of "housewife."

The authors outline more components of what could probably be called, "cyber-affairs:"

Online romances have a special appeal for married women. For one thing, you don['t have to leave the house. "You can come home from work, be exhausted, take a shower, have wet, dripping hair, have something fast to eat and the, if you're feeling lonely, you can go on the Internet," says Rona Subotnik, a marriage and family therapist in Palm Desert, Calif. On the Web, women can browse and flirt without being explicit about their intentions – if they even know what their intentions are (Ali & Miller, 2004: p 51).

If on-line romances have a special appeal for married women, this says more about the marriage than it does about the power of being "on-line," don't you think? As for not knowing that their intentions are, there is no doubt that they know. Even if its just what white people call "innocent flirting" (the black people I know don't play that), it's still an act that shows that what you've got is just not quite cutting it. So you wink, you brush up against someone, you give a smile. White women (and others) have been getting away with this for centuries. Many have gotten killed for it. But there is nothing to it until you interject that elusive variable of "marriage," "walking down the aisle," "jumping the broom."

Monogamous marriage forces the participants to go against their very nature. They marry while young and naïve in some cases, or marry for the economic security in other instances. This lasts for a while, but then you begin to think about it: waking up and going to sleep with the same person night in and night out. You look for outlets and in the age of technology, you find one: the internet. But it is a sad alternative because there is so much risk involved. The intentions cannot be anything even remotely honorable, because no matter how you dress it up or "eroticize" it, it's still going behind somebody's back who you swore you'd honor and respect.

Ali & Miller add that,

> Clicking past porn, women prefer to visit sites that dovetail with their interests such as chess, bridge or knitting, explains Peggy Vaughan, author of "The Monogamy Myth" and host of dearpeggy.com, a Web site for people with unfaithful spouses. "They find somebody else who seems to think like they do, and then they gradually move from that to an instant message, and then they wake up one day and they cannot believe it happened to them," says Vaughan (Ali & Miller, 2004: 51).

The system needs marriage because in order to do it, you have to purchase a marriage license. Marriages are expensive and this helps the economy. Marriage is the biggest racket in America. For this reason, it is therefore logical to use the Christian religion to push this "one man for one woman forever" madness. The fact that it doesn't work doesn't stop Hollywood and the rest of the media from publishing and promoting these bullshit stories that end with "happily ever after."

Moving from this, we find pimps who take advantage of those who are becoming aware of the shallowness of monogamous marriage. That is where people like the aforementioned come up with websites like those mentioned; that is why they write books. They may or may not believe in monogamous marriage, but being the pimps that they are, they know there is a growing audience that is SICK of being forced to marry someone and these people with the websites and the books are simply playing to that market.

What is described – moving gradually from finding someone to writing them an instant message and waking up not believing it can happen to them – is the same thing that happens with the myth of "romantic love"! Meet, eat, go to a movie, an evening date, and then have sex. How can you really get to know someone after even two or three years of this kind of shallow activity? And isn't the fact that over half of all marriage end in divorce yet another sign that monogamous marriage is going the way of the dinosaur, the pet rock and Beatle boots?

Women, labeled as being adulterers or being guilty of "infidelity," are just waking up to the marriage scam a lot faster than men. Again, Ali and Miller:

> Last year Vaughan did a survey of a thousand people who visited her Web site, and 70 percent of the respondents were women. Her results, though not scientific, are remarkable: 79 percent said they were not looking for love online. More than half said they met their online lover in person, and about half said the relationship culminated in sex. Sixty-percent said their spouses had no idea (Ali & Miller, 2004: 51-52).

Again, Ali and Miller rely on anecdotal evidence and conjecture. Also, by their own admission, the "survey" that they quote from are not scientific. So of what use then, is their article? A shrunken sample of twelve women, citations of irrelevant data, and quotes from women who have expertise in nothing more than sneaking around behind their husband's backs is what this Newsweek article was all about. But Newsweek is well-read and any chance people get to offer rebuttal must be seized. Hence, this counter-document.

This article is piecemeal, but does answer one thing: why the number of women being murdered is on the rise. Look at the preceding quote: 60% of the women on the internet said their husbands had no idea that they were having relationships on line which extended into real life. But guess what happened to the other 40%? Those are the ones whose husbands DID find out, and that is why so many women are checking into battered shelters and why so many morgues are filling up with female bodies. Think about it.

On the other hand, some women actually get fed up and just get away. Check out one example provided in the Newsweek piece:

> John LaSage was shocked to come home one day and find his wife of 24 years had disappeared. No note, no phone call, nothing. He'd bought her a computer four months previously, he says, and he knew something was wrong: she'd stay up until 3 or 4 a.m. browsing online. She told him she was doing research for a romance novel she was writing, he says, and after her disappearance, he hacked into the computer to investigate. "She had set up a chat room that was called … gosh … 'Smooth

Legs.' And so guys would come in there and flirt with her. I have transcripts. I can't tell you how excruciating it was to read the e-mails from people supposedly speaking with my wife, but she wasn't talking like my wife. That was just weird." Two weeks later he discovered she had left the country, he says, "I wasn't the perfect husband. I would have done a lot of things differently, but I never got the chance," says LaSage, who has since founded an online support group (chatcheaters.com) for people with spouses who stray (Ali & Miller, 2004: 52).

This scenario is worthy of some response.

First of all, John and his wife had been married for 24 years – more than enough time to realize the limitations of monogamous marriage. John purchased her a computer, and then began seeing signs of her wandering. When a married person is up until three or four in the morning, while the partner is sleeping, something is not right in most cases. When she told him she was writing a romance novel, that was his cue to offer her some "primary research sources" and start getting romantic. Did he? No. Only a white man would sit and smile while his woman stays up until the wee hours, claims to be writing a novel, and then not ask to see one single page of that book!

It's all about the white male ego: "it can't happen to me." And it's not as if he's making love to her all the time in every position. These white men think that because they buy her a diamond, then her own car and a home, or because they act "progressive" by watching as she roams the streets, that this is somehow a sign of "love." Just because she's accepting all these gratuities in no way means she's in love – it just means she's greedy as hell.

The hacking that this naïve man did after his wife left should have perhaps been done when she could not produce one page of the novel she was supposedly writing. Why, for instance, does she have her own private computer, anyway? Why can't they share? There has to be more to this story because there are gaps – either that, or John is the stupidest man on earth.

Indeed, he finds that she has a chat room called "Smooth Legs" and he reads what men were writing to his wife. He says that "she wasn't talking like my wife." No, she wasn't. He frames the statement incorrectly by saying that she wasn't talking like his wife. She was a woman before she became his wife. These white man – and far too many black men as well – think that having a "wife" means that the woman believes in the definitions of what a wife is. That marriage vow presents an illusion and serves as a façade for what will inevitably come to surface: the cry for freedom. She wasn't "talking like" his wife because she hadn't been his wife for a long time. He was married to his own sexist ideas of what a wife is supposed to be. And she wasn't having it.

He finds out she left the country and I'm willing to bet you it wasn't for or with another white man. She decides to start an online support group called "chatcheaters.com," because he knows he's not the only one out there. These white males need to undo all this ego and base what they feel on what they see and receive – not on what they're told. The fact is, she is just as deceptive as he has historically been.

We then move from incredibly bland case studies to a bit of history – or at least the superficial and spurious versions presented by Ali and Miller:

> In 1643 Mary Latham, who was 18 years old and married, was hanged in Massachusetts with her lover James Britton. Since then, adultery has been a crime in many states. A woman accused of adultery could, in divorce, court, lose her home, her income and her children. All that changed in the 1970s, when most states adopted "no fault" and "equitable distribution" divorce laws, in which nearly all the assets accrued to either partner during the marriage belong to the marriage and, in a divorce settlement, are split evenly. And unless a woman (or man) has been flagrantly or inappropriately sexual in front of the children, or has, in the frenzy of an affair, neglected them, infidelity does not legally affect settlements or custody. In researching her book "The Price of Motherhood," journalist Ann Crittenden found, however, that an implicit bias against female adultery still prevails in the country's predominantly male courtrooms – and that when it came to settlements, that bias was costly to women. "There may be no fault as grounds, but fault has not left the system," she says (Ali & Miller, 2004: 52).

Adultery as a crime? Only in a gender biased society would the female be the one primarily punished while men receive slaps on the wrist. Only in a gender biased society would the white man attempt to curtail the activities of his wife while he was having liaisons with women on the side, and in the southern part of the country, sneaking out back to rape African women being held captive.

The Newsweek article continues:

> Unearthing infidelity is shattering to any spouse. Men can be just as traumatized as women by such a revelation; they can also be more surprised. David, 39, a government worker in Washington, D.C., discovered his wife was cheating the day she told him she wanted a divorce. "Never in a million years did I think it was possible." He found out later that his wife had stated seeing someone at work, someone David knew fairly well because the two couples often met socially. Once the reality set in, he couldn't get images of his wife and the other man out

of his head. Beset by nightmares, he stated taking
antidepressants. "I felt shamed for what had happened, like I
couldn't keep a person happy enough to stay with me." Now,
eight months later, Davis is beginning to date again. His divorce
should be final this month (Ali & Miller, 2004: 52).

How can the authors say that men can be "as traumatized as women" by learning about a spouse's infidelity? A more in-depth explanation is needed. The fact is, men and women might both be traumatized, but I assure you, it is for much different reasons.

For instance women might be traumatized to learn about a husband being unfaithful, but the society's ideology of "boys will be boys" and "all men do it" might quash some of that astonishment. And although she is hurt, she is still a woman in a male society that will do her harm if she decides to leave. In most divorces, women end up in a worse situation than men do (including custody of the kids, which is no picnic), and the status of men actually improves. This is what she has to look forward to in addition to her trauma. So many of them cave in, accept him back and forgive him. But few of them ever forget (therefore paving the way for "payback" infidelity somewhere down the line).

But for men, I say that any "trauma" that is felt is much different. For these men, it is like losing a mother figure. The woman cleans, takes care of the children and handles bills and, even if she does work outside the home, she still performs these duties in most households. His is a kind of "how am I going to explain this to the fellas" kind of trauma. If a woman walks out on a man, the man's ego may be bruised, but in being "single," it is easier for him to pick up the pieces and move on. Women not only have the children to think about but also the stigma of the "housewife gone bad."

The male must align his immense ego with his limited abilities. We men tend to think that the sun rises and sets on us just because a woman bats her eyes and tells us so. Those are those tools that she uses to assuage the fragile male ego. When she's angry, and you're arguing, listen closely to what she says about you at THAT time – that is how she REALLY feels.

In light of this, David's statement of "never in a million years" did he think his wife would leave him, seems understandable. He never thought about it; he thought he was handling his business when, in reality, he was just being set up for her painful departure. Now, he is dating again. But this time, the dating process will be longer and hopefully, he'll see the problems inherent in monogamous marriage. His wife sho' did.

Moving on:

> Just over half of all cases of female infidelity end in divorce, says
> Susan Shapiro Barash, a professor of gender studies at
> Marymount Manhattan College and author of "A Passion for
> More: Wives Reveal the Affairs That Make or Break Their
> Marriages." But that number may be shrinking. The
> conservative-marriage movement, as well as recent books like
> Judith Wallerstein's "The Unexpected Legacy of Divorce," have
> created a backlash against separation and raised consciousness
> about the seriousness of its effects on children. (Ali & Miller,
> 2004: 52).

What else would expect a pro-system magazine like Newsweek to conclude? Of course it's going to say that the divorce rate is declining and of course it's going to offer hope. But my thesis makes more sense when one considers the character flaw issues of the dominant culture, in general, and the irrational justifications used to explain the importance of monogamous marriage. If fifty percent of ANY other institution in America failed – fifty percent of the schools, fifty percent of the medical facilities, fifty percent of the legal profession, fifty percent of the military – there would be a movement afoot to re-tool, revamp and overturn that institution, right? Then why not marriage? Is it not an "institution" as well?

The fact that half of all cases of female infidelity in divorce is no good sign on a number of levels. Not only do the children suffer, but those women who divorce their husbands and remarry remain the same women they were before. Or are we to believe that "second time's a charm"?

The authors continue:

> Therapists who see the overworked professional set say they've
> noticed an interesting trend: people who have children and marry
> late in life tend to be less interested in cheating than their
> contemporaries who married earlier – and more willing to work
> it out when a woman (or man) does stray. These women have
> spent a lot of time along, and they're wise to the benefits of
> companionship. They've also waited a long time to have families
> and have a realistic sense of what's at stake. "I think people try
> to stay together," says Alvin Mesnikoff, a psychiatrist with a
> private practice in New York. In spite of the temptations,
> "Women want a relationship, and they're willing to work hard at
> it" (Ali & Miller, 2004: 52).

The authors seem to believe there is a "trend" that shows that people who have kids and who marry later in life are less likely to "cheat" than those who married earlier, and are also more likely to work it out with a woman does cheat. That makes sense. As you get older, you abandon the fantasy and the exoticism that surrounds being married. You understand that people make mistakes and that the system of marriage is, for the most part, only good for giving a child "a name." You have a more profound understanding of human nature and you realize the role that peer pressure and the media play in providing "outside temptations." The older you get, the more likely you are to be religious and at least one religion teaches the importance of forgiveness.

But that doesn't mean that marriage, as a system, has any additional merit. The stereotypes and myths that surround the "importance of marriage" can weigh on people. As they get older, they feel the pressure of finding someone to propose to them or to propose to. Most of us have heard the mean things that are said about people who get into their '30s and '40s and have never been married. The assumption is that the person is either gay, has some sexual dysfunction, or hates children.

As for the statement that these late bloomers or late marriage decision makers have a more realistic concept of what's going on, that is not necessarily the case. Because if they had a better understanding, they wouldn't get involved in the situation at all. Marriage, American style, is farcical, which is why more than half of them end in divorce. And infidelity is not always the reason why. California, for one, has this concept of "irreconcilable differences," a point made emphatically and popularized in the 1984 "child divorces the parents" movie by the same name.

Even with all the evidence that I have presented herein, Ali and Miller interview a psychiatrist who claims that she believes that she thinks "people try to stay together." That is foolish. People "try" to do things every day, but we need to assess situations and relationships based on what is accomplished. A man who "tries" to respect his wife but who, instead, beats the living crap out of her everyday – what are we going to judge him by: what he TRIES to do or what he's actually done? Once again, this article falls far short on reliable information that can elevate human relationships to a higher level.

Without interviewing one single child, the authors instead rely upon the claims of individuals who may or may not be credible. These therapists and psychologists would lose their jobs if much of what is true about the human condition were ever actually shared or even dealt with. So they benefit from perpetuating the myth of marriage as some kind of ultimate norm. For instance, note the following information:

> Divorce or no, how do responsible parents protect the hearts of
> their children when they're in the midst of heartbreak
> themselves? Therapists say kids don't care whether it's Mom or
> Dad who fools around – all they care about is known they're safe
> and that their lives will remain stable. It's difficult, but parents
> who are dealing with a revelation of infidelity need to protect

young kids from the facts of the case, as well as from their own anger. "There are very few things I will be a solute about, and this is one of them," says Katz. "Everything [children] ask for is not something they want. And if they ask, you should say, 'Yes, you're right. Things are tense around here, but this is between Mom and me'" (Ali & Miller, 2004: 54).

Hide the lack of character from your children. Hide your sluttishness and backstabbing behavior from the ones whose lives you want to influence. This is the advice that these therapists give out. And it is because of this kind of duplicity, this kind of perfidy, that today's children – white and black – are rebelling against their parents, much of that rebellion rooted and revolving around the "lies" that their parents told them.

And as most people know, you can lie in one of two ways. You can tell an outright fabrication, which is lying by *commission.* But you can also lie by keeping something from someone, hiding an important fact. That is called lying by omission. This is what you do when you betray your family, go out and do what you want to do despite the vows you took. This is what happens when you believe in a marital situation that doesn't even make sense, and in realizing that, you go out and give love to someone else. And then, after you've done that, come home and hide it from the children. If you're so ashamed of it you can't tell the kids, then why in the hell did you do it in the first place?

And if we are to believe the information provided by Ali & Miller, then you don't even tell the kids who are old enough to understand. You tell them SOME things, but generally, you don't tell the whole story. Here is how they explain it:

> Explaining infidelity to older children is somewhat more complicated. If a 15-year-o0ld turns to his mom and asks, "how long has this been going on?" a truthful answer may be in order, says Berger, the Elkins Park psychiatrist. And if he asks, "how could this happen?" "It may be responsible for Mom to say, You don't understand, dear, that Dad has been cheating on me," Berger says. Sometimes correcting the record is all right. "There's nothing gained by one parent being a martyr to the other parent's mistreatment." What parents need to avoid at all costs is to wrap the children into the drama by treating them as confidants" (Ali & Miller, 2004: 54).

"You don't understand, dear – Dad has been cheating on me." This is the advice this silly psychiatrist offers? A fifteen year old will immediately hate the father and perhaps attempt something violent. And if the mother is the one cheating, the children will react with even MORE hatred because the mother is the one that they trust the most.

Here is what I think you should tell the child, and I'm going to lay it out in the exact form that should be used:

> Son (or daughter): Marriage is difficult and the only reason anyone should get into it is so that the children will have a name and some semblance of long-term security. You have had a good life, and your mother and I are proud of you. But sometimes people lose interest in things and your mother has lost interest in me. This loss of interest has prompted her to begin seeing another man. That's what happens with marriage: it forces people to pretend that they love each other even when they do not. At least your mother was honest with her feelings and remained committed to you kids. But she just doesn't see the need to remain with me. She has her own reasons, and I hold no malice toward her. I hope you won't either.

Now doesn't that sound more mature, more "everybody wins" oriented than the lies by omission proposed by Ali, Miller and the so-called therapists that they look to for guidance?

With that "avoid reality" foolishness out of the way, the authors offer up yet another "case study:"

> Nadine grew up in a small, Midwestern town, and when she was 13 years old, her mother cheated on her father, moved to a town two hours away and married the other man. "There weren't any fights, nothing crazy," says Nadine, who at 28 lives in a big city and works in finance. "We sat down at Christmas. We discussed that Mother was leaving; it was nothing we had done." She and her siblings continued to live with her father; her mother went to school conferences and games as they had always done. Her parents remained, as she puts it, "best friends." But Nadine's teenage years were difficult. She never warmed up to the new man. She felt abandoned (Ali & Miller, 2004: 54).

Before moving on, let's agree on one thing: Nadine's mother and father, as she put it, were NOT best friends. If she thinks they were that can be attributed to youthful naiveté. There is no way that this man, if he ever cared for that woman who had his children, can be "best friends" with her when she ran off and married someone else and then had the nerve to live in close proximity. Maybe he's got the children bamboozled, but not me. They might be associates and they might be buddies, but they are not "best friends." Since the mother has remarried, her "best friend' had better be her new husband. If those kids remained with the father, this means that the mother was either ruled unfit or, for some reason, the father was established as being the best parent. In that case, his CHILDREN ought to be his best friends, not a woman who now has another significant other.

But the story continues:

> In retrospect, Nadine understands what pushed her mother to be
> unfaithful. Beautiful and intelligent, her mother was stifled by
> her life's low horizons, and her father, a standup guy, was
> probably a little bit boring. The new promised travel, wealth and
> adventure; her father was the kind of guy who'd say, "Why go
> around the world? You'll get plane-sick." And although she and
> her mother have made a kind of peace – "I got tired of making
> her cry," she says – she thinks the affair eroded any kind of trust
> she has in marriage or love. She can't stay in long relationships.
> "Ever since I could date, all I could think was, 'I will never, ever,
> ever do what my mom did.' I will never have a man take care of
> me. I have been called an ice princess in the past. I feel in
> someway my mom sold out and kind of fell for something" (Ali
> & Miller, 2004: 54).

How selfish, silly and shallow are Nadine's statements.

Nadine says that she "understands what pushed her mother to be unfaithful." When phrased this way, the true ignorance of the writers, as well as that of Nadine, comes to surface. Someone who rejects monogamous marriage is someone who is moving based on logic; that is not the same thing has "being pushed to be unfaithful." When you phrase it this way, marriage is still the moral standard and in such a context, the individual is made out to be some kind of criminal. This should not be the case. Nor should someone who is a slut or a man-whore from the get-go, be trying to use "I strayed" as an excuse for exercising their total lack of character.

Secondly, the writers poetically state that Nadine's mother "was stifled by life's low horizons. Two points here. First of all, this is a white woman. If she is "beautiful and intelligent," as the authors claim, then she has the essential criteria for success. In fact, in America, you can be white and not even be intelligent. Doesn't the president of the United States clearly show this to be the case? The same goes for white women: you can be plain, drab and dumb as a doorknob, but if you have white skin, a white system, on some level, is going to look out for you. It's what Christine Sleeter and other scholars have come to call, "white privilege."

Another point along the same lines is the concept of "life's low horizons." Life has no low horizons. Life's horizons are the same for everyone; it's just that some people, based on discrimination or low self-esteem, are held down from seeing those horizons, are stifled from reaching them. If her life had low horizons, it is because she settled for what came her way. The writers then, should not make an excuse for a white woman who can't make it in majority white America.

The writers claim that the father was a "standup guy" but was "probably a little bit boring." There was a time when that boring guy was the family norm. Many fathers, especially those of the blue collar variety, were so tired form performing menial labor that they came home, flopped down in the chair and had a better. On the weekend, they might have one day with the family and then Sunday was a day to rest up and prepare for that Monday. Boring, yes. But it was the norm until technology advanced to the point where work became easier and where unqualified white men were promoted and left the difficult work to blacks and Latinos.

Another variable that lends itself to the father becoming "a little bit boring" is the media and the fast pace that America has shifted in to. With the images the media bombards families with, the father has to be a "super dad:" a joke cracking dunce, a workaholic, a super lover in bed, a volunteer and of course, a counselor, tutor and advisor. The regular father, the one that has to work at the blue collar level, can't meet these standards. So in the final analysis, by comparison, he becomes boring to the woman who married him believing that "romantic love" and "monogamous marriage" would make him a stud for life. She was wrong.

Her mother's affair supposedly ended "any kind of trust she has in marriage or love"? Why? Her mother acted based upon an understanding that there had to be something more than monogamous marriage to someone she no longer loved. Why should she be a hypocrite? Why should she pretend to be happy and live a lie for her children – including Nadine – to imitate? Nadine is being selfish and foolish: she claims she will never have a man to take care of her. And that is alright because no one wants to be dependent. But that independent spirit has to go further than just personal relationships; white folks are going to have to come to grips with the fact that the system that they control is oppressive and that more people are hurting than just themselves. Once they grasp that, change can begin taking place to correct problems in political and ideological relationships that will then trickle down to the flaws personal relationships.

The writers and the people they interviewed, appear to have the wrong definitions of the variables they are discussing. Check out the following:

> Who said being married and raising kid was easy? The good
> news is that the wounds inflicted on a family by a woman's
> infidelity are not always critical. Therapists say couples often can
> – and do –get past it. Sometimes the husband sees it as a wake-

<blockquote>
up call and renews his efforts to be attentive. Sometimes,
especially if neither party is too angry, too defensive or too far
out the door, the couple can use it as an opportunity to air
grievances and soothe old hurts (Ali & Miller, 2004: 54).
</blockquote>

For one thing, the preceding passage has a distorted statement that reads, "the wounds inflicted on a family by a woman's infidelity are not always critical." The wounds were not inflicted by the woman being "unfaithful;" the wounds are self-inflicted. The very concept of monogamous marriage is a wound, it is what Maulana Karenga (1978) would refer to as being "hacked into hostile halves." It is divisive and restrictive. That is where the wounds lie – the ideological and structural wounds inflicted upon human kind by the concept of monogamous marriage.

The American tendency is to teach people to suffer "peacefully." Malcolm X once talked about black folks are always taught to suffer peacefully, akin to the Novocain that dentists put in your teeth. This can be applied to marriage and this Newsweek article. Note where the typical therapeutic claim is "couples can get past it." Doesn't the therapist understand that wanting to be free IS an attempt to "get past it"? It "it" is not the affair itself, the "it" is the restrictions imposed on people by marriage itself! Suffer peacefully and endure the marriage even with its still existent sex role stratifications; accept marriage and the "boys night out" and "girls night out", one day acknowledgements that "one mate forever" just doesn't work.

Suffer peacefully. That is what the preceding passage was about. The husband's "wake up call" is construed as returning to the same strained relationship. The concept of "working past it" means getting back into the daily grind of legal social confinement. The issue of soothing "old hurts" means making up and promising to be good little boys and girls even when you're bored to the point of screaming.

And in the final analysis, marriage is really nothing more than the economic arrangement that it was back in the days of Europe, Africa, Asia and other cultures. The idea of being pre-arranged might have been problematic, but at least the foundation was based on something tangible – not on some *sui generis,* spiritual concept of "romantic love."

But some cling to silliness at all costs. Observe the statements permeating the following paragraph:

<blockquote>
Sometimes the woman sees the dalliance for what it is, a fling,
and takes it with her to the grave. In her study of good marriages,
Wallerstein found that an affair did not necessarily damage
family life – especially if it fell into the category of a "one-night
</blockquote>

stand." "In good marriages this doesn't dominate the landscape, and the kids don't know," she says. She remembers interviewing a 30-year-old man, who said that when he was 9, his mother had an affair, but his father assured him that they would stay together. The man said: "I learned from my father that anything worth having is worth fighting for." When lunch is over and the wine wears off, most women will admit that if they were the prize in a fantasy duel between an imperfect but loving husband and a handsome stranger, they'd root for the husband every time (Ali & Miller, 2004: 54).

Of course an "affair" should not damage family life. But on the other hand family life should not be rooted in a belief that a married person cannot have other relationships with other people.

Seeing a "dalliance for what it is" is not the issue. The issue is why it has to be defined as such and why so much import is placed on these "flings" in the first place. As the older sisters used to say, "as long as he comes home to me." But men, being as fickle, shallow and hypocritical as we are, don't want anybody else in bed with our women. Since that is the case, you would think we would try a little harder to make sure that didn't happen – like treating every day as if it is our last. Karenga talks about the African concept of "hofu ni kwenu," which translates to mean "my fear is for you." Imagine if we lived our lives according to this principle rather than, "when you get home I'm gonna kick your ass."

From the way these women are defining it, a "one night stand" is not as bad as a long-time fling. But I say this: if you are going to get married, then you're forced to abide by the rules of marriage. In that constricting context, a cheater is a cheater, whether it's a one-time indiscretion or an affair that lasts for months or years. In either case, you are forced to lie, cheat and jeopardize your "marriage." That's why I say it's all a crock, aimed at forcing people to spend money on licenses, wedding gear for the bride and groom and the maids of honor and all those other people. You rent a church or center, purchase cakes and hire a musician and a photographer. All this feeds into the system and creates or maintains jobs for somebody. That is why marriage is being promoted: it generates money.

Even the ideas for the TYPE of marriage become a competitive thing, the way many things do in a capitalist society. The ideas for location, style, format has become like a game show. One article claims that "brides and grooms are increasingly finding friends "borrowing" ideas for their special day" (Lipton, 2004: 1E). The article provided some interesting statistics:

> As if wedding planning weren't stressful enough, this year's 2.3 million marrying couples have something new to worry about: copycats. With the $43 billion wedding industry increasingly

> pushing elaborate nuptials, more couples are finding that the
> most special day of their lives isn't so special, because friend and
> acquaintances are appropriating their ideas. It's not just the food
> or flowers getting double exposure, but also those creative extras
> couples count on to make their weddings unique …
> Occasionally, the "something borrowed" could mean the entire
> ceremony (Lipton, 2004: 1E).

In a capitalist society, everybody is a commodity, and lives are determined by what you buy, whether or not you can afford certain things and so on. This, of course, impacts on the concept of "marriage" and what it is supposed to represent. That piece of paper, the marriage certificate, ties you to the State. The money you pay goes into State coffers. The vows you take, as a result of these two acts, are secondary. That's why people are allowed to write their own vows. You're making a commitment to capitalism and European tradition – not just to another human being.

A great many institutions are behind pushing this marriage concept in America:

> The me-too "I do's" are the result of the boom in the wedding-
> oriented TV and magazine industry, as well as the growth of the
> wedding –planning business. The past year or so has seen a
> proliferation of TV shows with meticulously detailed weddings,
> from Lifetime's " 'I Do' Diaries" to MTV's "Til Death Do Us
> Part: Carmen & Dave." More than a dozen new bridal magazines
> have debuted since 2000, resulting in more competition to spin
> out new cake styles, reception venues and memorable moments
> … In 2002, the latest year for which figures are available, the
> cost of the average first-time wedding in the United States hit
> $22,360, up 18 percent from 1999, according to Fairchild Bridal
> InfoBank (Lipton, 2004: 2E).

Spending all this money for what? To show others that you can afford to spend the money! Many say it is to declare your love to the world, but it's not "the world" that you're marrying, or who you're going on that honeymoon with. What it is, in my view, is a gigantic, capitalist ego trip on the part of two people who want to flaunt themselves to the world, placing the onus of paying for the wedding on the FATHER of the bride. What kind of bullshit is that?

> As a result, there is always a group of vultures
> ready to pounce on any trend or fad. As one article
> informs us,

> The number of U.S. wedding planners has also grown, rising 25

percent in the past 18 months to 7,000, the Association of Bridal
Consultants estimates. Although these coordinators are supposed
to come up with ideas, some say clients hire them just to winnow
through stacks of magazines. "A lot of times they get
overwhelmed – 'Oh my God, there are 50 billion choices' – and
start freaking out," said Pasadena, Calif., planner Marley
Majcher. Some couples just give up, planners say, and pick ideas
they've seen work before (Lipton, 2004: 2E).

Wedding planners, three- and four-tier cakes. Rentals of tuxedos and
purchases of gowns – white gowns when most of the women being married haven't
been virgins for years! But the concept of white being representative of virginity is
another one of that racist "color codes;" white being virginal and black, of course,
being decadent, negative and inferior.

Ultimately, what do we have? Once again we find the "economics" of
marriage becoming the ultimate reality. As in days gone by when arranged
marriages were based on economic considerations, so it is today; they might not be
arranged, but marriages are still about money. And like money, marriages are
consumable and fluid – not stable.

"Suppressed Promiscuity:" The Movies, White Women and Adultery

Sluttification is the result of what I call, "suppressed promiscuity." The fact
is, such behavior has existed in American culture in general, and in the movies in
particular, for a number of decades. When Doris Dowling died in 2004, the
headline in the New York Times read, "Doris Dowling, 81, Is Dead; Known for
Classic Films of 40s." The article outlined the movies she was a part of, and at one
pointed cited the following: "In 'The Blue Dahlia' (1946), a Raymond Chandler
thriller starring Alan Ladd, *she was the faithless wife who is murdered* (Saxon,
2004: A17). It was not the only movie dealing with adultery during those so-called
"Golden Years" of the American cinema – all the way up to the present-day
Hollywood-manufactured productions.

Double Indemnity

What about 1944's "Double Indemnity"? Fred MacMurray plays Walter
Neff, an insurance salesman and Barbara Stanwyck is a woman who met her

current husband by nursing his wife (who she killed, according to her stepfather). At any rate, Neff calls to renew the husband's car insurance but he's not home – but she is, standing at the top of the stairs in nothing but a towel. They get together and Walter sells her a $50,000 double indemnity policy. All they have to do is arrange the death. And they do, but she's tricked him and in the end, they get busted.

The Postman Always Rings Twice

In 1946 there was "The Postman Always Rings Twice," which was remade in 1981 with Jack Nicholson and Jessica Lange playing the lead roles. But in both, the central theme was a married woman (Cora) and a drifter (Frank) who lusted after each other and had wild sex behind the husband's (Nick the Greek's) back. They tried several times to kill the Greek, but failed the first time. The second time worked like a charm and the Greek is killed in a car accident. On their way home to celebrate, Cora falls out of the car (pregnant with Nicholson's kid) and is killed. He gets blamed for both murders.

Many will argue that Nicholson's character, Frank, got what he deserved for plotting behind he husband's back and taking that man's wife. I view it differently: Nicholson was punished because he rewarded that woman's cowardice. She should have come clean and admitted that she was not happy. Or perhaps they could have just run off – there were no children to worry about. But she not only felt alienated, but then meets someone else then goes one step further – let's kill the husband. This is where the real crime came in.

Sex, Lies and Videotape

What about the 1989 flick, "Sex, Lies and Videotape"? A lawyer screws his wife's sister, and then the lawyer's college roommate shows up and guess what? The neglected wife screws him. This is being done far more than white folks want to let on, because the white woman is already out of control as it is; if she knew that there were millions like her, women willing to talk about their frustrations and sexual lies on videotape – she would go nuts! And the white man knows this!

Consenting Adults

Then there's 1992's "Consenting Adults," which featured "adultery" galore. This is the movie that confirms what many black scholars believe: that white folks, in their suburban hideaways, commit all kinds of weird perversions that they want to keep between themselves. They are engaging in wife-swapping, kiddie porn, viewing snuff films and other sicknesses. This is why, according to the logic, segregation is so important: in the presence of equitable living arrangements, we would be able to see what the white man is REALLY like – and that includes the way that he REALLY feels about his "mate."

In this case, Richard and Priscilla Parker are living an ordinary suburban life (oxymoron?) until some new neighbors, Eddie and Kay Otis, move in next door. According to the reviews, "the two couples become friends until some mate-swapping is suggested by the men." Actually, this is a simplistic explanation of how director Alan J. Pakula allows the relationships to unwind.

I have noticed white folks and how they treat other couples. I am not sure if this is indicative of the majority of them, but the television implication infers that when they host company, the white woman kisses the man and the woman at the door. When one couple greets another, they exchange more than pleasantries, but also hugs and kisses again. When the white wife is at home alone, the white male neighbor is free to come over and visit, even though the husband may be out of town or at work. This is the kind of shit that sets the stage for what Ali and Miller are writing about. But their cowardice in mentioning the context of what leads to infidelity is yet another shortcoming of their Newsweek piece.

In "Consenting Adults," what we find are deceptions within deceptions; Eddy (Kevin Spacey) wants Priscilla (Mary Elizabeth Mastrantonio) and is really the instigator. So he and Richard are supposed to switch beds that night. Eddie comes over that night and gives Richard the signal to go on over – he goes upstairs and does nothing. Meanwhile, Richard goes up to Eddy's place and there is his wife, on the floor, brutalized, blood and dead. He is charged with the crime. Eddie convinces a more than willing Priscilla that Richard and Kay were having an affair all along. Then, Eddy shacks up with Priscilla. See how simple that was?

One of the Ten Commandments teaches, "Thou shalt not covet thy neighbor's wife." But how can you not do it when that wife is smiling in your face, kissing you and hugging you with her husband's apparent approval? This is white culture at its best. Even with the charges of black and Latino men being "macho" and "sexist," one thing is for sure; this shit don't go down in OUR households! But at the root of all this "free love" by white folks is an implication that they just don't care that much about each other. Take away the mortgage, the jobs and cars, the suburban lifestyle and kids, and what you've got is two strangers who are living together. That's how it appears to me.

<u>Indecent Proposal</u>

What about 1993's "Indecent Proposal"? The plot is simple enough: Diana and David have been high school sweethearts and may or may not be married. But in the emotional sense, they are husband and wife. David gets the idea to go to Vegas and try to win some money to save their house, a masterpiece that he designed (he's an architect). While in Vegas, Diana catches the eye of John Gage, a billionaire. He offers them a million dollars if David will let Diana spend the night with him. They reluctantly agree, but David shows he can't handle it once the act is complete.

Damage

What about another flick from 1993, titled "Damage," which addresses infidelity in another way. A man and a woman see each other and fall in love right away. The problem is, the woman is the fiancée of the man who has fallen for her. During one scene, a dinner party, some of those present include the son, the fiancée, the father and other relatives. Some of them can see something is different (the father has already been to bed with the boy's fiancée several times) but cannot quite put their hand on it. The tension is almost unbearable, and this leads me to make an important point.

The real "affair" begins with coveting. And if a person who has character is experiencing that or is a victim of it, then this is the issue that should be dealt with – not just because one is locked into a legally-sanctioned institution called "marriage." If a person sees young children and gets sexual urges every time he does, that feeling is what makes him or her a pervert, not the actual rape or sexual assault. In like manner, Americans are influenced heavily by the pleasure principle-orientation of this society. Some people say that "just looking" doesn't hurt anybody. That may be true, but in a society as sick as this one, just looking is usually a prelude for something else. And the limitations imposed by monogamous marriage makes "just looking" much more of an issue than it probably should be.

Woman's Guide to Adultery

In that same year, 1993, there was a TV-movie, lesser known. It was actually titled, "Woman's Guide to Adultery," and it starred Theresa Russell as a woman named Rose, who believes that affairs with married men are terrible things, and in fact, believes that anyone woman who has sex with a married man is committing a crime against her gender. This, despite the fact that three of her closest friends are having such flings. Then, she falls for a guy, her photographer instructor no less, who is married.

In this particular movie, the issue is that the women want men and seek out the men who are already married. To many, that makes the men the adulterers. But what of the women who target these men? This is a point that I make in another part of this book: these women have to make it known that they are available, or else no "affair" takes place! These men were able to "violate their marital vows" only because there are women out there who make it possible for them to do so! Women who do this will tell you that married men are more attentive, married men aren't hanging around all the time and, supposedly, they know more about pleasing women than single men. For whatever reason, adultery is a two-way street. While the Newsweek article focuses on wives, the point to be made is that being married in America is beginning to mean less and less in the age of cohabitation, swinging, and the "feminist movement." So why do we cling to it so?

Elsewhere in this paper I document how Malcolm X wrote about how when he was a pimp, one service he was paid to perform by white boys was to screw their wives, while they watched. Even to this day, prostitution is a billion dollar industry because, for the most part, white men are willing to pay women for sex. Many pay just for companionship. But the thing to remember is even those who are married and remain married may not be satisfied. So they sneak around, lie and "pretend." This is what monogamous marriage hath wrought.

The Affair

Courtney Vance, a talented actor (also married to Angela Bassett), is a black GI caught up in an interracial liaison with a married white woman in "The Affair" (1995). This is a powerful movie because they fall in love and her husband is a serious racist in World War II England, where Vance (a member of the Tuskegee airmen) is stationed. He gets caught screwing her one night by the husband and it is automatically considered rape. She testifies in order to save her husband and her son, believing that he will only get a few months in prison. But when she finds out that the real punishment is hanging, she admits that she loves him but by that time it's too late.

Caught

One of my favorite "infidelity flicks" is one starring Maria Conchita Alonso and Edward James Olmos as a long-time married couple whose lives change when young Arie Verveen enters their life in the 1996 movie, "Caught." In his review of the movie, which I've seen four times, Ebert captures a point most germane to this section of the book:

> Watching the movie has the fascination of watching a traffic accident; we know there is going to e a crash, cannot stop it, and cannot look away. But [Director Robert M.] Young and his

actors are able to lead us to the crash through a process that makes us care about people it happens to. And they are fearless in showing us the consequences of uncontrolled lust. When I think of sex in recent movies, I think of a joyless, calculated display of commercialized images, as in such movies as "Striptease," "Showgirls" … "Caught" is a throwback to a time when the movie thought about sex more simply, as something that people wanted so much that sometimes it overwhelmed their better senses. And that strong elemental power, coursing under the surface of the story, gives it a strength that elevates melodrama almost to tragedy (Ebert, 1996).

Almost to tragedy? In "Caught," the young study and the lovely wife have on-going affairs and finally, thanks to the son of the couple, the scheme is exposed. They planned to steal some of the money from the sale of the business and leave poor Joe behind. He goes berserk and in beating on Nick, has a heart attack and dies. Nick is later confronted during a rainy night by the jealous son Danny, and as Nick walks off, Danny stabs and kills him. So there was tragedy, and it intensifies the consequences of what happens when there is infidelity, old school style.

Rich Man's Wife

Another 1996 movie about adultery that dealt with a different "culture" is the flick, "Rich Man's Wife." In a strange twist, Halle Berry is married to a white man who is rich and drinks too much. She has an affair with another man who is secretly in cahoots with a third man. This third man, played convincingly by Peter Greene ("Laws of Gravity") meets her and gets her talking. One evening, over drinks, she admits that the "hates her husband sometimes;" she tells him that she signed a prenuptial agreement and Greene uses that to convince her that she needs to get rid of him; and the trap is set.

She and her husband unexpectedly mend fences but Greene has the impression that she wants him killed. And he does the deed – and then proceeds to blackmail her, telling her to get the money and give him some or he will tell the cops she was behind it. The man she is having an affair with, another white boy, is in it with Greene and wants Halle because he loves her. One thing leads to another and I won't spoil it for you. Here is the point.

Halle should have divorced that man. Even with a prenup, the Court would award her something, especially considering his incredible wealth. But she stayed and has been carrying on this long-term love affair with, of course, another white man. The race element clouds the central issue here, but it is clear that the belief in "marriage no matter" what, is what her biggest problem was. She only compounds it by going out with guys, sneaking around, submitting to blackmail, lying to the police, and eventually has to commit murder herself. The message in this context is clear: adultery pays.

One Night Stand

Then we come to "One Night Stand" (1997), a movie where, based on the title you would expect sexual trysts and maybe even an extramarital liaison. But in this case, both people are married. As was the case with "Consenting Adults," what you have are two couples. Max is black and has a white friend, Charlie, who has been hospitalized with AIDS (Robert Downey Jr.). While visiting him, he meets Karen, who tells him is ink pen is leaking. From that point on things develop, but they part company. When he gets back home he meets his best friend's brother – Vernon. Vernon is Karen's husband!

How does this movie end? In a shed, at a party. Karen and Max sneak off to knock boots and in the same shed are Vernon and Max's fine ass Asian wife, Mimi. Four "adulterers" and in the end, they end up having permanently swapped mates and lifestyles, so it seems.

Eve's Bayou

Another 1997 movie, this one also a black flick, was "Eve's Bayou." In this movie Eve is the youngest daughter of an affluent black family, her father, Louis, is the town doctor. He is respected but plays around on the mother. But the adultery of the female is he woman the father is messing around with. The young girl tries to intercept the husband from interrupting the nightclub rendezvous of the father and the woman, but the movie ends tragically.

The woman who was committing adultery (expertly played by Lisa Nicole Carson) had been meeting with the doctor for some time, while her university professor husband took the train to the school and spend days there before returning. On this particular night, he got back early, after an encounter with the young girl who hinted to him that his wife was slipping out. This film was very realistic and addressed adultery in a southern community – white women would do well to take notes, since this tryst did not involve technology or "sneaking around." The husband knew his hot wife was just that, but he trusted her. In the end, the only reason he killed the doctor was because the doctor disrespected him in public, not because the doctor was out with his wife.

American Beauty

Then there was the much-heralded "American Beauty" (1999). In this flick Lester Burnham is a man who is afraid to grow older, and is ignored by his wife. But as he lusts after a teenaged girl, his wife is having an affair as well. Lester finds out and the two of them have an encounter at movie's end, rooted in a mistake, that shocks the audience. I won't give it away. But let's deal with the movie's subtle message.

With the primary message being the husband's lusting after a teenaged friend of his daughter's, much is lost on the affair that the wife is having.

End of the Affair

On a lesser not is another 1999 movie, "The End of the Affair," which stars Ralph Fiennes as a man who meets the husband of his ex-mistress. The two men exchange notes only to find out that she is having an affair behind the husband's back – and this is what peeves Fiennes more than anything else. After all, he had five years with the woman (played by Julianne Moore), and she just broke it off. Here's the point:

Moore's character takes up with Fiennes even after being married. But Fiennes sees her as more than a concubine; he is in love with her. And this is another point that the Newsweek article only glossed over: the fact that in some of these "affairs," there is real feeling involved and yet the woman remains marriage. In most of the scenarios provided in Newsweek, she meets a man and they get together following a divorce. There are tens of thousands – maybe millions – of women out there, most of them white, who have TWO men that they love in their lives: the husband, and the man on the side. But the fear of the social scientists and the researchers may be that they don't want to document how monogamous marriage is breaking down; so they avoid the issue or take a different angle. But the facts speak for themselves.

Unfaithful

Then there's "Unfaithful" (2002), which was mentioned in the Newsweek article, and here's how sick this culture is: the Jews who run Hollywood give out Oscars to a woman if she's convincing in a fuck sequence. How else to explain Halle Berry's mediocre role (except for the sex scene with Billy Bob Thornton) in "Monster's Ball"? How else to explain Diane Lane's even MORE mediocre performance in "Unfaithful"? They both were depicted having orgasms given to them by white men. They were both lovely women and although Halle's husband had just been murdered by the state (the death penalty), the man who assisted in that murder was the same man she would be fucking! Are these women "wayward" or just legally recognized whores?

In "Unfaithful" we once again have a woman whose husband worships her. He even screws her. She has no reason to give up the booty other than because she wants to. Just like Clinton recently said he engaged in sex with Monica Lewinsky "because he could." This is all that is needed in American culture, and it hails back to that old "Laugh-In" produced slogan, "If it feels good, do it." Even today, people are being reduced to animalistic levels: "I'd Walk a Mile for a Camel," "Sometimes You Feel Like a Nut, Sometimes You Don't," "When You've Got It, Flaunt It" (Braniff Airlines),

And it continues on today with appeals to baser instincts: "Obey Your Thirst" (Sprite), "Just Do It" (Nike), or how about the white woman swinging her hair around and telling the audience, "Because I'm Worth It" (L'Oreal)? What does this have to do with infidelity, you ask?

In the final analysis, it's all about who accepts the "programming" and who doesn't. The title of this book is **Insanity By Any Other Name**, and that is for a good reason. Insanity, succinctly defined, is "a relatively permanent disorder of the mind." People in America have been brainwashed in a number of areas, and the issue of infidelity is only one of them. Karenga (1967) wrote long ago that, "The negro has been copying white culture so long, and has become so mixed up from doing so, he thinks that it is his own." But white folks have been brainwashed by the white supremacy machine as well. Despite seeing examples of how shallow and weak they are all around them, far too many of them still cling on to this concept of "white is right." And with this misconception as a foundation, that which they create will inevitably be similarly flawed.

"Obey your thirst," "Just do it" and the like are successful advertising slogans because they appeal to the brainwashing that permeates this society. Appealing to baser emotions and to the insecurities of the majority population is at the base of both taboos regarding interracial sex, dating and marriage as well as the " 'till death do we part" foolishness of monogamous marriage which, in turn, gives rise to terms and practices like "adultery," and "infidelity."

The movies are both a reflection and reinforcement of the brainwashed status that already exists. There is no "secret life" of the "wife." After taking her vows – which are a sham in the first place – if she still has "secrets" from the person she agreed to marry, then not only is the marriage a joke, but her status as "wife" does not exist. These are facts we have to accept in order to "de-program" this society so that it can face facts rooted in reality.

Casting Pebbles in the War Against Adultery: Response to a New York Times article by Jan Hoffman (May 18, 1997)

This 2004 Newsweek article was not the first time that the major media attempted to confuse the issue regarding so-called "adultery." In fact, a topical news story from 1997 provided fodder for discussions of who was being "faithful" and who was not; in this case First Lieutenant Kelly Flinn, a young single woman (26 years old) was court-martialed for military charges of adultery. Check this out: the guy she had he affair with, Marc Zigo, a soccer coach at Minot Air Force Base, was married to an enlisted woman, but told Flinn he was separated. Then, based on this lie, he had an affair with Flinn, who was also charged with "fraternization," lying to Air Force investigators, disobeying an order (to stay away from Zigo) as well as "conduct unbecoming an officer."

Flinn was later discharged and the country was angered because of the way she was treated. From that incident, involving yet another white woman, the article by Hoffman appeared in the May 18, 1997 issue of the New York Times under the headline, "Casting Pebbles in the War Against Adultery." Following are the main points of that article, and my analysis of it.

> To the Air Force, a 26-year-old bomber pilot who fell hard for a four-star bad boyfriend deserves to be court-martialed for a handful of military crimes including adultery, the quintessentially biblical sin. To most Americans, she does not. They have been reacting with amazement, not least because for decades, civilian courts have responded to adultery with a big yawn. It's not that adultery laws don't exist. It's that they're not enforced. Although 75 percent of Americans believe adultery is always wrong, the lack of enforcement reflects a certain ambivalence over whether the government should be peeping into bedrooms (Hoffman, 1997: 6E).

America primes its public for adultery and a form of acceptance of it as "alright." Oh sure, the claims are the opposite and there may be laws against it, and the Christian religion "forbids" it, but the popular culture media is a worthy enough opponent to override all of these. In fact, just the fact that there are laws and the Bible speaks of it and popular culture thrives on it proves how awesome a temptation "adultery" really is.

The previous excerpt claims that 75% of Americans believe that adultery is wrong. But just because they believe it's wrong doesn't mean that they don't admire those who practice it, worship those who promote it or are not engaged in it themselves. The temptation is just too great: too many sluts out there and too many man-whores who get "married" and then find out, too late, that marriage is a crock of shit. And when they find out that sleeping with the same person night in and night out for decades is about as boring as life can get (unless those people truly love each other), then they strike out on their own and seek sexual gratification with other people.

The debate over it, despite its dubious, unlawful and immoral nature simply reinforces its relevance all that much more. Check out the following:

> In half the states, adultery is still a crime. In some, including Oklahoma, Idaho, Michigan, Wisconsin and Massachusetts, it's even a felony. Professor Katharine B. Silbaugh of Boston University law school, a co-author with Richard A. Posner, a Federal judge of "A Guide to America's Sex Laws" (1996), said state laws vary according to which lover should be prosecuted: "The married one will always be guilty," she said, "but the question is whether the unmarried one is also guilty" (Hoffman, 1997: 6E).

This places the onus on a belief that marriage is somehow "sacred." Judge Judy (Judith Scheinlin) in all of her Jewish arrogance, often deals with cases of people living together. She usually prefaces her decisions with a statement like, "You two decided to live together without the benefit of marriage …" Benefit? Look at her own life: she had the "benefit" of being married for decades and her husband Jerry (also a judge). As one website told the story:

> The report of the television judge's betrayal came from *In Touch* magazine, which spilled details of the alleged affair in its most recent issue. The report claimed that Judge Judy ultimately found out about the "secret affair" and was enraged at her husband for sleeping with a woman 25 years younger … Judge Judy Sheindlin and her husband Jerry were first married in 1977. They split up in 1990, but ended up remarrying that same year.

You see? They all want to "roar as if they ruled" but if you live in a glass house (which is being married in the first place), don't cast stones.

Marriage as some kind of "sanctuary" is such bullshit, elevated by popular culture and religious (mythological) beliefs to the level of sacred observance. Marriage is a white man who claims to be a representative of God uttering some words from a book that is supposed to be the word of God, and getting two people to agree with some "vows" that are made in the name of God. Marriage is a way for the state to generate money and keep track of its citizens; you get two "slaves" for the price of one, and then further link people to the system. Now they've got to buy a house, get cars, file taxes jointly, plan vacations, have kids, clothe those kids and so on. It's all a giant scam aimed at generating profits for the system. If you love somebody, you don't have to be married to them. And look at the 70% divorce rate – all the people who got married who found out that when all was said and done, their "love" as sheer and shallow.

So from here, the issue of who is "guilty of adultery" is as somewhat twisted. If a "married" person goes to bed with someone else, there has to be a reason. If that person is not happy, is being abused, is not being sexually satisfied, or is just an outright slut, then that person – male or female – has the right to fuck someone else if they choose to. That person is guilty of nothing more than "seeking an alternative." And that is what marriage keeps you from doing: you are supposed to be happy with the person you're with "for better or worse," which is ridiculous.

If the person who is unmarried is involved with a person that is married, what's wrong with that? Both people have to consent and agree that they want to screw one another. If that agreement is made between two sane people, then who is the government to intervene in the arrangement. Look at all those unhappy housewives coming to the black community to pick up young black boys and fuck them – they're married. Look at the white coaches who molest and abuse young kids in locker rooms and elsewhere – they're married. Look at all the white men who come to the barrio and the ghetto looking for some ass – they're married. Think about it.

Enforcing the law on adultery is like passing a law against somebody because they don't know how to fuck. Even if you don't know how, that's not the system's call to make – it's up to the person that's getting the raw deal and in most cases, that's the woman. But my logic is based on sound reality, not bullshit game playing like the kind found in the following passage:

> … in Arizona, for example, both parties are guilty of a misdemeanor, as long as one is married. By contrast, the District of Columbia holds that when the act is between a married woman and an unmarried man, both parties are guilty, but that when lovers include a married man and unmarried woman, only the man is guilty (Hoffman, 1997: 6E)

Again, it seems that the issue is "marriage" and the "fidelity" that supposedly accompanies it. The rules change because people have different views of what adultery is and when people have ideas that come together, those ideas become policy – laws. This is why the issue of adultery is so flimsy and hypocritical: monogamous marriage does not make sense and was only created so that the fathers of the child could be identified. But leaving kids out for a minute, what fuckin' sense does it make to pledge yourself to a person "for the rest of your life" or "until death do us part"?

The rule makers just can't come to an agreement or consensus, it seems:

> Maryland has declared adultery a misdemeanor, but the punishment is just a $10 fine. (Some people have quipped that the state income tax could be jettisoned altogether if the fine were raised to $1,000 and platoons of officers unleashed to enforce the law.) And in Minnesota, the misdemeanor of adultery, said legislators in 1963, is an act between a married woman and a man other than her husband. Sex between a married man and an unmarried woman is not prohibited (Hoffman, 1997: 6E).

And then there is the gender bias, such as is the case in Minnesota. When men make laws, women are going to be disrespected. When men write books – like the Bible, for instance – women are going to receive short shrift. That's the name of the game, and adultery and the "laws" that govern it, are no exception. It's about money and about making the woman look like a slut while the man, if charged at all, becomes some kind of "super stud", "playa," or "mack daddy."

Moving on:

> Prosecutions, though rare, are not unheard of. Professor Silbaugh said they usually accompany another crime, or are used to go after troublemakers. And so in 1970 a Pennsylvania jury found a man guilty of adultery and bastardy, and the case, which resurfaced in the courts 13 years later, was used to compel the defendant to keep up his child support payments (Hoffman, 1997: 6E).

Child support payments. That's what it's about in some cases: paying the state, once again. First you get a blood test and then pay for a marriage license. Then you pay some lousy minister to perform the ceremony. Then you pay for all the shit for the wedding, which costs thousands and then you wear these buffoonish costume in front of all your friends. This is what marriage is all about, and cannot really be justified logically. If you love somebody, you love them. But that's not enough: the state wants evidence that the love is strong enough to keep those payments coming. Adultery threatens this system's money making apparatus and the bullshit myth of "love" that is at the root of getting married.

> In 1983, a Worcester, Mass., woman challenged the constitutionality of the state adultery law, for which she was arrested after police offices watched her get into a van with a man and have sex with him. But the Supreme Judicial Court of Massachusetts said that although her concerns about a right to piracy had merit, the state had an

interesting prohibiting conduct that would threaten the institution of
marriage (Hoffman, 1997: 6E)

And there you have it: "threatening the institution of marriage." And the
reason why these are threats is because they threaten the economics that surround
marriage and family. This is not a social issue: it is an economic and financial one.
It may become social after the economics are threatened, but believe me when I
say that marriage in the U.S. is a financial arrangement and the more people who
marry the more money (taxes and otherwise) this country can generate for itself in
both the short- and long-term.

More evidence follows:

> And in 1990, a 28-year-old Wisconsin woman was arrested for the
> felony of adultery after her husband swore out a criminal complaint.
> Charges were dismissed after she agreed to go for counseling, but the
> case created an uproar. A state legislator wanted to decriminalize
> adultery, but beat a hasty retreat when voters warned him they
> considered his proposal an affront to family values (Hoffman, 1997:
> 6E).

When adultery is "investigated," why don't the officers delve into the
marriage relationship? If the husband was not screwing his wife or if he was cruel
to her, don't these facts represent the kind of extenuating circumstances that would
justify adultery? In such a case wouldn't adultery be viewed as an alternative to
divorce?

The fact is, the Bible says that adultery is one of the main reasons, the only
reason, for divorce. But the Bible, being the sexist document that it is, was quick to
blame the female (just like she got the blame for what took place in the so-called
Garden of Eden).

The fact is, adultery is so common that the attitudes about it started to
change and what did I say about attitudes? I said that they tend to shape policy and
policy becomes law. Want proof? Take note of the following:

> Adultery is considered even less odious in divorce court than in
> criminal court. Following the divorce reform of the 1970s, all states
> have no-fault divorce, which means that a party no longer has to allege
> a specific fault, like adultery, as grounds. A minority of states also
> allow adultery as grounds, but that usually only serves to speed the
> process. In fact many heartsick spouses who fantasize that a judge will
> wreak vengeance on the philanderer are shocked to learn that when it
> comes to divorce court, the only cheating a judge cares about is on
> income reporting. And just a handful of states say that if adultery is at

issue, a judge may, but not must, consider it a factor in the division of marital property (Hoffman, 1997: 6E).

"Income reporting." "Marital property." These capitalists don't give a shit about sperm, hotel rooms, dick sucking or intimacy. They don't care that lives can be ruined because of an inane belief in "'til death do we part." No. They care about money, plain and simple. The change in the rules to "no fault" saved time and saved the courts money. Trials were too expensive and saving money is a key component of the system's smooth operation. So there you have it. White men change the system whenever their money is threatened. It's not an issue of morality or love.

In truth,

> … the Sixth Amendment just doesn't pack the same oomph anymore, The term "adultery" – as distinguished from the practice – has grown dusty from lack of use. Instead, today's descriptive language dilutes condemnation with a drop of wistfulness. Philanderer, rather than adulterer. A faithless spouse has wanderin' eyes, a cheatin' heart. Even more watered down – has an extramarital affair. Sex opinion surveys ask: "Have you ever had sex with someone other than your spouse while you were married?" A tenet of the anti-divorce movement is that couples should repair the breach of marital trust exposed by the affair, because divorce is a far greater family crime than adultery (Hoffman, 1997: 6E).

And not just that, but the whole idea of a "separation" is granted so that the people involved can have time to work out the issues without going into immediate divorce mode.

So what is all this about changing the terminology and the rules so that it sounds more palatable? It's about the concept of "temptation," and all humans suffer from being able to be tempted, do they not? The dictionary defines "tempt" as, "To entice (someone) to commit an unwise or IMMORAL act. To be inviting or attracted to. To provoke or risk provoking. To incline or dispose strongly (Berube, et al., p. 1252).

Wow! The dictionary says as its first definition that to tempt has to do with committing an unwise or immoral (sinful) act. Now these Americans who claim to be Christians want to use the Bible and use Scripture in order to buttress the points – that is until they come up against somebody like me who knows the Bible better than they do. So according to our language, *even Jesus sinned because the Bible says that he, too, was "tempted."* Do I need to prove my point any further? Okay, I will.

When a person is "tempted," he or she first has to think on it before they act on it. Many times we will ponder in our mind whether we should do something that we really want to do but first we will do the best we can to weigh the consequences of our actions. If our "will" is strong enough, we can resist the temptation of doing it. The point here is that we think, ponder and roll it over in our mind, first. Now, check out what Jesus said in Matthew 5:28-29:

> But I say unto you, that whosever looketh upon a woman to lust
> after her hath committed adultery with her already in his heart.

So it begins with the heart (the mind), just like it did back in 1980 when Jimmy Carter admitted that he had lusted in his heart "many times," remember that? So it's a mental thing, and that stuff about the "heart" is just a metaphor because the heart don't do nothin' but pump blood. So when the Bible talks about the heart, it is referring to the MIND. Got it? Good.

So then, we find that sin begins in the mind and Jesus s said *that if you think bad thoughts you've already sinned* and then Hebrews tell us that Jesus was TEMPTED, which means he SINNED, having thought it in his heart (Mind). This stuff is like an algebraic equation: you have to think and use your reasoning power. The formula is $S = T + T$, or "sin equals temptation plus thought. This is also why Jesus says, "Watch and pray that ye enter not into temptation: the spirit (mind and will) indeed is willing but the flesh (actions) is weak" (Matthew 4:1-10).

That's right my mindless little Christian soldiers: Jesus was constantly tempted, that is to say, he "thought" about it. Remember in Matthew where is says, "Then was Jesus led up of the spirit into the wilderness to be tempted of the devil" (chapter 4, verse 1). You mean to tell me that when Jesus saw all those kingdoms of the world that he could be king over, he thought about taking the devil upon his offer?? At least for a nano-second – that's what tempt means. Jeremiah 17:9 asks us all, "The heart is deceitful above all things, and desperately wicked: who can know it?"

Adultery. What a joke. Secret lives? Secret to those who don't want to know the truth. Marriage: a financial farce. Remember: you heard it here first.

Conclusion: Getting in Touch With Their "Mitches" – Mission Accomplished

Published so long ago, but still relevant but a day late and a dollar short. The search for, creation of an on-going exploitation of today's "mitches" has been a long process. But it appears on the verge of accomplishment. Today's men are more feminine as ever and today's women, replete with "kick ass and take names" approaches to running this white supremacist system, are taking control of the world and the nation.

"The Secret Lives of Wives" was the title of the 2004 Newsweek article. That was 14 years ago. It may have been a "secret" to those who saw it coming and didn't want to scare the hell out of the oppressive systems all over the world that were about to get turned on their ear, but it was not much of a secret for those of us who have watched, analyzed and seen the transformation taking place. America is another "European nation" and it values white nationalist history as much as anything else. Therefore the powdered wigs once worn in the European courts should have been a clue. Even American presidents and Supreme Court justices donned those hair pieces. And that's not the only indicator that shows that the "mitch" has truly arrived.

Maybe a secret to the men that these women are "playing on." But certainly not to the men who are screwing these women. And one point not dealt with is the number of these white housewives who are panting behind men of color while their white husbands play silly games of "slap the butt" at the workplace!

And it's not just the naïve and square bear white boy. Black men have been slowly lulled into accepting commands and orders, allowing themselves to be measured, assessed, run through the paces, called names and otherwise "beastified." In the neighborhood the conk may be gone and the jheri curl may be outmoded, but the "punk" still remains behind: double earrings, skinny jeans and a submissive attitude on any topic that even remotely smacks of politics or speaking truth to power. A race of sissified men no matter how many children they produce or how many touchdowns they run. Everybody can see it – but us.

Secret? The world knows that the American woman (translation: the white woman) is a slut! That is what Hollywood and the other media, that is what the advertising industry, the modeling runways and magazines galore have made of her. And most of them, the overwhelming majority, have conformed to this image. And sure, there is no secret about that.

Not only that, but any nation that has had a formal system of racial segregation and has opted under social pressure to disband it, has started off by "relaxing" the anti-miscegenation laws. The men in power by time by ordaining, "You can now interact with, date, screw and marry white women." After all, the global myth and media have held her up as the crown jewel. And she has brought into it. But in recent centuries, in America at least, she has bided her time, bedded the right people, and cut the right bargains. She has used what I call "gifts, gams and ideological game." Look around: she no longer needs her pale mate and men of color are nothing more than a sexual release and comic relief.

But these white women are a fickle bunch. If you tell it like it is, they will resort to denial and call you a misogynist. Personally, as a black man, I don't care what a white woman thinks about me. I know her history, and I know the role that her history played in the oppression of my people. She never, at any time, told her man that what he was doing was beast-like, bellicose or bombastic. Instead, she allowed him to do it in her name. And today she's saying, "move over, let me show you how it's done."

Now, we fast forward to the 21st century and these white women want to pretend as if they are "free" and "independent" and in a position to lead black women someplace. They are on television trying to tell the world how to dress, how to cook, how to apply makeup, how to raise children, how to clean a home, and so on and so on. But for the most part, she had to be mentored and tutored by women of color. Helen the housekeeper, Caterina the Cook, Nadine the Nanny and so on. Some say the reasons why many of them have flat asses is because they sat on them most of their lives throughout the centuries. But today she has under-alls, girdles, corsets, and fake-bun surgery. Nothing beats a failure but a try.

Be that as it may, one thing we know for sure: *the white woman's complicity in our oppression is no "secret."* And knowing this one major simple fact, we cannot believe that anything else is a "secret" either. After all, we've been there.

Works Cited

Adorjan, Michael, et. al. (2016, October). Stockholm Syndrome As Vernacular Resource." **The Sociological Quarterly** 53.3 (2012)

Aksamit, N. (2004, March 15). Excercisin' and socializing.' **Omaha World Herald.**

Ali, L. and Miller, L. (2004, July 12). The secret lives of wives. **Newsweek.**

Angier, N. (1998, June 21). Men. Are women better off with them, or without them. **New York Times**.

Barnett, R.C. and Rivers,C. (1996, November 17). Book: Working women lead healthy, happy lives. **Omaha World Herald.**

Barron, J. (1996, October 31). West Point acuses cadet of raping another cadet. **New York Times.**

Britt, D. (1999, June 14). Ebony and ivory. **Omaha World Herald.**

Campbell, B.M. (1985, October). The they factor. **Essence.**

Clines, F.X. (1997, June 1). America's jaded eye on sex in public life. **New York Times.**

DeBare, I. (1997, February 23). Love thrives in the workplace – despite '90s risks. **Omaha World Herald**.

Dowd, M. (2000, May 24). What a girl wants … What a girl needs. **New York Times.**

Ebert, R. (2003, August 29). Thirteen. **Chicago Sun-Times.**

Ebert, R. (2006). Caught. **Chicago Sun-Times.**

Elder, J. (1997, June 22). Poll finds women are the health-savvier sex, and the warier. **New York Times.**

Fix, J.L. (1994, October 17). Reversal of fortune: When women make more than men. **USA Today.**

Glaberson, W. (1999, February 14). Sex on the witness stand: Get used to it. **New York Times.**

Goodman, E. (1996, November 1). The rules of womanipulation. **Omaha World Herald.**

Hass, N. (1998, September 28). Hard times for strong-minded women. **New York Times.**

Hoffman, J. (1997, May 18). Casting pebbles in the war against adultery. **New York Times.**

Hooks, B. (1990). **Yearning: Race, gender, and cultural politics**. Boston, Massachusetts: South End Press.

Jet. (1985, December 16). Women who enjoy erotic books have sex more often.

Kakutani, M. (1997, June 10). Feminism lite: She is woman, hear her mate. **New York Times.**

Karenga, M. (1978). **Beyond connections: Liberation in love and struggle**. New Orleans: Ahidiana Publications.

Kilbourn, P.T. (1997, March 12). 5 women say sex charges in army case were coerced: NAACP suggests a racial motivation. **New York Times**.

Kirkland, B. (2001, August 14). Liz's first film kiss has place in the sun. **Toronto Sun.**

Kitroeff, Natalie (2012, May 3). Stockholm Syndrome in the Pimp-Victim Relationship. **New York Times**. Retrieved from https://kristof.blogs.nytimes.com/2012/05/03/stockholm-syndrome-in-the-pimp-victim-relationship/

Kolata, G. (1997, June 22). Women want control, just not all of the time. **New York Times**.

Kolata, G. (1998, June 21). Women and sex: On this topic, science blushes. **New York Times.**

Krauss, C. (2004, May 19). Morning-after pill in Canada: Prescription may not be needed. **New York Times**.

Kuczynski, A. (1998, May 4). Bosom foes together again. **New York Times.**

Lewin, T. (1998, March 12). All-girl schools questioned as a way to attain equity: Study finds no proof programs are better. **New York Times.**

Lipton, L. (2004, June 14). Me-too 'I do's'. **Omaha World Herald**

Mann, D. (2004, May 14). Extreme makeover: Coming to a beach near you. WebMD. Retrieved July 27 from http://aolsvc.health.web.md.aol.com/content/article/87/99363.htm?DEST=WebMD &conte …

Mann, D. (2004, June 11). The Stepford syndrome: Is the quest for physical perfection creating a nation of Stepford wives? Retrieved July 27 from http://aolsvc.heatlh.webmd.aol.com/content/article/88/100018.htm?DEST=WebMD&contentSRG=aolmain

Marable, M. (2004, August 26). Along the color line: A jobless future. **The Omaha Star.**

Morin, R. (1992, May 31). Survey: What if women ran the country? **The Milwaukee Journal.**

Mosendz, Polly (2015, November 15). Ronda Rousey Spends Night in Hospital after Losing UFC Matchto Holly Holm. **Newsweek.** Retrieved from http://www.newsweek.com/ronda-rousey-spends-night-hospital-after-losing-ufc-match-holly-holm-394717

New York Times. (1996, October 20). Nation's most common infections are sexual.

New York Times. (1997, March 21). Army officer pleads guilty in Aberdeen sex-abuse case.

New York Times. (1998, September 18). Fewer high school students having sex, poll shows.

Norment, L. (1997, March). Sex and sisters: What turns women on – and off. **Ebony.**

Oldenbourg, Z. (1965). **Catherine the great**. New York: Random House.

Omaha World Herald. (1997, February 13). A new message at the Citadel.

Omaha World Herald.(1997, August 15). Louisiana goes marching into new era of divorce.

Omaha World Herald. (1997, May 26). Pilot says she has lost trust.

Omaha World Herald. (1999, April 30). Survey: Sex more important than job.

Omaha World Herald. (2000, March 18). 3 years of divorces hardly shaking Ireland to its core.

Omaha World Herald. (2000, March 21). Study: Sexes navigate with different strategies.

Omaha World Herald. (2001, July 15). It's no joke: Blonde backlash turning culture on its head.

Omaha World Herald. (2001, August 5). 'First woman of Wall Street' says more doors are opening.

Omaha World Herald. (2001, August 20). Cohabitation numbers soar: Conservative regions see largest increases, census shows.

Omaha World Herald. (2001, August 27). 1 in 10 teen girls, 1 in 20 boys report abuse on dates.

Omaha World Herald. (2001, August 4). Why do married people cheat? Condit situation spurs therapists'analysis of adultery's causes.

Pappas, L. (1998, August 24). China's new family values. **Newsweek.**

Racine Journal Times. (1992, April 6). Marriage, kids buffer women from job stress: Study says family can protect working women.

Rich, F. (1998, December 26). Scandals sans bimbos need not apply. **New York Times.**

Sagan, D. (1998, Jun 21). Gender specifics: Why women aren't men. **New York Times.**

Saxon, W. (2004, June 28). Doris Dowling, 81 is dead; Known for classic films of 40s. **New York Times.**

Shank, A.M. (2012, September 9). Marriage and the wedding ring. Retrieved from http://www.bibleviews.com/wr.html

Sikes, G. (1998, April 5). Sex and the cynical girl: A gentler approach. **New York Times.**

Smith, D. (1997, May 1). Study looks at portrayal of women in media. **New York Times.**

Stein J. (2004, July 26). The strip is back. **Time,** 164, (4).

Taylor, S.L. (1982, January). Your beauty within. **Essence.**

Terry, D. (1996, November 14). Graphic testimony at army base, and a sentence for sex offenses. **New York Times**.

Welsing, Frances Cress. (1974, May). The Cress Theory of Color Confrontation. **The Black Scholar**.

Welsing, Frances Cress (1991). **The Isis Papers: The Keys to the Colors.** Chicago, Illinois: Third World Press.

Williams, A. (2004, July 15). Breezy image of infidelity is harmful. **Myrtle Beach Sun News.**

Williams, F. (1997, December 11). A house, 10 wives: Polygamy in suburbia. **New York Times**.

Wolf, N. (1997). **Promiscuities: The secret struggle for womanhood**. New York: Random House.

Zuger, A. (1998, June 21). What doctors of both sexes think of patients of both sexes. **New York Times.**

9 781986 467742